NINETY YEARS
CROSSING LAKE MICHIGAN

NINETY YEARS
CROSSING LAKE MICHIGAN

*The History of the
Ann Arbor Car Ferries*

Grant Brown, Jr.

THE UNIVERSITY OF MICHIGAN PRESS · ANN ARBOR

Copyright © by Grant Brown, Jr., 2008
All rights reserved
Published in the United States of America by
The University of Michigan Press
Manufactured in the United States of America
⊛ Printed on acid-free paper

2011   2010   2009   2008   4   3   2   1

A CIP catalog record for this book is available from the British Library.

Library of Congress Cataloging-in-Publication Data

Brown, Grant.
     Ninety years crossing Lake Michigan : the history of the Ann Arbor
car ferries / Grant Brown, Jr.
         p.   cm.
     Includes bibliographical references and index.
     ISBN-13: 978-0-472-07049-7 (cloth : alk. paper)
     ISBN-10: 0-472-07049-5 (cloth : alk. paper)
     ISBN-13: 978-0-472-05049-9 (pbk. : alk. paper)
     ISBN-10: 0-472-05049-4 (pbk. : alk. paper)
         1. Ferries—Michigan, Lake—History.   2. Ferries—Michigan—Ann
Arbor—History.   3. Train ferries—Michigan, Lake—History.
4. Train ferries—Michigan—Ann Arbor—History.   I. Title.
HE5778.B76   2008
386'.609774—dc22   2008015003

*Dedicated to the men who conceived, built, and later
fought to save the Ann Arbor car ferries, and to those who
gave them heart and soul, the men who sailed the boats*

Preface

* * *

As a young boy I was fascinated by the Ann Arbor car ferries. My parents owned a cottage on Crystal Lake, three miles north of Frankfort, Michigan, where we spent the summer months. When in town, I was thrilled to hear the unmistakable blast of the boats' whistles and to watch the big ships leave the harbor. Incidentally, the car ferry crews always referred to the vessels as boats, but they were in fact ships, 260 to 380 feet in length. I have used the terms interchangeably, and there should be no particular inference drawn from the use of either term at any particular place in the story.

My first trip across Lake Michigan occurred during World War II with my mother and sister. After what seemed an interminable wait in Manitowoc, we boarded the *Wabash* and started across on a stormy afternoon. Although the *Wabash* was less than twenty years old, she creaked and groaned as she lumbered through the big seas. My mother and sister were miserable. I loved it.

Later in life, I enjoyed the books about the Ann Arbor written by Captain Arthur Frederickson, but it wasn't until I retired and moved to Frankfort to live permanently that I had an opportunity to follow up on my interest. I have been fortunate to talk with five former Ann Arbor captains and several times as many crew members over the last nine years. Also I have researched some two thousand newspaper articles; valuable information from the Archives of Michigan and the National Archives;

logbooks from the Wisconsin Maritime Museum, Manitowoc, and the Historical Collections of the Great Lakes, Bowling Green State University, Bowling Green, Ohio; and annual reports from the Clarke Historical Library, Central Michigan University, Mount Pleasant, Michigan.

Everyone has been helpful, but there are a few people who have gone beyond helpfulness. Captain Bruce Jewell has taken time to teach me about ship handling and ice breaking and has answered every question I could think up in countless discussions in person and over the phone. William C. Bacon (former Ann Arbor superintendent of marine) and Leonard Kittleson (former Ann Arbor captain) have also given freely of their time and helped me consolidate what I learned. Each has brought me a wealth of knowledge and had the wisdom to tell me when I asked something he did not know.

Daisy Butler kindly allowed me to view and copy all of the information in her father's (A. C. Frederickson's) extensive collection of car ferry materials. Later, when she decided to part with the collection, I was privileged to purchase it from her. Jonathan Hawley helped me greatly improve my research skills. All I had to do was raise a question and Jon was figuring out how I could find the answer. Donald Riel helped me understand the last five years of the Ann Arbor's operation, its dealings with the state, and the influence of national legislation. Byron McClellan introduced me to Don and helped me in countless other ways. Bruce Ogilvie took the time to read the book several times and give me the benefit of his thoughts.

I would like to thank everyone at the University of Michigan Press with whom I have had contact. All have been exceedingly friendly, helpful, and professional: Mary Erwin, who thought the story should be published; Catherine Cassel, who walked me through the process of converting the story into a manuscript; Christina Milton and the copy editors, who gently pointed out inconsistencies and put my references into acceptable form. Each took time to answer a multitude of questions and provide guidance as I needed it. It has been a pleasure.

I wrote the book over a period of four years, which left ample time for critical appraisal. My sons, Neil and Ross, were most helpful, and my wife, Ginny, was invaluable. If Ginny liked it, I had confidence it was readable.

I have been most fortunate to have had the time and access to reference materials to research and write the history of the Ann Arbor car ferries. I have found it an intriguing story and hope you do as well.

Contents

✳ ✳ ✳

Introduction:
Ice and Ice Breaking

✳   ✳   ✳

When the Toledo, Ann Arbor and North Michigan Railroad first announced its intention to ferry railcars across Lake Michigan there were two major obstacles cited by those who felt the idea was unworkable. First, it was not possible to secure railcars so they would not roll back and forth or tip over in a storm, and, second, it was not possible to consistently cross Lake Michigan in winter. The railroad solved the first problem very quickly, but the second—crossing the lake during winter storms and entering harbors filled with ice—took a while longer. Indeed, it could be argued that it was never "solved." Eighty-five years after the line began operations a car ferry was denied entrance to Frankfort Harbor for nine days due to ice. To fully understand what the boats and their crews were up against it is helpful to have some knowledge of ice in its various forms, as well as how the boats broke ice, how they became stuck, and how they broke each other out.

The freshwater ice of the Great Lakes is dense and very difficult to break up—much more so than sea ice. Sea ice contains salt, which depresses the freezing point and lessens the density. Over time, as the ice remains frozen, the salt leaches out and the ice becomes more dense. It takes sea ice a year or more to become as dense as freshwater ice.[1]

Depending on who is doing the categorizing, there are anywhere from a few to twenty or thirty different forms of ice. There is some overlapping of definitions, and it is unlikely that any two captains will identify all forms the same way. The same is true for institutions such as the U.S. Coast Guard, the Canadian Coast Guard, and the National Weather Snow and Ice Institute. The U.S. Coast Guard and the Canadian Coast Guard have adopted definitions that do not closely relate to the terminology the car ferry captains used throughout most of their service. Since our interest is in car ferry history, we will follow the definitions that were commonly used by car ferry captains even though they may not fit some current definitions. Fortunately, we only need to be familiar with a few forms of ice to appreciate the challenges the car ferries faced and the stories of how they met those challenges over the years.

Sheet ice is formed when the water is very calm; it skims over and then gets thicker and thicker, depending on how long the temperature stays below freezing. Sheet ice can be anywhere from a fraction of an inch to several feet thick. The early car ferries, such as the *Ann Arbor No. 1, No. 2, No. 3,* and *No. 4*—those built through 1906—could plow through sheet ice about one and a half feet thick without having to stop. That was considered very good for the time. Later boats, such as the *Ann Arbor No. 5, No. 6, No. 7,* and the *Wabash*—those built through 1927—could plow through about three feet of sheet ice without having to stop.[2] The Ann Arbor's best icebreaker was the *Viking,* the 1965 rebuild of the *Ann Arbor No. 7.* When she was rebuilt, she was given a diesel-electric power system that produced 6,120 horsepower—over twice that of the *No. 5,* previously considered the best icebreaker in the fleet. The *Viking* was capable of forcing her way through four feet of sheet ice without having to stop. Variations of sheet ice include *ice floes,* which are made up of sheet ice that is not attached to something, such as the shore, and *ice fields,* which are made up of sheet ice that is attached to the shore.

Many newspaper articles in the 1890s referred to *blue ice* of various thicknesses. They were referring to sheet ice that was nearly transparent, made up of ice crystals very closely packed together with few impurities. Blue ice is very dense and difficult to break through compared to *white ice,* which is usually older and contains large quantities of air.

Anchor ice is so called because it is attached (anchored) to something such as a pier. Anchor ice often formed around the slips where the boats tied up and was difficult to break up because the normal method of simply ramming into the ice was not possible due to the damage the boat might do to the slips.

Pack ice is much like anchor ice in that it is attached to something, but

Sheet ice on Crystal Lake, an inland lake about three miles north of Frankfort. *(Photo from the author's collection.)*

Anchor ice lines the piers as the *Ann Arbor No. 2* enters Frankfort Harbor in the mid-1890s. *(Photo from the A. C. Frederickson Collection.)*

it forms differently. Ice is piled up against something—a pier, a breakwater, the shore, a harbor entrance—by a prevailing wind and becomes thicker with the passage of time. The ice at the harbor entrance in the following picture is not sheet ice even though it appears to be flat on the surface. It is attached to the two piers, extends to the bottom, and has

Pack Ice at the entrance of Frankfort Harbor. (*Photo from the A. C. Frederickson Collection.*)

been formed by wind pushing more and more ice into the harbor entrance. Because of the way it was formed, it should be called pack ice.

Windrows are formed when the wind shoves pieces of sheet ice together under pressure. Where there is a crack, the ice breaks into chunks that are forced up and down, forming a "wall," usually along a relatively straight line. That wall of ice, or windrow, may rise ten to fifteen feet in height and extend even farther below the surface, often to the bottom in water less than twenty-five feet deep. Windrows can be several feet across and extend for miles. Car ferries always had difficulty with windrows and often became stuck trying to break through them. Many times when they were stuck for hours or even days windrows were involved.

Slush ice is defined as "snow which is saturated and mixed with water on land or ice surfaces, or as a viscous floating mass in water after a heavy snowfall"—tiny ice crystals suspended in water.[3] Slush ice was often a problem in the basin between the breakwaters of Frankfort Harbor.

The standard method of breaking ice was for a car ferry to plow into it under full power until the ship could go no farther, back off, and try again. There were various recommendations on how far to back, but most car ferry captains liked to back off as far as they could in order to work up more speed before they rammed the ice again. While this was an

Ann Arbor No. 5 opposite a large windrow. *(Photo from the A. C. Frederickson Collection.)*

acknowledged method, it was (and is) not for everyone. Vessels not designed for some level of ice breaking can suffer serious damage.[4]

Another good method of breaking ice was backing. The backing method used the wash of the propellers to break up the ice and was particularly effective on anchor or pack ice, where ramming into it full speed ahead might damage whatever the ice was attached to. To break ice by backing, both engines were put in reverse to bring the boat close to the ice to be broken up; then one engine was put ahead and one astern to create a circular current, which acted on the ice and tore it up. Sometimes both engines would be put ahead to vary the direction of the current. The boat alternated having both engines in reverse and then one or both engines ahead. An advantage of backing was that a boat was less likely to get stuck due to the fact that it was always clearing space ahead of the stern. There was, however, a disadvantage. Because one engine was often ahead and the other astern, the turning force on the boat tended to swing the bow to one side or the other unless there was sufficient ice pressing against it to keep it in line. In some cases that was not a problem, but at times it could be.

Car ferries became stuck in ice due to surface friction, which resulted when:

1. They plowed into heavy ice, such as pack ice or windrows going all the way to the bottom, and found they could not back off

Ann Arbor No. 5 backing in ice on Green Bay. *(From the Roger Griner Collection. Photo courtesy of the Marinette Eagle Herald.)*

    2. They found themselves under pressure from ice pressing against their sides

    3. They got caught in slush ice

The boats became stuck while plowing into windrows or pack ice in an effort to break through. They found they had the power to ride up onto the ice but not to back off. The longer they stayed, the more the ice closed in around them. Often they needed the help of another boat to break out.

Pressure exerted by ice is best understood with an example. Picture an ice field extending from the Michigan shore several miles into Lake Michigan. Add to this picture a strong west wind pushing the ice against the beach. The ice is being pushed against the beach, but it is not moving onto the beach and inshore because the beach is pushing back with equal force. Now imagine a car ferry somewhere between the shore and the western extremity of the ice. The ice, pushed by the wind, exerts tremendous pressure on the sides of the ferry, as does the resistance

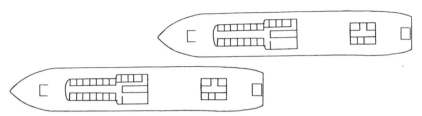

Car ferries passed very close aboard to break each other out of the ice. *(Drawings from the author's collection.)*

from the shore. Thus, the ice squeezes the ferry from both sides, developing a surface friction that it cannot overcome. The ship will remain stuck until the wind changes, relieving the pressure.

Slush ice presented more of a problem for car ferries than one might expect. It seems logical that a ferry could simply plow though the relatively soft slush ice, but that was not what happened. Instead, the ice stuck to the sides of the ferry, changing its effective shape to one that became very unstreamlined and creating a drag the ferry could not overcome. Slush ice blown into the harbor entrance at Frankfort was particularly difficult on occasions when it extended to the bottom. A boat could plow into the ice, but as it neared the piers the ice beneath it would be compacted, causing the ship to ride up as though there had been solid ice on the bottom. Before long, the ship would become stuck, much as it might if it had run onto a sandbar.

At times when a car ferry got stuck it required the help of another ferry to free itself. The standard method of breaking a boat out was to run alongside the boat that was stuck for its entire length, keeping the boats about ten feet apart. Ten feet seems very close for two ships 360 feet or more in length, but former captains say that unless they were that close the method would not work. Also, they say that the operation was not as dangerous as it sounds because once the pass was started even a foot or two of ice between the boats was enough to keep them apart. The skill was in starting the pass. Over the years, there were some accidents. Log entries such as "Ran into boat 4 near the stern. No damage done" or "Hit boat 3 near the bow" occurred from time to time. The boats were solidly built and could take considerable abuse, though there were times when they required repairs.

A second good method of breaking boats out was backing. A boat could use the circular current created by putting one engine ahead and

Spudding around the *Ann Arbor No. 1* at the entrance to Frankfort Harbor in the early 1900s. *(Photo from the A. C. Frederickson Collection.)*

one astern near the boat that was stuck to break up the ice around it. This method was effective but not always practical because of the potential to lose control of the bow.

A third method in use from the early days through the 1930s was spudding. Crew members went out on the ice and used spuds (long poles with a wide blade at one end) to create cracks in the ice. In some cases, they used ice saws to remove blocks of ice in an attempt to loosen the ice around the boat. Modern captains say that spudding could not have worked as the forces pressing against the boats were too great. One can easily see the merits of their view, particularly in situations involving boats under pressure from the ice, but, correct or not, the Ann Arbor used the method as late as 1940. Perhaps the best view is that of Arthur Frederickson, an Ann Arbor captain and the author of three excellent books on the company's history, who said, "Sometimes this worked, and others it was necessary to wait for a wind shift."

ONE ✻ The Beginning

November 24, 1892, dawned cloudy and cold with a light north wind as sixty-eight-year-old James M. Ashley, president of the Toledo, Ann Arbor and North Michigan Railway Company, boarded the *Ann Arbor Car Ferry No. 1* in Frankfort Harbor.[1] After conferring with the captain, he settled down for the five and a half hour voyage across Lake Michigan to Kewaunee, Wisconsin. The ship carried a cargo of four railcars filled with coal—the first loaded freight cars to cross the lake, ever. In doing so, Ashley culminated fifteen years of personal effort and initiated ninety years of cross-lake service by the company soon to be known as the Ann Arbor Railroad Company.

No one knows when Ashley first decided to build car ferries to cross Lake Michigan. It certainly wasn't in 1875, when he moved to Ann Arbor from Toledo. A prominent Ohio congressman during the Civil War, he had been defeated when the war was over and, after a disastrous stint as governor of the Montana Territory, moved to Toledo. He practiced law for a few years and then moved to Ann Arbor so his oldest son, James Jr., could attend law school and his next oldest son, Henry, could do undergraduate work at the University of Michigan.[2] Once he was an Ann Arbor resident, he recognized a long-standing civic problem: the city needed a second railroad. The city had been served by the Michigan Central since 1839, but residents were convinced that the railroad, with its monopoly on freight and passenger service, set its rates much too high. There had been attempts by Ann Arbor citizens to build a railroad to Toledo, but the endeavor was in limbo with a mostly graded roadbed but no track, no cars, and no engines.

With little money of his own and no experience in railroading, Ashley sensed a business opportunity and stepped in to fill the breach. He traveled to Pittsburgh to see an old friend, T. A. Scott, a former assistant secretary of war under Edwin Stanton in the Lincoln administration and president of the Pennsylvania Railroad. Scott told Ashley that he could buy rails and other materials on credit if he could find the funds to begin the operation. Ashley raised nearly $80,000 in pledges from the Toledo/Ann Arbor area, mortgaged his property in Toledo for $114,000, and went to Boston to seek money. He returned with enough to buy and complete construction of the Toledo and Ann Arbor Railroad. Within a year he had finished grading, laid track, and bought cars and engines.[3] On June 21, 1878, his first train rolled into Ann Arbor.[4]

Ashley made his railroad a family affair, installing his twenty-three-year-old son, James Jr., as vice president and his twenty-one-year-old son, Henry, as general manager. James and James Jr. were both big men. James was about six feet tall and quite heavy with white hair that reached down to his collar. He was powerfully built, an impressive speaker, and well suited for his role of raising money to build the railroad. Deeply religious, he believed that no one should work on the Sabbath, and while he was president he made sure that none of his trains ran on Sundays. James Jr. was even taller, about six feet four inches. He weighed 250 pounds and was very strong and quite willing to use his physical strength when other persuasive methods failed. He stuttered at times, but his physical presence and visible strong will marked him as a leader of men. Henry, two years younger, was less impressive but, ironically, remained with the railroad long after his father and brother were gone.[5]

With the railroad up and running, Ashley immediately began expanding to the north. He had something to offer—a connection to the East through Toledo—and that was a significant enticement to small towns without service. In fact, most towns throughout the Midwest were eager to have a railroad, believing rail service was essential to their survival. Roads were still "unimproved" and nearly impassable in wet weather. Even when conditions were good, travel was slow and the shipment of goods in volume impractical. Railroads were fast and comfortable and could accommodate goods in almost any quantity. Towns with rail service flourished while those that were bypassed often died.

After some false starts Ashley extended his railroad north and west,

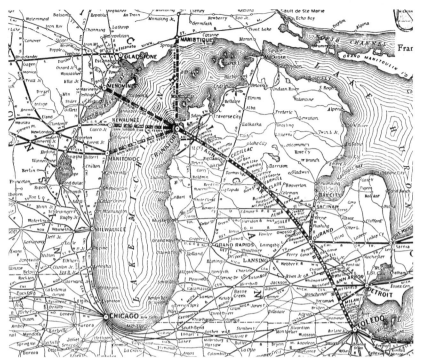

An early map of the Ann Arbor's route northwest from Toledo to Frankfort and across Lake Michigan. The Toledo, Ann Arbor and North Michigan began operations by shipping to Kewaunee, the port directly across the lake from Frankfort and the shortest route to Wisconsin.

partially through new construction and sometimes through buying existing trackage. Ashley placed James Jr. in charge of construction, and, though young, he rose to the occasion. James Jr. gained the trust of his men and became adept at extracting right-of-way agreements from small towns and farmers. When his negotiations failed, he usually went right on grading and laying track, willing to fight disputes in court.[6] In 1883 Ashley announced plans to extend the line to Mount Pleasant and mentioned a "proposed" route all the way to Frankfort. In 1884 he changed the name of the company to the Toledo, Ann Arbor and North Michigan Railway Company, and in 1887 his railroad reached Cadillac. In 1889 he expanded to Copemish, a little over twenty miles from Frankfort and the Lake Michigan shore.[7]

Ashley was constantly short of money. With almost no resources of his own, he bargained for free right-of-way agreements where he could, secured local aid from villages and counties, and sold mortgage bonds, intending to pay the interest with the profits of the railroad.[8] He counted on James Jr. to secure right-of-way agreements, and his son did not disappoint him. Both men were well known and highly respected in Michigan—and in New York City, where financial institutions were most interested in the development of railroads across the country. Railroads provided access to new markets and were considered vital to the growth of the country—not to mention that the men who controlled them could make a great deal of money.[9]

In 1890 the Ashleys hired a new chief engineer, a young man by the name of Henry E. Riggs. Riggs came to the company with about four years' experience with the Burlington and Santa Fe systems and a fertile mind. Given a complete tour of the line, he was appalled at the quality of construction. To Riggs, the railroad resembled many of the logging railroads in use at the time—one-track, built with lightweight rails, not well ballasted, and not well graded.[10] Most logging railroads were not meant to last. After the land was cut bare the roads were torn up or simply abandoned. That was not the expectation for the Toledo, Ann Arbor and North Michigan. At the end of his tour the kindest thing he could say was that all but one of the bridges were safe.[11]

Riggs only stayed with the company for a few years, but while he was there he had an impact. At the time he was hired the company had twelve to fifteen lawsuits pending, mostly brought by contractors who claimed that the work had been underbid or they had been underpaid. Riggs was told by Henry Ashley that he had only one responsibility—to dispose of those claims. Ashley had hired a Cadillac lawyer, Eugene F. Sawyer, who he described as "a small town lawyer," to handle the cases. The first case involved Mr. J. Fuery, a contractor who had graded two miles of roadbed south of Cadillac. He claimed "a) gross underestimate [of cost by the company engineer]; b) only partial payment of the engineer's estimate."[12]

Mr. Sawyer believed that the best way to win cases was through thorough preparation. He and Riggs decided to find all the pertinent information concerning the estimate and contract and to make another estimate based on the information they developed. After several months of work digging out files from boxes that had been sent to Toledo for storage, they found all of the original estimates, vouchers, and correspondence. When they completed their own estimate, they were within 3 percent of the original. They located the contractors who had worked on each side of the roadbed Fuery had graded and found that they were fully satisfied with their treatment by the Toledo, Ann Arbor and North Michigan. They also unearthed a letter from Mr. Fuery acknowledging the final payment and thanking the company for its courteous treatment. When the case went to court, a jury of twelve farmers delivered a verdict of "no cause for action" after thirty minutes of deliberation. All other cases against the railroad were dismissed.[13]

While Ashley was building his railroad to Copemish in 1889, a group of Frankfort businessmen, in an effort to promote the use of Frankfort Harbor, were building the Frankfort and South Eastern Railroad from Frankfort to Copemish. While there is no written record, it is probable that they had hopes of connecting with Ashley's railroad or allowing Ashley to purchase theirs.[14] When it was completed, the lines did connect, and it is likely that soon thereafter Ashley began negotiations to acquire the Frankfort and South Eastern because the following year (1890) he made plans for the construction of two car ferries.[15] On May 15, 1892, he took possession of the Frankfort and South Eastern and soon began laying track through South Frankfort, now Elberta, to a point near the harbor entrance where he would dock the car ferries.[16]

In 1890 Frankfort was a small lumber town with 1,175 residents. It was located on the shore of Lake Michigan, with an unusually good natural harbor, and its economy was made up of five lumber mills and an ironworks. The resort and fruit industries that would later drive the economy had yet to arrive. Frankfort has little recorded history before the mid-1800s, though it is now believed by many that the French missionary Father Jacques Marquette died at the harbor entrance in 1675. Frankfort Harbor was "discovered" by one Captain Snow in the fall of 1854 when he found himself on Lake Michigan in a November gale with some bleak choices. He could either beach his schooner, which would undoubtedly destroy it but perhaps save his life and those of his crew, or he could stay in the lake and take his chances with the storm. He decided to beach the ship, but as he approached the shore he saw a depression in the bluffs and headed for it. Before he knew what had happened he was inside the harbor. He spent the winter there and in the spring told the vessel's owner, who lived in Buffalo, New York, about the remarkably protected harbor on the Michigan shore.[17] Before long the area was surveyed, settlers arrived, and a town was born.

In the spring, summer, and fall, Frankfort was connected to the outside world by lake boats, mostly sail, which carried lumber to the major

t Pass. Train in Benzie Co. July 4 1889

A Frankfort and South Eastern train in 1889. *(Photo courtesy of Roger Griner.)*

cities and brought supplies in return. In the winter the town was largely cut off, though in the 1870s and 1880s there was stagecoach service to Traverse City, forty miles north and east. Travel by stage was unreliable due to the poor roads, which in wet weather were hardly passable, but if a traveler was willing to endure the trip he or she could board a train in Traverse City that would connect to Chicago or Detroit. The completion of the Frankfort and South Eastern Railroad in 1889 gave Frankfort its first railroad, which ran to Copemish where it connected with the Toledo, Ann Arbor and North Michigan. A traveler could walk or hire a horse and carriage to cross the few miles from the station in Copemish to Thompsonville, where he or she could board a train to Chicago.

In the early 1890s the Great Lakes were crowded with commercial vessels, more than would ever ply the lakes again. In 1892 some 2,926 vessels operated on the lakes. Steam had overtaken sail as the preferred means of propulsion, though there were still 1,226 sailing craft in operation.[18] Manufactured goods from East Coast cities reached Chicago and the West by rail, but commodities normally shipped in bulk, such as grain, ore, and lumber, were transported by water. Chicago, after the great fire of 1871, was rebuilt with lumber shipped from ports that lined the shores of Lake Michigan. The Great Lakes were heavily trafficked

An early picture of Frankfort Harbor taken from the South Frankfort (later Elberta) side before 1890. The depression to the right of the tree-covered hill on the left side of the picture marks the original channel where Captain Snow entered the harbor in 1854. *(Photo courtesy of Roger Griner.)*

with commerce, but navigation on them was dangerous and no one had attempted anything close to what Ashley had in mind.

Ashley's plan was to establish a rail and water transportation route from the east to the northwest (Minneapolis/Saint Paul). His route would take days off the time needed to ship goods through Chicago and would reduce the potential for damage. Railcars were handled roughly in the Chicago yards, and damage was common. Tonnage was already being shipped across Lake Michigan by a method known as break-bulk, but it was expensive. Trains ran to ports such as Grand Haven and Ludington where the cars were unloaded. The cargo was then reloaded aboard a boat, shipped across the lake, off-loaded, loaded onto new cars, and sent on its way. By shipping fully loaded cars across the lake without touching the cargo inside, Ashley could reduce the loading and unloading cost of six to twelve dollars a ton to about two dollars a ton.[19] If he could pull it off, he could make a handsome profit.

But pulling it off involved some daunting business and technical challenges. The major business challenge (other than finding the money to build the ships) was to find a trading partner on the Wisconsin side of Lake Michigan with whom he could develop east-west traffic. While Ashley was bargaining for control of the Frankfort and South Eastern Railroad to gain access to Lake Michigan, the Kewaunee, Green Bay and Western Railroad was being completed to Kewaunee, linking the Wisconsin port with a generous portion of the Midwest grain belt (all the way to Omaha).[20]

Almost directly across the lake from Frankfort, Kewaunee was a lumber town with a population of 1,251 in 1890 and a deepwater harbor at the mouth of the Kewaunee River, which was navigable up to six miles inland. A major settlement of the Potawatomi Indians for six hundred years, Kewaunee was first visited by the French explorer Jean Nicolet in 1634. Father Marquette said a mass there on November 1, 1674. The area's later history began in 1836 when an unknown explorer discovered what he thought was gold near the mouth of the river. Elaborate plans were laid for a city intended to rival Chicago with plots (even in the middle of a swamp) selling for five hundred to a thousand dollars. The bubble soon burst when no gold was found, but settlement began in the years following and by the early 1890s Kewaunee was a lumber port with eight hundred vessels entering and leaving each year.[21] Like Frankfort, Kewaunee did not have a railroad until late in the century (1891), but as early as 1862 residents could reach the outside world by traveling twenty-nine miles to Green Bay and catching a Chicago and North Western train to Chicago or Milwaukee.

The Kewaunee, Green Bay and Western Railroad began shipping grain across the lake via break-bulk steamers operated by the Flint and Pere Marquette Railroad to Ludington, Michigan, bound for destinations in the East and abroad, but the service was dropped due to a railroad war involving Vanderbilt interests. The Kewaunee, Green Bay and Western route east required shipping grain across the lake on a Flint and Pere Marquette steamer to Ludington; by rail via the Flint and Pere Marquette to Port Huron, Michigan; across Canada to Buffalo on the Grand Trunk Railway; and to New York City on the Delaware, Lackawanna and Western Railroad. The Delaware, Lackawanna and Western was a competitor of Vanderbilt's. The Flint and Pere Marquette was allied with the Vanderbilt interests and did not want to funnel any business to a competitor, so it stopped sending steamers to Kewaunee. Thus, the time was right for Ashley. He crafted a route to the East Coast that included his car ferries across the lake; the Toledo, Ann Arbor and North Michigan; and the Delaware, Lackawanna and Western.[22]

With the new route in place, the Kewaunee, Green Bay and Western did not wait for Ashley to build his car ferries. The company chartered the 183-foot wooden break-bulk steamer *Osceola*, which began crossing the lake in mid-January 1892. That the ship was not up to the task be-

Kewaunee Harbor saw about eight hundred vessels enter and leave each year before the Toledo, Ann Arbor and North Michigan began service in 1892. *(Photo courtesy of the Kewaunee County Historical Society.)*

came apparent within a few weeks as she suffered one mishap after another. On January 27 she missed Kewaunee and wound up in Ahnapee ten miles to the north. On her next trip she encountered a winter gale that drove her off course toward the Sturgeon Bay Ship Canal where she ran aground. After she was pulled off, she was found to be leaking. She returned to Frankfort where, while tied to the dock, she took a severe pounding in a high wind and an engineer, W. P. MacDonald, was scalded to death when a steam pipe burst.

In February a northwest gale forced the *Osceola* north of Kewaunee again. She made three attempts to enter the shelter of the Sturgeon Bay Ship Canal but struck a pier head instead. A fire broke out, adding to the vessel's woes. A day later the weather moderated and the ship found her way to Kewaunee. During her first four weeks of service she completed only three trips across the lake due to winter storms. In the spring the Kewaunee, Green Bay and Western hired the *City of Marquette,* a wooden steamer about one-third the tonnage of the *Osceola.* It was agreed that the Toledo, Ann Arbor and North Michigan would share the cost (and risk) of her operation. She was a new vessel and amassed a much better record than the *Osceola,* but her value was limited due to her small size

The package (break-bulk) steamer *Osceola* suffered greatly in storms during the winter of 1892. *(Photo from the A. C. Frederickson Collection.)*

and the necessity of loading and unloading the contents of freight cars for each crossing.[23]

Knowledgeable people in the shipping industry felt that the technical challenges of crossing the open water of Lake Michigan with fully loaded freight cars could not be met. First, there was the problem of seaworthiness. Car ferries had operated for nearly forty years across rivers at Detroit and Buffalo and more recently at the Straits of Mackinac—all sheltered waters. Most car ferries in operation at the time had little freeboard (distance from the waterline to the first exposed deck) and were loaded at the bow, two factors that would render them unsafe for cross-lake service. The gales of November often produced waves nine to fourteen feet high—ample to swamp and sink the boats—and some storms produced waves much higher. The railcars would have to be carried above the waterline, raising concerns about the stability of the vessels. Another major concern was how to secure the cars so they would not roll back and forth (and perhaps right off the boat) or tip on their sides when the boat began to pitch and roll in the large waves that would build with a strong wind. That was a problem that had to be solved. Otherwise, the boats would be unsafe to operate in anything but the mildest weather.

A typical river car ferry. Note the low freeboard and open sides. *(Photo courtesy of the Historical Collections of the Great Lakes, Bowling Green State University.)*

Then there was the problem of ice. Ashley knew his boats would have to cross the lake year-round if his route was to be considered legitimate. That meant operating in ice, particularly on the eastern side of the lake. His biggest concern would be keeping Frankfort Harbor open in the winter months. While the western shore of Lake Michigan was consistently colder, the prevailing winds were from the northwest, pushing the ice across the lake and against the Michigan shore. He saw a danger that the harbor might fill with ice and lock his boats out for the winter. While that never happened, there were times when the entrance filled with ice to the bottom and it was very difficult for the car ferries to get in and out.

Ashley attacked his problems by hiring a well-known naval architect, Frank E. Kirby, who had had success in 1888 with the design of the *St. Ignace,* an ice-breaking car ferry that operated at the Straits of Mackinac. The *St. Ignace* was unique in that she had a bow propeller, an innovation Kirby worked out with L. R. Boynton, a renowned captain famous for his ice-breaking abilities. The idea was to suck water from under the ice, making it easier to break up. Also, the propeller could be used to direct a powerful stream of water toward ice that extended many feet below the surface, helping to break it up. The boat was designed to rise in the water as ice pressed against her sides, preventing her from being crushed. She was given trim tanks, which allowed her to rock from side to side when needed to break up ice on either side. The innovations worked,

The narrow entrance to Frankfort Harbor could easily fill with ice in a strong westerly wind. *(Photo from the A. C. Frederickson Collection.)*

and the *St. Ignace* was a very good icebreaker.[24] A few years later officials from the Russian navy visited the Straits to observe the *St. Ignace* and her successor, the *Sainte Marie*. They were so impressed that they contracted for a vessel based on the design of the *Sainte Marie* to be built in England, dismantled, and shipped to Siberia where it was reassembled and put into use.[25]

Kirby designed two car ferries for Ashley, the *Ann Arbor No. 1* and *No. 2*, to be built in 1892. Nearly identical, the boats were heavily constructed of wood using five-inch oak for the outside planking at the bow. The bottom was sheathed in steel to 4 feet above and below the waterline for protection from the ice.[26] The *No. 1* was 260 feet long with 53 feet of beam. The *No. 2* was 4 feet longer. Both were powered with three horizontal compound steam engines developing 610 horsepower each. The boats had two propellers aft to facilitate docking and one forward for use in ice breaking, making them the first triple-screw ships in the United States.[27] Both boats originally had two stacks, one aft for the two engines powering the propellers at the stern, the other forward for the engine powering the bow propeller.

Kirby solved the basic seaworthiness problem by enclosing the bow and sides, but left the stern open for loading. His design was much bet-

Ann Arbor No. 1 tied up in South Frankfort in the early 1890s. Note the two stacks, the rectangular windows, and the swept back bow for ice breaking. The ship is tied up alongside the dock. The apron for loading and unloading is opposite the stern. *(Photo from the A. C. Frederickson Collection.)*

ter than that of the earlier car ferries, which loaded at the bow, but it still left an Achilles' heel that could be dangerous in a storm. A following sea could roll across the car deck and, in time, sink the boat. The Toledo, Ann Arbor and North Michigan countered the concerns of its captains by telling them to keep the boats headed into the wind during a storm, but that was not always possible—and not always sufficient.[28]

Whether through innovative design or overstatement in the first place, the stability problem did not materialize. Both boats were quite stable when loaded and able to ride out heavy storms. The Toledo, Ann Arbor and North Michigan developed a novel way to secure cars through the use of extra rails, jacks, turnbuckles, and sometimes chains. While not infallible, the system in large measure solved the problem of securing cars and allowed for different levels of security depending on the weather. The method was described in the first issue of *Marine Engineering* in 1897 and was adopted by all of the Ann Arbor's competitors as they began cross-lake service.

Both car ferries were built to be icebreakers. The bows were designed to slant sharply aft a few feet above the waterline so that the boats could ride up on the ice and use their weight to crush it. The idea was successful and was incorporated in all later Ann Arbor boats with the exception

Ann Arbor No. 2 from the stern. Note the height of the man and his closeness to the water. Ann Arbor captains had good reason to be concerned about their vessels' safety in a following sea. *(Photo courtesy of the Benzie Area Historical Museum.)*

Ann Arbor No. 1 at the slip in South Frankfort. *(Photo from the A. C. Frederickson Collection.)*

of the *Ann Arbor No. 6,* which was already under construction when the railroad decided to buy her. Over fifty years later, the Coast Guard embodied the same principle in the design of the cutter *Mackinaw* in 1944.[29] To address the problem of the harbor filling with ice while the car ferries were across the lake, the company purchased a small tug, the *G. B. Doane,* whose job was to move around inside the harbor and keep the ice broken up.[30]

The wood construction of the *No. 1* and *No. 2* was in some ways an advantage (though not from the standpoint of longevity) because the boats were very limber, able to give when stressed and withstand greater shocks than similar, steel-hulled boats. That was important because during the first several years the boats suffered a number of groundings and occasionally hit the piers while entering Frankfort Harbor due to the shallow channel. The wooden boats escaped relatively damage free whereas more brittle, steel-hulled boats could have sustained serious damage.[31]

Each boat was built to hold twenty-four railcars and had an electric arc searchlight along with a limited electric light system—a luxury the city of Frankfort would not enjoy for another year. Unlike later boats, the crew slept in cabins on the main deck. The deckhouses and sides were constructed with rectangular windows rather than portholes. Construction of the *No. 1* began at the Craig Shipbuilding Company in Toledo on June 10, 1892, and the ship was launched on September 29 of the same year. She arrived in Frankfort on November 16 ready for her historic trip across the lake to Kewaunee on November 24.[32]

TWO ✳ *The Testing*

As the *Ann Arbor No. 1* neared the Wisconsin shore on her first trip across the lake, she found herself in a heavy fog and, due to the poor visibility, ran aground north of the harbor. Realizing the potential for a public relations disaster, Ashley acted quickly, sending a message ashore via nearby fish tugs to telegraph all available tugs for help. Captain Martin Swain from Cheboygan, Michigan, arrived in two days with the tug *Favorite*. At first he had difficulty getting near the *No. 1* because of the other boats around her, but soon he was able to pull her off the bottom. Several vessels had shown up to help, but none was large enough to have much effect on the 260-foot ship.[1]

Despite her inauspicious introduction to the Wisconsin shore, the *No. 1* entered Kewaunee where she made a solid impression on the local populace. The following day's headline in the *Kewaunee Enterprise* read:

THE ANN ARBOR NO. 1
The Monster Ferry Boat in Which Freight Trains Will Be
Transported Across Old Lake Michigan.[2]

On the return trip, the *No. 1* carried twenty-two railcars of flour from the Pillsbury Mills in Minneapolis bound for England. Thus began a trend that would prevail throughout the next ninety years—relatively full eastbound cargoes and less full westbound shipments due to the difficulty of securing westbound traffic from carriers at Toledo.

Later it was said that the *No. 1* ran aground because she was faster than the crew expected and therefore was farther across the lake than they thought. Captain Edward "Tim" Kelly said that they had made about ten miles per hour on the trip from the builder to Frankfort but, as the machinery broke itself in the ship must have picked up speed. The explanation made sense but lost a little of its legitimacy when the *No. 1* ran aground again on her second trip to Kewaunee![3] Captain Kelly and the crew probably did require some time to adjust to the new vessel, but it is also likely that they made some mistakes.

In Captain Kelly's defense, captains in the 1890s did not have the benefit of the navigational aids of today. There was no Loran, no direction finder, no ship-to-shore phone, no radar, no global positioning system (GPS). A captain left port with less than reliable charts, a magnetic compass, a lead line, and a log line with which to measure his speed. Magnetic compasses were subject to error due to the presence of iron on the ships. A lead line was useful but only in relatively quiet circumstances. A captain couldn't send a man forward with a lead line to measure the depth of the water in a howling gale, even though he might badly need the information. A cone-shaped log, trailed behind the ship and built with a rotator that turned as it passed through the water, recorded the rotations on dials that converted them into distance and speed. Logs were a tremendous help to captains but were far from precise, as they were subject to error due to wind, wave, and current—and of course they measured speed and distance through the water, not over the bottom.[4]

Navigation on the Great Lakes was (and still can be) dangerous. In 1893, the first full year of Toledo, Ann Arbor and North Michigan operation, 325 vessels (about 11 percent of all ships operating on the Great Lakes that year) were wrecked and 102 sailors and passengers lost their lives.[5] The numbers are even more telling when one considers that the overwhelming majority of vessels operated only eight months a year, laying up in late November and starting up again some time in April, depending on the weather. Ashley fully intended his boats to operate nonstop, year-round, and he had done his best to construct boats that were up to the task. He knew his boats had to be very good icebreakers, as well as seaworthy, but he could not have imagined how quickly they would be tested.

The winter of 1892–93 was one of the coldest of all time on the Great Lakes.[6] Only four winters were colder in the next century. The testing began on December 8 when the *Ann Arbor No. 1* left Kewaunee for Frankfort. There had been a storm on the lake, and, though the wind was down, the seas were still high. By the time the *No. 1* was about ten miles out she began rolling so badly that Captain Kelly turned around and went back to Kewaunee, departing the next day.[7] Exactly why he turned around is not known. Captains knew how to deal with the large seas that built over the length of the lake with a north or south wind. Instead of heading straight across the lake and putting their ships in the trough of the waves, they headed into the seas, quartering the waves until they could turn and run downwind to their destination (in this case, Frankfort). Captain Kelly was presumably an experienced captain aware of his options—so he must have had a reason for turning back. Possibly he did not trust the gear to hold the cars in place, perhaps he was uncomfortable with the thought of running downwind with an open stern, or perhaps he simply thought he could not get into the two-hundred-foot-wide harbor entrance at Frankfort in the high seas. Given that he had only two weeks' experience crossing the lake with the *No. 1* and had no example to follow, one can understand how he might not have wanted to assume the risk of three potential threats, any one of which could sink his ship.

At 3:00 pm on December 24, 1892, Ashley's second car ferry, the *Ann Arbor No. 2*, left the Craig Shipyard in Toledo, beginning what would become a tradition among Ann Arbor boats—completion of construction late in the year and a difficult passage to Frankfort. Under the command of Frank A. Dority, who had given up his command of the *Osceola*, the *No. 2* plowed through five inches of sheet ice across Lake St. Clair, loosening some of the steel plates that were meant to protect her from the ice. After stopping at a shipyard in Port Huron for repairs, she started up Lake Huron toward Frankfort. Three times she was forced to anchor due to bad weather before reaching Frankfort on New Year's Eve.[8]

At 11:00 a.m. on New Year's Day, 1893, the *No. 1* left Frankfort and started across the lake to Kewaunee. She soon ran into heavy snow and a strong westerly wind, which increased to gale force as the day went on. About 7:00 p.m. the ship reached the Wisconsin shore near Ahnapee, about ten miles north of Kewaunee. Captain Kelly turned south along the shore toward Kewaunee, but the snow, driven by the high wind, was so heavy that he could not find the harbor. After several tries, he gave up and continued south. By the next morning he was near Sheboygan, over fifty miles south of Kewaunee. When the storm finally moderated, he steamed north and entered Kewaunee Harbor. He told newspaper reporters the wind was so strong that no one dared go out on deck for fear

Ann Arbor No. 1 and *No. 2* at the Frankfort Harbor entrance. In an effort to keep the harbor entrance from filling with ice, the Toledo, Ann Arbor and North Michigan tried to have a boat enter and leave the harbor as often as possible in the winter months. *(Photo from the A. C. Frederickson Collection.)*

of being swept overboard. The boat had rolled unmercifully, but the six cars of coal onboard arrived intact—a convincing affirmation that the system of securing cars worked under extreme conditions.[9]

On the night of January 8, gale force winds from the northwest began shoving slush ice into the entrance of Frankfort Harbor. More and more ice was pushed into the narrow opening as the night wore on. The powerful winds continued the following day, and the temperature dropped to single digits. Snow fell all day and the surface froze solid with slush ice extending all the way to the bottom. A day later (January 10) the wind moderated but the snow and very cold air continued. Captain Dority arrived from Kewaunee with the *No. 2* and tried to force his way between the piers, but he soon became stuck. In her brief period of operation since late November, the *G. B. Doane* had already shown that she was not up to the job of keeping the harbor ice broken up, so the Toledo, Ann Arbor and North Michigan had chartered the tug *Saugatuck* for the work. Early the following morning (January 11) the *No. 1* arrived and began working to break open a channel with the help of the *Saugatuck* and the *City of Marquette*, the break-bulk steamer hired by the Kewaunee, Green Bay and Western in the spring of 1892. The three vessels broke a channel, and both car ferries were at the dock by early afternoon. They had fought their first battle with ice and won.[10]

Less than two weeks after his stormy trip to Kewaunee, Captain Kelly found that the Wisconsin port was not always accessible even when it was within sight. On January 12, the *Ann Arbor No. 1* left Frankfort for Kewaunee in the aftermath of a strong south wind with heavy swells that had built all the way from Chicago, but by the time she approached the Wisconsin shore the wind had switched to the north-northeast and was blowing hard with snow. The Kewaunee Harbor entrance was fully exposed to the waves, making it foolhardy to attempt entry. Captain Kelly knew he could not make the harbor and turned south toward Manitowoc, which was protected by Two Rivers Point. The boat took a beating in the cross-chop, but she reached Manitowoc safely, entered the harbor, and waited out the storm. Some of the crew members were so shaken by the trip that they left the ship and did not return. The *No. 1* was three days getting to Kewaunee.[11]

Despite the storms, ice, aborted trips, and missed harbors, the *Ann Arbor No. 1* and *No. 2* were enjoying success. The two car ferries transported six hundred railcars across the lake in the first twenty days of the new year.[12] Also, they were attracting attention. The *New York Times* ran an article in which it stated that the car ferries would make excellent warships should the need arise. The article further explained that the very strong decks and sides of the vessels meant that the navy could mount guns on them without additional strengthening. Oddly, the article mentioned that such an armed vessel "can justly be expected to silence any craft the British are able to send through the Welland or St. Lawrence River canals."[13] Ashley's car ferries were dissected in articles published in several European countries. A Liverpool newspaper said that if the boats proved successful soon there would be full trains sent across the Atlantic and Ashley would be known as the Christopher Columbus of the nineteenth century.[14]

The winter became increasingly cold, but the boats held their own. Storms were a threat. One week in February the *No. 1* made only a single trip and the *No. 2* only three due to bad weather. By February 10, ice covered forty-two of the sixty-two miles across Lake Michigan. Also in February it became apparent that the *No. 2* required additional steel plating

Ann Arbor No. 2 leaving Frankfort Harbor in 1894. *(Photo from the A. C. Frederickson Collection.)*

to protect her sides and bow. The original plating did not extend far enough above the waterline to protect the wood planking from the ice. The boats were proving to be good icebreakers and were successfully getting in and out of Frankfort Harbor in what everyone knew was a very cold winter. The February 3 edition of the *Kewaunee Enterprise* reported that the *No. 2* had crossed the lake through "a field of blue ice which was ten miles wide and about fifteen inches thick" at a rate of four miles per hour—an impressive demonstration of the boat's ability to perform under difficult conditions.[15]

In March the same newspaper reported that a load of freight cars containing flour had reached New York from Minneapolis in five days via the Toledo, Ann Arbor and North Michigan. Later in the month the *No. 2* set a record for crossing the lake, leaving Kewaunee at 5:00 a.m., crossing to Frankfort, unloading and reloading in fifty-five minutes, and arriving back in Kewaunee at 5:10 p.m. The paper pointed out that the boats running from Milwaukee to Muskegon took eight hours one way *in the summer.*[16] The paper also reported that the Toledo, Ann Arbor and North Michigan boats were making another impression on Kewaunee

Harbor, one that no one foresaw or intended—the propellers were killing fish. Each time the boats turned around in the harbor and docked, quantities of dead fish rose to the surface. They didn't stay there long because seagulls quickly arrived for the unexpected feast.[17]

In the spring and summer both the *No. 1* and *No. 2* went to a Milwaukee shipyard for extensive strengthening. Although they had successfully operated throughout the winter, it was obvious that they needed extra hull strength to fight the ice, especially since, though the winter had been very cold, ice conditions were not as bad as they might be another year. For several months the Toledo, Ann Arbor and North Michigan operated with just one boat while the other was being strengthened.[18]

With the *No. 1* and *No. 2* successfully ferrying railcars across the lake, James Ashley was planning for the future. Early in 1893 articles appeared that described his plans to build two car ferries to operate between Buffalo and Toledo, each to carry forty-eight railcars.[19] The company announced that it would begin service to Menominee, mostly to transport iron ore from the Upper Peninsula of Michigan to steel mills in Ohio.[20] There was also talk of two more car ferries to service Kewaunee, but Ashley's good fortune was coming to an end. Three events conspired to hurt him badly: the economic downturn that resulted in the panic of 1893, the line's first strike, and a precipitous drop in the company's stock. On April 26, John Craig, owner of the company that built the *Ann Arbor No. 1* and *No. 2*, brought a bill of complaint against the Toledo, Ann Arbor and North Michigan to the U.S. Circuit Court of the Northern District of Ohio, Western Division, stating that the company owed $135,000 in payment for the ships and was not keeping up with the payment schedule. He further stated that the company could not make interest payments on its secured bonds and that it carried about $1,000,000 in unsecured debt for which it did not have funds.[21] By April 28, 1893, the company was in receivership and both James and his oldest son, James Jr., were on their way out.[22]

The court placed the company in the receivership of Wellington R. Burt, a wealthy lumberman from Saginaw, Michigan, and a member of the Toledo, Ann Arbor and North Michigan Board of Directors.[23] The only remaining Ashley in the company was Henry, James's second-oldest son, who had married Burt's daughter. Henry had been general manager under his father and retained that position. Gone were the plans for additional car ferries, but Burt followed through on the promise to pro-

vide service to Menominee. The company was reorganized into the Ann
Arbor Railroad Company in 1895 but remained in receivership until July
1897. Burt turned out to be a very good influence on the company. A
self-made, astute businessman, he put the company on a more sound
financial footing and brought about improvements in track, bridges, and
roadbed that lifted the railroad from near "logging railroad" quality into
legitimacy.[24]

In the first year of their existence, Toledo, Ann Arbor and North
Michigan car ferries established a pattern of carrying flour east and coal
west. Navigation was an adventure. Most harbor entrances on the lakes
were too narrow, too shallow, and inadequately marked, making them
nearly impossible to enter in a storm and difficult even in good conditions. Frankfort and Kewaunee were no exceptions. While there were
many dedicated people working to keep navigational aids (lights and
bells) operating, they were not always as reliable or as powerful as they
would become later. Captain Alexander Larson, who began working on
the boats as a deckhand, rose to the rank of captain, and enjoyed a forty-
seven-year career with the Ann Arbor, described early conditions in a letter to the company on his retirement.

> There was no fog whistle on the piers at that time [1894]. A big bell
> was located on the south pier which was rung by the light keeper, pro-
> viding that gentleman was in good condition to get out and do it. I am
> reminded of an entry once made in a dense fog by Captain Dority
> (Steamer No. 1). When unable to locate the piers, he had a boat
> (lifeboat) lowered with three men and sent them in to locate the en-
> trance. For a signaling device they were given a large bread pan and a
> wooden mallet. Finding the piers, they beat upon the bread pan and
> the vessel was guided in safely. After landing in the slip, we found that
> everyone connected with the railroad had gone home, as the agent,
> Mr. L. E. Vorce, had advised that the No. 1 could not get in and that
> it was useless to remain there.[25]

Not all improvised piloting techniques worked exactly as planned. In
1903, Captain Rydt was bringing the *Ann Arbor No. 3* into Manistique in
Michigan's Upper Peninsula, a difficult entry, even under good conditions, because there were rocks on either side of the channel.[26] There
was a heavy fog, and, after finding the general location of the harbor
through the use of a lead line, he sent a few men aboard a lifeboat to find

The light and bell at the south pier of Frankfort Harbor. It is easy to see how the light keeper might have found it difficult to ring the bell at times. *(Photo from the A. C. Frederickson Collection.)*

the harbor entrance and signal back to the ship. The men rowed in and began yelling that they had found the breakwater, but about the same time the locomotive that was used to load and unload the ship began blowing its whistle. The captain took a bearing on the whistle and made his way to where the harbor entrance should have been. Before he knew it, he had run onto the beach south of the harbor. It turned out that the engine was not in its usual place at the end of the track near the mouth of the river, where it would normally be positioned to load and unload; instead it was much farther back on the track. The railroad men did not realize how much the captain would rely on the exact position of the locomotive. After about twelve hours, Captain Rydt got the *No. 3* off the beach without damage. The *Door County Advocate* stated shortly thereafter, "Manistique is one of the worst places on the lakes to get in and out of even in clear weather, say nothing of when it is thick. This port should have a fog signal station."[27]

As the two car ferries continued to cross the lake, problems began to surface. There was not enough clearance between the car deck and the cabin deck on the boats, with the result that some damage was done to cars while loading and unloading. The sides near the stern pinched too far in with a similar result. To solve the problem, the railroad cut back

Ann Arbor No. 1 and *No. 2* in ice off the Michigan shore in the mid-1890s. Note that the deck of the *No. 1* has been cut away near the stern. *(Photo from the A. C. Frederickson Collection.)*

the cabin deck by fifty feet, leaving that part of the car deck exposed to the elements. At first it left an elevated walkway from the cabin deck to the stern so the captain could walk to the stern to direct docking. Later that was removed, so captains found themselves standing on the tops of freight cars with a line in each hand to signal the operation of the ship's engines.[28] Far from an ideal arrangement in any weather, docking could be particularly challenging on nights when there was heavy rain, sleet, or snow or the temperature fell below zero, as it often did on the Wisconsin side of the lake in winter.

Another significant problem was posed by the entrance to Frankfort Harbor. There were two piers, two hundred feet apart, which extended about a thousand feet into Lake Michigan. The channel was approximately fourteen feet deep, which was nearly identical to the draft of the ships when fully loaded. Worse, there was usually a sandbar at the entrance between the piers. At times, the boats had to "dredge" their way out, plowing into the bottom, backing off, and then plowing into it again until they cleared the harbor entrance. Captain Larson described an early trip.

My first departure from Frankfort through its present harbor was in November, 1894. I was then privileged to be one of the three deckhands of the crew of the Ann Arbor No. 1, which was the first carferry to cross Lake Michigan. A deckhand then received the munificent salary of $15 per month. Any young man who could obtain a job of that caliber and salary considered himself most fortunate as I did.

We left the slip late of an evening with a cargo of eight cars on board for Kewaunee. A fresh south wind and moderate sea prevailed at the time. We were three hours in reaching deep water, due to the fact that a sand bar formation extended across the pier entrance. We kept plugging away. Each time the vessel rose with an incoming swell or wave, we would gain a few feet, finally getting over the bar into the lake.

Once outside, the course was set for Kewaunee, but after a short run the wind and sea increased to such force, it was necessary to square away and run to the shelter of the Manitou Islands, where we remained for two days. A total of five days was consumed in making the round trip. Apparently no one seemed to know where we were. I do remember that on arrival at Frankfort, that I saw Supt. W. F. Bradley shake hands with the captain and heard him remark, he was glad to see us back again.

Fortunately, we had no schedule to contend with. It seems we had more time than money in those days.[29]

Getting into the harbor in a strong west or southwest wind could be nearly impossible because the waves accentuated the problem of the shallow water. A wave could drive a boat into the bottom, causing it to lose headway and control; then a second wave would slam it against the north pier. There were times when the boats laid off the harbor entrance or remained on the Wisconsin side of the lake for hours, and even days, waiting for the waves to lessen. Fortunately, the heavy wood construction of the boats was an advantage. They were strong and limber enough to flex and bend when they accidentally hit one of the piers, whereas a ship constructed of steel might have sustained severe damage. It was said that they often did more damage to the piers than they absorbed themselves. Again, Captain Larson tells us:

I recall an occasion when, attempting to make the Frankfort piers with Steamer No. 1, we struck the bottom and got hung up crossways on the north pier. The wind and sea was southwest and the port side of the ship was pounding severely on the corner of the pier.

Sailing ships were still much in evidence in the late 1890s as the *No. 1* steamed toward Frankfort. *(Photo from the A. C. Frederickson Collection.)*

We remained in that position for ten hours, and it was thought by all on board that the vessel was badly damaged, that holes had penetrated the ship's side. After reaching the slip, an examination was made. We were amazed to find that only a small portion of planking had been damaged and that some of the black paint had rubbed off. However, fifty feet of the end of the pier was damaged, but no report of such minor damage was reportable in those days. Later when the inspector from the U.S. Engineering Office came around, after discovering the damage, and inquiring as to which carferry had caused it, no one could recall a carferry being near the damage in question.

I recall suggesting to Captain Dority that perhaps some windjammer (sailing schooner) had caused it, and such was the final disposition of the matter.[30]

In 1893, the Toledo, Ann Arbor and North Michigan tried to solve the problem of running aground in the harbor channel by laying pipes to the ends of the piers and pumping oil into the lake—an undertaking approved by the government and watched closely by other shipping companies on the Great Lakes. The thought was that the oil on the surface of the water would calm the waves, which it did—but it also increased the distance from peak to trough, creating a greater probability of a boat's hitting the bottom. That, and the fact that the pumps continually became clogged with sand, persuaded the Toledo, Ann Arbor and North Michigan to abandon the practice soon after it began.

In 1894 the bow propellers and forward engines were removed from the two boats. The propellers were said to have been ineffective, possibly due to the beating they took when the boats dredged their way out of Frankfort Harbor and perhaps because they had not yet encountered the type of ice against which the propellers would be most effective. The removal of the propellers speeded up the boats by one mile per hour to fourteen miles per hour, a 7 percent increase.

In the same year, the Toledo, Ann Arbor and North Michigan began service to Menominee, in the Upper Peninsula, via the Sturgeon Bay Ship Canal with a stop in Sturgeon Bay for passengers. Ships ran three times a week to both Menominee and Kewaunee. In the summer of 1895, the newly formed Ann Arbor Railroad Company added a fourth trip to Menominee and began service to Gladstone, nightly from Frankfort, stopping in Escanaba for passengers. In July 1896 the Wisconsin Central Railroad completed a slip in Manitowoc, allowing the Ann Arbor to begin service to a port that would be more accessible than Kewaunee in northeasterly winds.[31]

The car ferries were now offering service to four ports on the western side of the lake, but that was not very satisfactory. For two boats to call at each port with sufficient frequency, they needed to stop at more than one port while on that side of the lake. A normal pattern was to call at Kewaunee, then steam nearly thirty miles south to Manitowoc, take on additional cargo, and cross the lake to Frankfort. The difficulty was in maintaining proper weight distribution on the boats. The car ferries were very sensitive to changes in weight distribution, so once a boat was loaded and balanced it was not a simple matter to add cars. At times, the entire cargo had to be rearranged, and the time involved was costly.[32]

The system developed by the railroad for securing cars was effective but not foolproof, as Captain Charles Moody discovered in 1895. A renowned captain on the Great Lakes and master of the *Ann Arbor No. 1*, Moody was approaching Frankfort from Kewaunee in a northwest gale. Because of the high wind and its direction, the only practical way to enter the harbor was from the northwest, heading straight for the north

Ann *Arbor No. 2* on an excursion from Sturgeon Bay. *(Photo courtesy of the Door County Maritime Museum.)*

pier knowing that the wind would blow the boat into the center of the channel as she reached the harbor entrance. Attempting entrance from the west or southwest would result in the ship's being blown into the south pier by the crosswind.

While he was still some distance out in the lake Captain Moody realized that he was already south of where he needed to be to enter the harbor. He could not just head slightly more north to correct his position because the boat would roll too much in the trough of the waves. He would have to turn the *No. 1* into the wind and quarter the waves in a northerly direction until he could again turn and run straight downwind to Frankfort. While he was making the turn to head upwind, the ship rolled so badly that much of the security gear that held the cars in place was dislodged and several cars broke loose. Four cars of flour and three of butter rolled over the stern into Lake Michigan, and some of the cargo wound up on the beach north of Frankfort. Rather than explain the mishap to the railroad, the captain resigned and took a job for the winter as captain of one of the Flint and Pere Marquette package boats out of Ludington. Captain Moody continued to be well known and respected on the Great Lakes, commanding the famous whaleback ship *Christopher Columbus*.[33] Over the years, there were other isolated incidents of cars tipping over or breaking loose, but by and large the system

The Toledo, Ann Arbor and North Michigan used a combination of clamps, jacks, turnbuckles, and chains to keep the railcars from moving independently of the ship. *(Photos from the author's collection.)*

was remarkably successful. Often, though not always, a problem occurred when the crew set the system for moderate weather and then got
caught in a storm.

While the Ann Arbor boats were having their adventures in the ice,
weathering storms, and simply getting in and out of harbors, the business itself—transporting railcars across the lake—was slowly growing and
gaining acceptance. Wellington Burt, who was appointed the receiver of
the railroad in 1893, applied his considerable business acumen to the
company. Already wealthy from his lumber interests in Saginaw, he was
not afraid to spend money. This contrasted with Ashley, who had never
had much money of his own and tended to spend as little as possible.
Burt ran the company through the receivership and became president of
the newly formed Ann Arbor Railroad Company in July 1897, keeping
his son-in-law, Henry Ashley on as general manager.

The financial picture was grim at first, with both boats tied up for the
winter of 1895. Company officials realized that with a reduced amount
of freight available the ships would not be able to run often enough to
keep Frankfort Harbor open. While it was in receivership, the company
showed a deficit for two years and a small profit for three.[34] During that
time, Burt plowed $1,227,000 back into the company in the form of bet-
ter grading, 26 miles of additional mainline track (which *reduced* the
overall length of the railroad from 302 to 292 miles), upgraded bridges,
heavier rails, and better equipment and terminals—all of which improved the quality of the railroad and put it in a position to become
more profitable.[35]

By 1898 business was improving. The major eastbound traffic was
made up of lumber, logs, and grain; the westbound traffic of coal and
manufactured goods. With the increased traffic and the need to service
the four ports on the Wisconsin side of the lake, the company ordered a
new steel car ferry, the *Ann Arbor No. 3*. The new ferry would expand the
Ann Arbor's capacity at what was considered a moderate cost. Car ferry
engines cost only slightly more than locomotive engines to maintain,
and they did not require track. The new boat was 258 feet long with 52
feet of beam, about the same size as the *No. 1* and *No. 2*. She was built of
steel for greater strength and longevity with a double bottom to protect
her from damage should she run aground on rocks or shoals.[36] Given
the early experience of the *No. 1* and *No. 2*—dredging their way out of
Frankfort Harbor and slamming against the bottom on the way back in—
the Ann Arbor had ample reason to be cautious about the construction

Ann Arbor No. 3 as she was initially built, with two stacks. *(Photo from the A. C. Frederickson Collection.)*

Area above the pilothouse of the *Ann Arbor No. 3*, where in the early days crew members stood watches, a holdover from the days of sailing ships. Modern captains say it was too cold to stand outside for any significant period of time in winter. The crew member on the right is Samuel Nelson. *(Photo courtesy of William R. Olsen.)*

Samuel Nelson by the wheel of the
Ann Arbor No. 3. *(Photo courtesy of
William R. Olsen.)*

of a steel ship. Ironically, the *No. 3*, which was better protected than any
of the other boats, before or after, had a nearly perfect safety record
throughout her sixty-two years of operation, running aground only
once.[37]

The company used the two engines that had powered the bow propellers on the *No. 1* and *No. 2* to power the *No. 3* and included a hold forward (in the space used on the *No. 1* and *No. 2* to house the forward engines) so she could carry grain in bulk as well as freight cars. Grain was
loaded in Manitowoc and unloaded to a grain elevator in Frankfort.
Both operations were conducted while the ship loaded and unloaded
freight cars, so no extra time was needed. Also, the *No. 3* was given two
large gangways in her side so she could carry package freight. Built in
Cleveland by the Globe Iron Works, she maintained the Ann Arbor tradition of bad weather on her trip to Frankfort, arriving on November 20,
1898, after four days, complete with snow and a forced anchorage at the
Straits of Mackinac.[38]

In 1900 the Ann Arbor transported nearly twenty-six thousand railcars across the lake.[39] In the following year's annual report, Wellington Burt discussed the need for a fourth car ferry. In 1902, the company obtained a ferry landing and track terminal privileges at Manistique, on the southern side of Michigan's Upper Peninsula. This netted two more rail connections and access to several districts that produced iron ore. Manistique Harbor, though in the Upper Peninsula and farther north than Menominee, stayed open during the winter months because the prevailing northwest winds tended to take the ice out into the lake.[40] The company was getting stronger but had yet to face the full power of Lake Michigan in winter.

THREE ❦ *The Perils of Green Bay*

Although the Toledo, Ann Arbor and North Michigan's first winter of operation, 1892–93, was one of the coldest on record, the ice conditions confronting the car ferries became much more difficult in the years to come. Starting in 1897, the Great Lakes suffered unusually harsh winters for the next ten years.[1] While the captains and crews did everything they could to fight the ice, they were at times overmatched.

In February 1897, the *No. 1* and *No. 2* got stuck in windrows between Arcadia and Manistee, Michigan, about seven miles offshore. While trying to free herself, the *No. 2* broke the pin on her rudder stock, rendering the rudder useless. On car ferries, the chief engineer is accountable for the operation of all things mechanical, so the chief on the *No. 2* was responsible for fixing the rudder pin. He could not possibly fix the pin onboard the ship, so he picked up the broken pin, climbed down a ladder onto the ice, and began *walking* toward shore. The "walk" was anything but easy—seven miles of ice and windrows. When he reached the beach, he turned south toward Manistee. Hours later he reached the town and sought out a blacksmith who could make a new pin. Then he purchased supplies for the boat and arranged for men with horses and sleighs to carry them back to the *No. 2*.

After what one can only hope was a good night's sleep, he set out the next morning, leading the men and their teams of horses and sleighs north along the beach—then seven miles across the ice to the boat. Although he could ride on one of the sleighs much of the time, he said the trip back was even more difficult than his walk to Manistee. He and the

Ann Arbor No. 1 and *No. 2* stuck in the ice outside Frankfort in the mid-1890s. *(Photo from the A. C. Frederickson Collection.)*

men spent hours chopping a path through the windrows with axes and iron bars so the horses could pull the sleighs filled with supplies to the ship. Unspoken was his assumption that it was all part of his job.

It was twenty-three days before the wind shifted to the east and relieved the pressure on the two ships, freeing them at last. Other than the broken rudder pin, the boats were not seriously damaged and returned to service.[2]

In early 1899, the *Ann Arbor No. 3*, the company's flagship, had her own bout with Lake Michigan ice between Frankfort and Point Betsie, three miles to the north. The log entries tell the story.[3]

February 16	Trip 21. Left Frankfort 6:25 a.m. Wind SSE Fresh. Got fast in ice and drifted down to Point Betsie. Got clear and came up to about Frankfort and got caught in ice again and drifted down to Point Betsie again.
February 17–18	Still fast in ice. Got her nearly cut out and it shut in over us again.
February 19	Got clear of ice 8:30 a.m. Stood to the southward. Got fast again.
February 20	Got clear of ice 3:40 p.m. Arr. Manitowoc 9:40 p.m.

The log entries give some idea of the frustration but little of the danger in the situation. The *No. 3* was not going to be crushed by the ice. Her steel construction was too sturdy for that. But the fact that the crew did not have control over her movements was inherently dangerous. Had the ice taken the ship ashore or across the shoals extending outward from Point Betsie, she would have run aground and probably capsized—and the crew would have been helpless to prevent it.[4]

Over the years, Kewaunee and Manitowoc, on the Wisconsin shore of Lake Michigan, had stayed relatively clear of ice even though the temperatures averaged several degrees colder than in Frankfort. While ice formed readily, the prevailing west and northwest winds pushed the ice across the lake to the Michigan side.[5] Menominee, however, was another matter. Located on the western shore of Green Bay, the harbor was never open for the entire winter. The shallow water of Green Bay froze much more quickly than the rest of Lake Michigan and remained frozen longer.

During the winter months the ice would get so thick that it was almost treated as an extension of the land. From the early 1890s through 1914, stagecoaches ran from the town of Sturgeon Bay on the Door Peninsula straight across the ice to Menominee, some twenty miles away. As many as fourteen teams a day crossed the bay with cargoes of farm products for Menominee and groceries and hardware for the residents of Door County. Discarded Christmas trees were used to mark the trail. A "portable hotel" was erected partway across the bay to shelter and feed travelers. While the stages ran on a regular basis for much of the winter, crossing the twenty miles of Sturgeon Bay and Green Bay to Menominee was not necessarily "safe." Witness the story of two travelers in 1903 as reported in the *Door County Advocate*.

> Mr. Hansen met Mr. Glass in Sturgeon Bay, and as the latter was coming to Menominee and he also wanted to get to this city, the two men hired a horse and cutter at the livery stable of Mr. Putnam, the stage man, who runs the line across the bay.
>
> The two men started about the middle of the afternoon and succeeded in crossing all of the cracks in the ice until they reached the last one, about four or five miles from Menominee. They had followed the route laid out for the stages, marked out by small evergreen trees, but about half past four o'clock, the men say, it became foggy out on the bay, and they could see but a short distance ahead, barely being able to make out the trees along the road.

When they reached the last crack about three or four feet wide, their troubles began. The horse attempted to jump across but landed on the other side only with his fore feet, the hind feet going into the water. Mr. Hansen said the horse backed up instead of trying to go ahead and went into the water. It was finally gotten out and Mr. Glass then got out of the cutter and started to find a place where they could cross with safety. He had not gone far before he fell into the crack himself, and the traveling man then went to his rescue and succeeded in pulling him out of the water.

He was soaked from head to foot and fearing he would freeze to death with all the water in his clothes, the lap robe was spread on the ice, and there, in almost zero weather, with the aid of Mr. Hansen, every strip of clothing was stripped from the drenched cigar maker. There he stood for fully five minutes, wearing nothing, not even a pleasant smile, while the other wrung the water from his clothes. The wet clothing was then put back on and the men hurriedly planned on what to do.

Hansen had never been across the bay on the ice before and it was decided that Glass should start for town for aid. He started and walked the four or five miles in his wet clothes.

Hansen, who was left behind, said this morning: "I never expected to see him alive. I thought he would freeze before reaching the shore and that if ever I were able to find my way I would find his dead body on the ice. We dared not attempt to get the horse over the crack again, as it was by that time so dark that we could not see and we were afraid of running into another one from which we would not be able to get out.

I waited there from half past four until eleven o'clock last night, waiting for Glass to come with help, and by the time they arrived, I was about done for. If they had been ten minutes later in reaching me I should have been frozen. I had never been on the ice before and did not know anything about it, so I feared to make the attempt to reach the shore. I could see one of the trees a short way off and I walked, leading the horse between the tree and another spot to keep from freezing. The poor horse was shivering and always kept his nose right to my back, seeming also to fear that he should be precipitated into the water again. Finally, I became stiff with cold and walked almost like a drunken man.

Way late in the night I saw lights coming from the shore. They

Afternoon Stage
——Betweeen——
Sturgeon Bay and Menominee.
Stage leaves Sturgeon Bay for Menominee
from the Union Hotel at 1 o'clock p. m.
 Leave Menominee for Sturgeon Bay from
the American House, at 1:30 o'clock p. m.
 Good comfortable rigs and careful experi-
enced drivers.

Anderson & Moeller,
'Phone 118-2.   'Phone 15.

Putman & Baldwin
Stage to Menominee.
Leave Sturgeon Bay at 8 a. m   Leave Me-
nominee at 8 a. m.
 Last stop at Waldo Hotel
Take the Early Stage.

These advertisements appeared in the February 11, 1905, issue of the *Door County Advocate.*

came nearer and nearer, and seemed to be going about the ice as though some were looking for me. At last I could hear the men hollering to me and I tried to answer two or three times, but could only do so in such a weak voice, which could not have been heard one quarter of the distance. I was about to give up and lie down, not caring whether I died or not, when the men reached me. I have been a steward on ocean steamers and have crossed the ocean many times and had many experiences, but never one such as this. I shall never forget it and hope I never have another one like it."

Glass showed great endurance in reaching the shore in his wet clothes. He arrived at Menominee about nine o'clock and telephoned the livery stable of Spencer and Riley at once, informing them of the state of affairs. Fred Baldwin and Mr. Putman, two stage men who know the road thoroughly, went with Mr. Glass after he had changed his clothes, to find the other man. They half expected to find him frozen, but about eleven thirty o'clock they reached him and he was brought in and taken to the National Hotel. Icicles several inches long were hanging from his moustache and he was shivering and nearly frozen. He was given a good drink of brandy and warmed up and was soon all right again.

He left this noon for Green Bay on business and expects to return to Menominee again next week, but says he will never cross the ice again, even if he has to wait until flying machines are in use to get to the other side.[6]

The winter stagecoaches were an integral part of life on Green Bay but were not to be taken for granted—there was always some danger. They usually continued running into the spring until an unlucky horse fell through the ice or suffered a "near miss."[7] Residents of Menominee enjoyed ice skating, and later iceboating, on the bay, and in the spring there were occasional incidents of people accidentally falling through the ice.

Most commercial shipping on the Great Lakes came to an end in December and resumed in the spring—in April or May depending when the Straits of Mackinac was clear of ice. An added incentive to shut down operations for the winter was that most insurance coverage ended with the closing of the Straits. The Ann Arbor car ferries did not conform to that practice. They could plow through one and a half feet of sheet ice and ran year-round to Kewaunee, Manitowoc, and Manistique. They continued running to Menominee into early January, officially ending the navigation season on Green Bay with their final departure. Then, in the spring, they opened the season with their first visit, often taking two or three days to get through the bay. Their progress and arrival made headlines in the local papers.

In 1900 the Ann Arbor ships continued making trips to Menominee through January, longer than usual. Near the end of the month the *Ann Arbor No. 3* had a most difficult trip, so when Frank Butler, the captain of the *Ann Arbor No. 1*, left Frankfort for Menominee on February 2 he must have known that he would face severe ice conditions. Even with that knowledge, he could not possibly have imagined all that was in store for him. The trip across Lake Michigan and through the Sturgeon Bay Ship Canal was uneventful, but as he started across Green Bay he began running into windrows. He continued across the bay, fighting his way through each one, but as he neared Green Island, about five miles off Menominee, he encountered a windrow he couldn't conquer. He was stuck.

Captain Butler asked for assistance from the 127-foot railroad ferry *Algomah*, which was owned by the Mackinac Transportation Company and classified as an "ice crusher." The *Algomah* and the *No. 3* had fought their way across Green Bay together the previous week. Whether the *Algomah* was a better icebreaker than the *No. 1* is open to question, but she did have the advantage of being free while the *No. 1* was stuck; however, while approaching the *No. 1*, she struck something beneath the surface of the water that tore two blades off her propeller. Soon the *Algomah* was as immobile as the *No. 1*.

As the two boats remained in the ice it became clear that they would be there for the winter. The crews stayed aboard and passed the time as

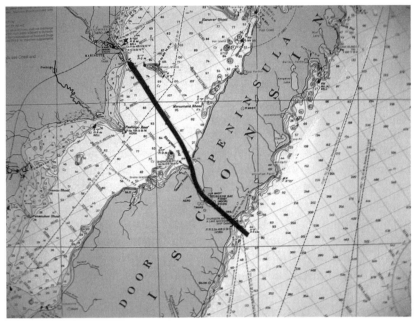

The chart shows the route the ferries followed through the Sturgeon Bay Ship Canal and across Green Bay. The winter stagecoaches followed the same route until they stopped running in 1915. *(Photo of U.S. government chart by the author.)*

The "Ice Crusher" *Algomah. (Photo courtesy of the Historical Collections of the Great Lakes, Bowling Green State University.)*

best they could. Some fished. One lamented the lack of reading matter. They were far from isolated because the Sturgeon Bay–Menominee stage passed within a few hundred feet several times a day, bringing supplies and mail and allowing crew members to stay in touch with their families. Captain Butler, an avid sportsman, trekked across the ice to Green Island where he hunted rabbits. Winter on the bay went on as usual. Fishermen staked out their positions for fishing through the ice, and residents of Marinette and Menominee skated on the bay for pleasure.

With the passage of time and the constant pressure of the ice against her sides, the *No. 1* began to leak. Her pumps were adequate to keep the water from rising, but they had to run twenty-four hours a day to keep up, which precipitated another problem—lack of fuel. The *No. 1* was burning about five tons of coal a day. It was possible to bring coal from Menominee by sleigh, but it was not an easy matter to load it aboard the ship. Normally the crew loaded coal by running coal cars onto the car deck and dumping the contents into bunkers. Now everything had to be done by hand. On March 10, the *Door County Advocate* stated, "According to all reports, the No. 1 could not stand much of a squeeze in her present condition and if she should happen to get caught in an ice jam it would probably end her career."[8] In mid-March the Coast Guard shut down all the navigation lights on Green Bay.[9]

On April 5 the *Ann Arbor No. 3* left Frankfort bound for Menominee, her mission to free the *No. 1* and the *Algomah* and then open the port of Menominee. When she reached the town of Sturgeon Bay, the second mate went ashore and telegraphed Frankfort to send the *No. 2* as well. The *No. 3* bucked the ice all that night, but there were heavy windrows and the going was agonizingly slow. At 6:00 a.m. the following morning the *No. 2* arrived, and the two ships began fighting their way across Green Bay. In the next six hours they made only two miles, but then their progress improved. At 5:50 p.m. they passed the *Algomah*, and twenty-five minutes later they were breaking out the *No. 1*. The *No. 3* transferred a gondola of coal to the *No. 1* and then led the *No. 2* into Menominee while the *No. 1* began towing the *Algomah* back to Sturgeon Bay.[10] The going was relatively easy for the *No. 1* because she could follow the ice channel created by the *No. 2* and *No. 3*, but the next morning the *No. 1* struck a submerged object that sent one propeller and shaft straight to the bottom of the bay.

Now Captain Butler had a new problem because the *No. 1* had damaged her rudder while stuck in the ice and he had been manipulating

This picture is said to be of the *Ann Arbor No. 1* when she was stuck in Green Bay, though she is riding high for a ship carrying a full load of freight. It is possible that the picture was taken in 1904 when the *No. 1* was stuck off Kewaunee for about a month. *(Photo courtesy of Barbara J. Butler.)*

her two engines to steer. With only one propeller operative, he could no longer do that; however, the *No. 1* was still in the channel made by the *No. 3* and *No. 2*, and for a while the pressure of the ice on each side of the boat kept her moving in the right direction. As the ships entered Sturgeon Bay the channel opened up, which meant the men on the *No. 1* could no longer steer. So they did the only thing they could: they brought the *Algomah* alongside the *No. 1;* lashed the two boats together; and, using the power of the *No. 1* and the rudder of the *Algomah,* limped toward the ship canal. When they neared Hills Point, they stopped and laid in the ice, waiting for the *No. 3* to return from Menominee.[11]

Late in the day the *No. 3* returned, towed the two boats to the canal, and dropped off the *Algomah.* The plan was for the *No. 3* to tow the *No. 1* back to Frankfort, but the fates were not smiling on Captain Butler. A strong north wind was blowing, and, while a car ferry could easily cross

Ann Arbor No. 1 and the *Algomah,* lashed together, limp into Sturgeon Bay. *(Drawing by Chris Patterson.)*

Lake Michigan on its own (the *No. 2* was already on her way), it was not safe to attempt crossing with a tow.

The two ships lay in the canal all of the following day and the day after until 6:00 p.m., when they decided to make a run for Frankfort. The north wind was still blowing hard, so their plan was to go northeast along the Wisconsin shore to Pilot Island and then head southeast toward Frankfort. In that way they would never be in the trough of the waves and would not be subject to the severe stresses that occur when boats roll heavily. Just after midnight, as they arrived off Pilot Island, the towline parted. In the next hour they passed another towline to the *No. 1* but then realized that the ship was running short of fuel. If anything were to go wrong on the trip across the lake and the *No. 1* ran out of fuel, she would surely sink. So, with more than a little frustration, they turned around and took the *No. 1* back to the ship canal.[12] The *No. 3* went on to Frankfort, and the *No. 2* towed the *No. 1* to Frankfort the following day.

When the *No. 1* arrived, she was thoroughly beaten up by her ordeal. Her stern had been chewed badly by the ice. Much of the steel that was wrapped around her bottom to protect her from the ice had been torn off. One propeller and one shaft were gone, and her rudder was inoperative. The ship had been stuck in the ice for sixty-three days and had been gone from Frankfort for sixty-seven days. On the bright side, she

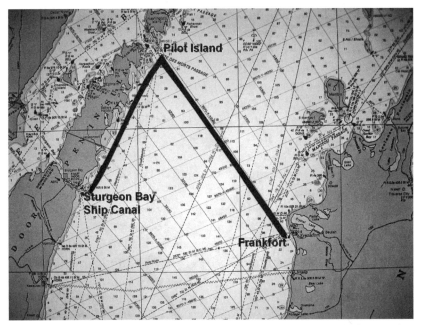

Ann Arbor No. 3 planned to tow the *No. 1* northeast along the Wisconsin shore and then southeast to Frankfort, thereby avoiding the trough of the waves. The chart shows the planned route. *(Photo of U.S. government chart by the author.)*

had survived. Crew members could return to their families, and Captain Butler still had a ship to command. The *No. 1* was taken to Milwaukee for major repairs but was back in service by mid-May.[13]

A week after the *No. 1* was released from the ice, the *Door County Advocate* reported that Henry Ashley, general manager of the Ann Arbor, still believed winter navigation was possible across Green Bay. He was said to have favored the use of a small "ice crusher" to bring railcars across Green Bay where they could be transferred to the car ferries at Sturgeon Bay. The smaller vessel would make trips across the bay with greater frequency than the car ferries and thereby keep the channel open. While there was some merit to the idea, it was never pursued.[14] For the next twenty-four years (until 1925) the Ann Arbor was forced to discontinue service to Menominee for at least part of each winter, usually shutting down in early January and starting again in April.

The winter of 1904 was one of the coldest of all time and the coldest in the Ann Arbor's ninety-year history. Lake Michigan froze from shore to shore, and the conventional thinking that prevailing west and northwest winds would push ice off the western shore of Lake Michigan, keeping the Wisconsin ports open, was thoroughly discredited. The Ann Arbor suffered much greater losses that winter because its problems extended beyond Green Bay to the normally open port of Kewaunee. The difficulties began when Captain Bernard Tulledge and the *Ann Arbor No. 1* set out from Frankfort for Kewaunee on February 9 after an exceedingly difficult trip from Manistique to Frankfort during which the ship had been locked in the ice for eight days. She plowed across the lake through solid sheet ice the entire distance, verifying that the lake was completely frozen, but reached Kewaunee with surprising ease. The weather in Kewaunee was bright and clear, with a very light north wind, and cold, about ten degrees. Late in the day, after unloading her cargo and loading another for the return trip, the ship left Kewaunee, but instead of heading straight across the lake she headed south to Manitowoc, most likely to take on more railcars before crossing the lake to Frankfort. In the meantime the wind had begun blowing from the northeast, shoving the lake ice against the shore. Soon Captain Tulledge and the *No. 1* were stuck, pinned by the pressure of the ice pushing against the Wisconsin shore.

The following day, the *No. 3* and *No. 2* were sent from Frankfort to break the *No. 1* out. By the time they reached her, the wind had backed to the north and dropped to almost nothing; but it did not help. As the *No. 3* got close enough to break a channel, she became hopelessly stuck. The crew of the *No. 2*, realizing that they could not help, left while they still could and returned to Frankfort.[15] Two days later (February 12) the *No. 2* crossed the lake and tried to enter Kewaunee, but the harbor was effectively closed by two large windrows that blocked the harbor entrance. The *Pere Marquette No. 15*, a wooden car ferry operated by the Flint and Pere Marquette Railroad from Ludington, was trying to get in as well. She was a larger boat but underpowered. Neither could force a passage. The *No. 2* briefly became stuck but extricated herself by using the wash from her propellers to break up the ice and again returned to Frankfort. That was fortunate because the next day (February 13) it "blowed a gale from the southeast accompanied with snow," shoving more ice against the harbor entrance. On February 14, the wind shifted to the northwest, creating some open water off Kewaunee harbor, but the windrows blocking the entrance didn't move. Local people said conditions were the worst they had ever seen.[16]

The *No. 3* and *No. 1* remained stuck and were carried south by the ice.

Ann Arbor No. 3 and *No. 1* opposite the Royal Frontenac Hotel, Frankfort, in the mid-1900s. *(Photo from the A. C. Frederickson Collection.)*

A group of people from Kewaunee visited the boats and learned that while they had no chance of breaking loose, they were in good shape. Both ships had plenty of coal (the *No. 1* had three hundred tons and the *No. 3* four hundred), and they could readily get supplies from shore. The crews passed the time playing cards and visiting the town of Two Creeks, about three miles to the south. They constructed iceboats to make the trips to shore easier and faster. Captain Tulledge reported that the ice went all the way to the bottom for about two thousand feet in each direction from the boat. As time passed, the captains wisely made no attempt to break out. The Ann Arbor suspended cross-lake service, holding the *No. 2* at Frankfort.[17]

On Saturday, February 27, the *No. 2* went back across the lake to break out the *No. 1* and *No. 3*. With light and variable winds on Sunday, and temperatures in the midthirties, she worked her way to within a half mile of the two ships but could go no farther. A blizzard struck from the northeast on Monday, and the attempt was aborted. On Tuesday, temperatures rose to the forties, and that night the *No. 3* broke loose and went to Manitowoc. On Wednesday, March 2, the *No. 3* returned and began working with the *No. 2* to break out the embattled *No. 1*. Overnight a gale developed from the northwest, relieving the pressure, and by morning the *No. 1* was free.[18]

Kewaunee Harbor opened for traffic on February 28, but the harbor eluded the Ann Arbor boats well into March. The *No. 1* left Frankfort on Thursday, March 10, with a west wind blowing, which had cleared the Wisconsin shore of ice, but by the time she crossed the lake the wind had shifted to east-southeast and increased to twenty miles per hour with rain, shoving the ice back to the Wisconsin side. The *No. 1* fought her way into the huge ice field, but progress was slow. On Friday, temperatures dropped to the twenties and the wind swung to the northeast, continuing to push ice against the shore. Kewaunee residents watched throughout the day as the *No. 1* fought her way toward the harbor. When she was about one-half mile off the entrance, she became stuck in a large windrow.

Saturday turned bright, clear, and cold, but the wind remained steady at twenty miles per hour from the northeast. The crew freed the *No. 1* from the windrow, but she was unable to move farther because of pressure from the ice. On Sunday, the wind moderated, but the *No. 1* remained stuck. The *No. 2* arrived from Frankfort but could get no closer than a mile off the harbor and a half mile from the *No. 1*. On Monday, March 14, the Kewaunee Life Saving Station log stated that "a genuine blizzard raged all day from the NE and the two Ann Arbors are still stuck fast in the ice." That night the ice began moving, carrying the two ships south. The wind swung to the northwest, freeing the *No. 1,* but the *No. 2* was carried ten miles south of Kewaunee. The *No. 1* entered Kewaunee early Tuesday afternoon, March 15, the first time an Ann Arbor ship had entered Kewaunee since February 8. The *No. 2* finally freed herself and arrived the next day.[19]

It had been the most difficult winter the Ann Arbor had endured since the beginning of cross-lake service in 1892 and the fourth coldest ever (before or after) on the Great Lakes.[20] Considering the conditions, the boats emerged remarkably unscathed. The *No. 1* resumed her duties immediately, in sharp contrast to her state after being stuck in Green Bay for sixty-three days in 1900. One can only surmise the reason why she fared so much better, but it is likely that she was not fully loaded (she was en route to Manitowoc, presumably to take on more cargo) and would have been floating higher in the water than a fully loaded vessel. That may have materially changed the way the ice acted on her sides. The sides of a car ferry are essentially perpendicular to the water but are rounded where they enter the water. When less than fully loaded, the ice would push against the rounded portion of the ship, causing it to rise rather than simply squeezing it. The *No. 1* was sitting a full six feet above her waterline just before her release.

The survival of the *No. 1* and *No. 3* with minimal damage was a great plus, but the year-round reliability of the system had come into question—and, of course, the ships still faced the opening of Green Bay and Menominee. The first Ann Arbor boat to reach Menominee in the spring of 1904 did not arrive until May 4, and the last ship to call before ice shut off navigation for the winter almost didn't reach port. The *Marinette Daily Eagle Star* article, dated December 29, 1904, tells the story.[21]

ANN ARBOR IS LOCKED IN ICE

The Big Carferry is Blocked at the Mouth of the River and Cannot Move—Cars in Boat are Smashed During Storm

The big steel carferry Ann Arbor No. 3 lies at the Point Menominee Lighthouse this afternoon, stuck tight in a great mass of packed ice, about two hundred yards from the docks which she has been trying in vain to reach. The Ann Arbor is in bad condition. She left Frankfort at twelve o'clock Tuesday night to cross the lake and she had the worst experience in the entire history of the boat since that time. One of the most terrific winter storms in years lashed the waters of Lake Michigan into waves that washed over the big boat, and for fifteen hours she struggled bravely against the terrific gale.

TERRIBLE EXPERIENCE ON LAKE
It was a terrible experience for the crew of the steamer, and as they tell the story today, it is evidently one that they will never forget. The boat was so dashed about in the sea that the cars in her hold became loosened, and were dashed against each other, and against the sides of the boat, making terrible confusion, and, raising havoc among the freight. Several of the cars on board are badly damaged, while one that ran loose is entirely smashed up. There is considerable freight damaged.

JAMMED IN ICE FIELD
At seven o'clock the Ann Arbor got into this port and within one quarter mile of the lighthouse. Then her troubles began again, and

she is having as much trouble with the ice of Green Bay as she did with the waves of Lake Michigan. From seven o'clock Wednesday evening [December 28] until seven o'clock this morning, was required for the boat to force her way through the ice as far as the end of the lighthouse, and there she stuck and there she still lies.

CARFERRY MAY NOT ENTER PORT

It is an open question whether she will ever be able to enter port and land her cargo of freight. There is even a possibility that she can not get out of the difficult position in which she now lies. She can neither go ahead nor back up, and the ice is making it very hard for her machinery to operate. If the ice was hard, the big boat could go through it much easier, but it is soft and slushy, and forms a terrific barrier both in front of the boat and behind it. Many people visited the boat from the shore, walking out on the mass of ice that is packed around her.

While the *No. 3* may have been defeated, the crew wasn't. The men went out on the ice with axes and literally chopped a path to the dock. The *No. 3* unloaded quickly and within a half hour began her trip back across Green Bay. This time the going was much easier because of the channel she had carved out on her way to Menominee. She arrived in Frankfort in normal time without mishap.

The *Ann Arbor No. 3*'s return in the spring of 1905 was only somewhat better than her departure in December of the preceding year. Headlines in the *Marinette Daily Eagle Star* and the *Menominee Herald Leader* explain.

April 8   Ann Arbor No. 3 Coming Next Week

April 12   Coming of Ann Arbor Delayed

April 13   Ice Still Remains in the Bay

April 15   Carferry Will Arrive Here Monday at 5:00 p.m.

April 17   Ann Arbor Tonight

April 18   Carferry's 20 Hour Battle with Ice; Ann Arbor Arrives

FOUR ✻ *A Dangerous Lake Michigan*

The Ann Arbor boats in the 1890s and early 1900s were large and sea-worthy for the time but rather small and underpowered by today's standards. As noted earlier, each was about 260 feet in length and pow-ered by two steam engines developing a total of 1,200 horsepower. That paled in comparison with the power of later boats such as the 360-foot *Ann Arbor No. 5*, with 3,000 horsepower, and the *Viking*, with 6,120. Ac-cordingly, the early boats found the lake more treacherous and had some close calls in conditions that would not have threatened the later boats to the same extent.

In early January 1901, the *Ann Arbor No. 1* was somewhat run down due to constant operation and was in need of general maintenance. There was too much play in the steering system, she had lost two pro-peller blades in heavy ice on Green Bay, and her pumping system was not operating properly. She could pump water from her holds in the aft part of the ship but not at the forward end. Some of the limber holes (holes cut in the bulkheads to allow water to run forward and aft) were clogged. There was a chain extending through the holes that a crewman could pull to keep them clear, but the chain was rusted and broken. In sum, the ship was in no condition to battle a storm on Lake Michigan.[1]

On January 8, at 5:30 a.m., the *No. 1* left Manistique for the run back to Frankfort. All had been going well for about an hour when a gale force wind hit from the south and the temperature began falling. As the seas increased, the ship took water forward and ice began forming on her deck and superstructure, adding weight and putting the bow lower in the water. The storm may have been unexpected because the cars on the port center track came loose and began rolling back and forth, indicating that the crew may not have used the maximum security gear before leaving port. The *No. 1* had electricity but not on the car deck. The men had to use lanterns to see when they were away from the stern—a frightening and dangerous situation with the unstable cargo.

The crew managed to put blocks on the tracks, inadvertently causing some of the cars to derail. That turned out to be a benefit because the wheels of the derailed cars pierced the wooden car deck, which kept them from rolling back and forth and may have saved the ship. As the seas continued to build, the stern started digging into the waves when the bow rose to meet a new wave, resulting in water coming over the stern. Now the boat was filling with water and ice was forming at the stern. The Ann Arbor management had thought its boats, with their open sterns, would be safe in high winds if the crew kept them headed into the wind; but that was not entirely true, as the crew of the *No. 1* and later boats that found themselves in the similar circumstances could testify.

The *No. 1* fought her way past Frankfort (she did not dare try for the entrance in the high seas) and worked her way close to the shore south of the harbor in an effort to take advantage of the lee of the bluffs. Then the steering quadrant came loose, and the key came out of the rudder stock (post). A steering quadrant is a half-round-shaped piece of iron or steel, several feet in diameter, the center of which fits over the rudder stock. It is bound mechanically with a pin that fits through the quadrant and the rudder stock. Thus, when the quadrant turns, the rudder does too. The circumference of the quadrant is lined with teeth that mesh with gear teeth from two steering engines, one on each side. The engines are mechanically linked with the wheel in the pilothouse so that when the wheelsman turns the wheel one of the engines is activated, turning the rudder. If the quadrant is not mechanically linked to the rudder, as when the pin is broken or comes out, the crew can no longer steer the ship with the wheel. The only option is to rig a steering tiller that fits over the end of the rudder stock at the level of the car deck.

The officers steered by manipulating the two engines while most of the crew went to the stern and began chopping through the ice so they could reach the end of the rudder stock and rig an emergency steering

The two-hundred-foot-wide entrance to Frankfort Harbor became quite narrow in a blow. *(Photo courtesy of Roger Griner.)*

tiller. Steering by the engines was a difficult and dangerous practice in the best of conditions. The officers in the pilothouse had no direct control over the engines but communicated commands to the engine room through the use of Chadburns, devices that could send signals to the engine room that could be heard over the noise of the machinery. Of necessity, there was a lag from the time a signal was sent to the time it was acted upon. The deck officer sending the signal had to be very sure of what he wanted because he could not easily undo his command. Working in such a manner required greater skill than in later years, when it was possible to operate the throttles directly from the bridge. With high seas and a powerful wind behind them, there was considerable risk. On the other hand, there was no choice.

In time the crew was able to clear enough ice at the stern to rig the steering tiller, though it is doubtful they actually steered the ship with it. A steering tiller has very little mechanical advantage on the rudder, making it nearly impossible to steer by hand. It is possible to fasten chains to the end of the tiller and connect them to steam winches on either side of the ship, which would have sufficient power to move the tiller and the rudder, but the arrangement is awkward, and it is more likely that they simply lashed the tiller in the middle so the rudder wouldn't interfere with their efforts to steer with the engines, giving them some semblance of control and allowing them to ride out the storm. After thirty-eight hours on the lake, the *No. 1* limped into Frankfort at 7:30 a.m. January 10, low in the water and by all accounts the survivor of a very close call.[2]

Four years later, in early January 1905, Captain Alexander Larson left Manitowoc Harbor with the *Ann Arbor No. 1,* bound for Frankfort. A strong north-northwest wind was blowing, which meant he would need to follow the Wisconsin shore north and east until he was far enough north to turn and run for Frankfort in a southeasterly direction with the wind. In that way, the ship would never have to be in the trough of the waves, which would cause her to roll badly, probably damage the cargo, and possibly cause her to capsize. There were eleven cars onboard (about half a normal load), which caused the boat to float higher in the water and made her more difficult to handle. Weight adds stability, and the *No. 1* was light.

The second mate was on watch in the pilothouse and misjudged the wind, turning for Frankfort too soon. As the *No. 1* neared the Michigan side of the lake and Captain Larson could see the shore, he knew his course with the wind would take him south of Frankfort. By now the wind was gale force, the temperature was well below zero, and there was light snow. To enter Frankfort Harbor he would have to haul into the wind and head north until he could square before the wind and approach the harbor. He was in a very similar position to that of Captain Moody when he lost seven cars of butter and flour over the stern ten years earlier.

Three times Captain Larson tried to bring her bow into the wind, but each time the *No. 1* lacked the power to stay there. The wind and waves pushed her bow to the side, and each time she drifted nearer the shore. The *No. 1* was already south of Frankfort, and unless Captain Larson did something soon she would be blown onto the beach and wrecked. Knowing the danger, the captain stopped fighting the wind and laid the *No. 1* off toward the south, heading with the wind and quartering the waves so he could make some progress away from the shore. He continued running with the seas, making what progress he could into the lake, until he wound up all the way across the lake off Sheboygan, Wisconsin. He entered the harbor and remained there for three days while the storm blew itself out and then returned to Frankfort with no serious damage. His good judgment and skill had prevented a certain catastrophe.[3]

A little over two years later, in late February 1907, Captain Charles Frederickson found himself in a comparable and even more dangerous situation with the *Ann Arbor No. 2.* He had left Manistique for Frankfort at 4:00 a.m. on the twenty-fifth with a light east wind and cloudy skies. Four hours into the trip, the wind backed to the northwest and increased to gale force with snow.

Approaching Frankfort harbor, he knew his only chance of getting through the narrow entrance was to use full power to achieve maximum steerage. The entrance was always treacherous in a sea because of its narrowness and the shallow water near the end of the piers, which intensified the force of the waves. Just as the *No.* 2 reached the piers, a very large wave slammed her bow into the end of the south pier, tearing off most of the crib at the end of the pier. The shock was so great that it knocked everyone off his feet and caused a freak accident that nearly sank the ship. A heavy block of oak fell through the wooden grating in the car deck and landed on the crosshead slide of the port engine, jamming the slide, preventing movement of the piston, and shutting the engine down.

The *No.* 2 was now drifting south of the pier with a northwest gale pushing her toward the shore. It was nearly the same position in which Captain Larson had found himself two years earlier except that Larson had been infinitely better off. He had had two engines operating and could run downwind, away from the waves. With only one engine operating, Captain Frederickson had to turn downwind, but he could not outrun the waves. He immediately headed south along the shore, but the waves began overtaking the boat and rolling across the car deck. Unless the crewmen could fix the port engine, the ship would either sink or he would have to put her on the beach. Either way, the *No.* 2 would likely be a total loss and the lives of the crew in great jeopardy.

Sam Arnerson, the first assistant engineer, went straight to the task of freeing the block, and he got help from most of the crewmen, who realized they must fix the engine or sink. There was no chance of simply removing the block—it was jammed too tightly—so they began chipping away at it with anything they could find. The work was agonizingly slow, but they had no alternative. As they worked, the water continued to roll in over the car deck. In the engine room the water was knee deep and extremely cold, a degree or two above freezing. It was so deep that the wooden grates covering the manholes that led to the holds began floating away. A man inadvertently stepping into one of the holes would find himself over his head in ice-cold water.

By the time Sam and his men finally loosened and released the block, the steam pressure was dangerously low—barely enough to turn over the engines and run the pumps. The water was almost up to the firebox. If it rose much higher, the ship would be lost. Much of the coal was wet, so the crew had to carry dry coal by hand from the tops of the piles through waist-high water to fuel the boiler.

As the steam pressure gradually increased, the *No. 1* gained speed and began pulling away from the waves. Now the pumps could begin to reduce the water in the boat rather than simply slowing down its rate of increase. With better control of the boat, but still an inordinate amount of water in her, Captain Frederickson knew he had no chance of fighting his way back north to Frankfort but he thought he could get into Onekama, twenty miles south of Frankfort. He knew that the steamer *Oscar T. Flint* had recently entered the harbor drawing eighteen feet of water. With so much water in the *No. 2*, she probably drew about the same, so he had a good chance. In spite of the high wind, but perhaps helped by the deeper draft, he made the entrance and found his way to the lumber dock, where he tied up.

The *No. 2* stayed at Onekama for twenty-four hours, running the pumps for the entire time. At about 2:00 p.m. the following day, she left Onekama and arrived at Frankfort a little over two hours later. A number of the crewmen suffered from colds and bruises. Sam Arnerson, who was credited more than anyone with the ship's survival, was hospitalized for several weeks, suffering from swollen limbs, the result of prolonged exposure to the ice-cold water. He returned to the Ann Arbor to become, in time, a well-known and highly respected chief engineer. A few days after her return to Frankfort, the *No. 2* went to Milwaukee for an assessment of the damage and to make repairs. Much to everyone's amazement, there was very little to fix—only a few cracked timbers aft. The resilient wood hull had fared much better than could have been expected from a steel ship—and much better than the south pier. The *No. 2* was back in service in a week.[4]

Life on the boats was not always filled with battles against storms and ice. On the contrary, the vast majority of trips were uneventful, and at times the crew—even the captain—needed something to liven up the days. One November afternoon in 1907 Captain Bernard Tulledge was bringing the *Ann Arbor No. 4* into the Sturgeon Bay Ship Canal when he looked across the bow and saw the head of an animal. Thinking it was a deer, he slowed the boat down and brought out his hunting rifle, which he just happened to have in his cabin. As the steamer approached the animal, he realized it was a wolf. With one shot to the head, Captain Tulledge had a trophy. The wolf was unusually large, a fine specimen. The crew surmised that the wolf had probably followed a deer into the water where the more agile deer had escaped. The lifesaving crew at

The Royal Frontenac Hotel, built by the Ann Arbor Railroad Company in 1902 and destroyed by fire in 1912. *(Photo courtesy of Kelene Luedtke.)*

Sturgeon Bay helped get the dead animal aboard the ship. It is not clear whether deer were in season, but there was always a bounty on wolves.[5]

Early in 1901 the Ann Arbor began construction of a luxury hotel in Frankfort that was meant to rival the Grand Hotel on Mackinac Island. The new hotel was named the Royal Frontenac after the French governor of Quebec at the time Father Marquette was said to have died near the mouth of Betsie Bay. The structure was built by C. I. Hoertz and Son, the firm that built the Grand, and it was impressive—five hundred feet long and three stories tall with 250 rooms, each with two double beds, hot and cold running water, and a telephone. The rooms were lavishly appointed, and all were said to have lake views. Students from Fisk University were imported in the summer months to staff the hotel as waiters, busboys, and housekeepers. The hotel opened in June 1902 and was immediately successful, drawing people from Chicago, Detroit, Toledo, Saint Louis, and Kansas City—all trying to escape the midwestern summer heat. Many came by rail—the Ann Arbor station was a few hundred feet away—while others arrived on lake boats such as the *Petoskey* and the *Missouri,* which sailed from Chicago and called at several Michigan ports on their way to the Straits of Mackinac.[6]

Hotel guests could gamble in-house, walk out the front door to the Lake Michigan beach, play golf on the nine-hole course at the east end of Frankfort, or ride the Ann Arbor's ping-pong train, so-called because it ran back and forth between Frankfort and Beulah, a small resort town at the southeast end of Crystal Lake. There guests could swim in the exceedingly clear (and often cold) lake and enjoy its deep, blue water and bright, sandy beaches. The ping-pong train consisted of one locomotive and one coach; it ran several times a day between the two towns with stops at the golf course, the outlet of Crystal Lake into the Betsie River, and a private resort. Because there was no place to turn around in Beulah, the locomotive pulled the coach to Beulah; then pushed it back to Frankfort. The hotel was good for business. The July 1903, Ann Arbor's annual report showed a 20 percent increase in passenger traffic over the previous year.[7]

In the early 1900s, the Ann Arbor attracted attention from a major railroad powerhouse, George Gould. Having inherited a railroad empire from his father, Jay Gould, George controlled trains that ran on ten thousand miles of track in the United States—but he wanted more. Specifically, he wanted to extend his Wabash line from Toledo to Pittsburgh, a city of 325,000 inhabitants and the largest shipping center in the country. Fueled by the need for huge quantities of iron ore and the production of iron, pig iron, and steel in the mills built by Andrew Carnegie, as well as a variety of manufactured goods, Pittsburgh generated three times more freight than any city in the world and more than the combined freight of Chicago, New York, and Philadelphia. The city was a railroader's dream, and most of the business went to the Pennsylvania Railroad.[8]

George Gould was not the astute businessman his father had been, but he had an excellent railroad man to help him. Joseph Ramsey, born in Pittsburgh in 1850, a civil engineer and in the railroad business since age nineteen, became general manager of the Wabash in 1895 and president in 1901.[9] Ramsey and Gould saw the Ann Arbor as a way to deliver iron ore from Michigan's Upper Peninsula and Minnesota to the Wabash in Toledo and on to Pittsburgh while shipping iron and steel westward. They did not attempt to buy out Wellington Burt and his group of investors, but they did acquire enough stock to install themselves on the Board of Directors in 1902.[10] Ramsey became president of the Ann Arbor in 1903 while he was also president of the Wabash Railroad. In that year, the Ann Arbor made a trackage agreement with the Wabash, and Ramsey expressed the need for another car ferry in the annual report.[11]

Gould and Ramsey completed their Pittsburgh connection by building a new railroad and securing a controlling interest in another in

1904, but business did not develop as they had expected. It was a year before they shipped any iron ore from Lake Superior or steel from the mills built by Andrew Carnegie. In the meantime, they were having a falling out. Ramsey, the astute railroad man, saw things he felt should be done, but Gould didn't want to commit the money. In October 1905, there was a proxy fight and Ramsey lost.[12]

In the same year, Gould gave up his interest in the Ann Arbor and the line came under the control of the Detroit, Toledo and Ironton Railroad. Eugene Zimmerman was president of both railroads for the next five years. Surprisingly, Joseph Ramsey, now out of the Gould empire, stayed as vice president of the Ann Arbor. The Detroit, Toledo and Ironton was a north-south railroad running between Detroit and Ironton, Ohio, a small town on the Ohio River across from Kentucky and close to the West Virginia state line. The Detroit, Toledo and Ironton needed a route to the west, and the Ann Arbor provided it with its cross-lake service, while the Ann Arbor needed the westbound traffic the Detroit, Toledo and Ironton could supply. The Ann Arbor had another new president, and the home office moved to Detroit (the Detroit, Toledo and Ironton's home town).[13]

Eugene Zimmerman recognized the same need for another Ann Arbor boat that Ramsey had seen, and in 1906 construction of the *Ann Arbor No. 4* began at the Globe Iron Works in Cleveland. Construction was completed in the fall, and the ship left Cleveland for Frankfort on Thanksgiving Day, November 28, 1906. Maintaining the Ann Arbor tradition, she ran into a winter storm and anchored at the Straits of Mackinac for three days.[14]

The *No. 4*, built of steel, was 259 feet long with 52 feet of beam, about the same length as the earlier Ann Arbor ships and about the same power. Probably due to the good experience with the steel-hulled *No. 3*, the *No. 4* was not given a double bottom. Ironically, she could have used one. While the *No. 3* was nearly accident free during her entire life, the *No. 4* suffered numerous groundings, some of which put her in danger of sinking, and she could have benefited greatly from the protection a double bottom would have afforded.

It has been said that the highest form of flattery is imitation. If that is true the Ann Arbor was deserving of praise because other lines began initiating cross-lake rail service based on the Ann Arbor's achievements. In 1895, the Pittsburgh, Shenango and Lake Erie Railroad built two wooden car ferries, the *Shenango I* and *Shenango II*, to operate across Lake Erie to Port Dover, Ontario. They were similar to the Ann Arbor boats—designed by Frank E. Kirby—but larger and not nearly so successful. Both were underpowered and, even with their bow propellers, were not up to the task of fighting Lake Erie ice in winter. The *Shenango I* burned in 1904.[15] The *Shenango II* was leased to the Flint and Pere Marquette Railroad at Ludington and renamed the *Pere Marquette No. 16.* Even the Ann Arbor leased her for a short time. In 1907, while leased to the Ann Arbor and chartered to another company, she suffered a disastrous trip en route from Peshtigo, Wisconsin, to South Chicago in which she lost control of most of her cargo, smashed her stanchions, and broke many of her steam connections, disabling the engines. The crew finally brought her to port under her own power, but her career as a self-propelled car ferry was over.[16]

The management of the Flint and Pere Marquette Railroad followed the experience of the Ann Arbor, the car ferries at the Straits of Mackinac, and the boats on Lake Eire with great interest. They had been in the business of running break-bulk boats across the lake from Ludington since 1875, at first chartering and then buying boats of their own. By 1895 they had five boats crossing the lake, and they decided to act—contracting to build a 337-foot steel car ferry designed by Robert Logan, a well-known naval architect from Cleveland who would have a profound effect on car ferry design in the years to come. Meanwhile, the Flint and Pere Marquette Railroad negotiated with the Wisconsin Central Railroad to build a branch line from Neenah, Wisconsin, to Manitowoc, giving it an east/west connection. The line was completed in June of 1896, and, ironically, the Ann Arbor was the first to use the connection. The Flint and Pere Marquette's new boat, the *Pere Marquette,* did not begin service until February 1897.[17]

The winter of 1908 was not particularly severe. The stagecoaches that ran across the ice of Green Bay operated for only five weeks and shut down in late March after horses went through the ice on two trips, thoroughly frightening the passengers.[18] It was time for the Ann Arbor to open navigation on Green Bay. On April 1 (perhaps there was a message in the date) the *No. 3* and *No. 2* left Frankfort for their first spring trip to Menominee.

The preferred (and shortest) route from Frankfort to Menominee was through the Sturgeon Bay Ship Canal, but in the early spring and near the end of the shipping season in January the best route often was

Ann Arbor No. 2 in Manitowoc. The Ann Arbor was the first to use the new connection developed by the Flint and Pere Marquette Railroad. *(Photo from the A. C. Frederickson Collection.)*

through Death's Door. The "Door" was the first natural passage from Lake Michigan into Green Bay at the north end of the Door Peninsula, about forty miles north of the Sturgeon Bay Ship Canal. Named Porte des Morts by the French in the 1600s, the Door was a narrow passage between several islands with many rocks and shoals. It was particularly hazardous to sailing vessels because of its strong current but also to steam vessels under conditions of limited visibility or in a storm.[19] The exact number of shipwrecks caused by conditions at the Door is subject to error, but an 1870 proposal to Congress to build the Sturgeon Bay Ship Canal stated that an average of eight vessels were lost each year.[20] The added distance and inherent danger of passing through the Door were major factors in the decision to build the canal, which was opened to large vessels in 1890 and taken over by the federal government in 1893. The Door was usually clear of ice earlier than the canal, so it was the first choice in the early spring.

After twenty-four hours of battling their way into the Death's Door passage the *No. 3* and *No. 2* were defeated. The ice was four feet thick, and that was simply more than they could handle. They retreated and went north to the passage around Washington Island, a much wider passage, which, while farther out of their way, should have been easier.[21] Again they could not force their way through, so they returned to Frankfort, arriving three days after they had left port.[22] Three days later the *No.*

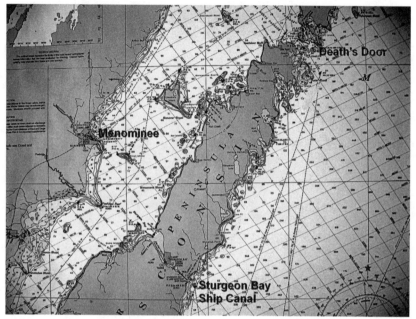

The Ann Arbor boats often found it easier to reach Menominee through Death's Door in the early spring. The chart shows the route. *(Photo of U.S. government chart by the author.)*

3 and the *No. 2* again set out for Menominee with two soon to be famous captains in charge, Alexander Larson on the *No. 3* and Charles Frederickson commanding the *No. 2.* This time they got through the Door but ran into very heavy ice in Green Bay along with a gale that could have done serious damage to both boats. When the boats arrived, they received a greeting fit for the *Queen Mary* or the *Queen Elizabeth* (neither of which had yet been built). The Menominee fire whistle gave several prolonged blasts, and then whistles and horns from all of the factories and mills near the harbor joined in. Hundreds of people lined the docks to see the vessels, some even going out on the ice to get a better look. The *Menominee Herald Leader* interviewed Captain Larson and reported his story as follows.[23]

CAPTAIN TELLS HIS STORY

When interviewed in his cabin this morning, Capt. Larson told an interesting story, or rather series of stories, for the three battles which the boats fought are each a chapter in themselves.

"After finally fighting our way back to Frankfort last week, after we found it impossible to work through the ice at Door Bluff, we remained in Frankfort until midnight of April 6. Then with a crew of seventy-five men, not including the officers, the two boats left the dock, so as to reach the ice fields bright and early in the morning. We made Plum Island about 7 o'clock and found no ice there, but as we worked our way toward Cedar River, we began to encounter resistance."

ICE PILED MOUNTAINS HIGH

"Here, in ice twenty-four inches thick, we made the southern turn. *No.* 2 took the lead, with the prow of the second boat pressing against the stern. With both vessels using every ounce of power possible, we moved through the ice at a snail's pace and hardly had proceeded ten miles when we began to encounter the windrows. The wind had piled the thick blue ice up twenty-five feet in our course so there was nothing to do but attack it and that we did. *No.* 2 would back and then ram ahead at full speed, only to get stuck fast and hard in the mountainous mass. The second boat was then obliged to circle about it, cautiously chipping away at the ice until the sister ship was released."

ICE HOLDS UP BOAT

"Again and again and again this performance was repeated, the windrows growing higher and thicker as we crept toward Chambers Island. At nine o'clock Tuesday night, both crews exhausted from their hard work, we concluded the fight for the day. Promptly at five o'clock in the morning, just as the sun arose, we began Wednesday's battle and let me say that nearing Chambers Island I never before encountered such ice in my marine career. On one occasion *No.* 2, after a flying start, leaped partly upon a windrow, and so powerful was the ice that the boat remained on its side for five minutes before the support gave way."

ESCAPED FORCE OF BLIZZARD

"By the way, we were partly out of the path of Tuesday night's blizzard, although the wind and snow tore across our decks with such force that the boats were shaken from stem to stern. Not the slightest damage resulted, however, as there was no open water on any side of us. Slowly but surely we needled our way toward Chambers Island yesterday and during the afternoon when about 16 miles from Menominee, we noticed that the ice grew weaker. At nine o'clock last night we were about 15 miles from the city and having the race practically won, we took things easy and rested until daybreak."

END WAS CHILD'S PLAY

"Five o'clock this morning the engines again began to pound and the ice to crumble away. Let me say that for the benefit of many people who watched the last few miles of our journey, that the ice bucking in that territory was child's play compared to what was near Chambers Island. Not a steel plate on either boat was wrenched or a particle of machinery jarred. We used about 500 tons of coal in the last fight and about 300 tons on our first attempt. That was the biggest portion of the expense, but I can not state definitely how much it cost the Ann Arbor people to open navigation. It was over $1,000, however.

We will return to Frankfort late this afternoon and expect four days of hard work to make the return trip. If the channel has become solid again we shall have practically the same job cut out for us as the one we completed today."

Fortunately for the two ships and their crews, Captain Larson was mistaken about the difficulty awaiting them on the return trip. They departed Menominee the same evening, passed through the Sturgeon Bay Ship Canal without difficulty, and arrived at Frankfort the next day.

FIVE ✳ *From Out of the Blue*

Mrs. Wilson, a cabin maid on the *Ann Arbor No. 4,* was lying on her bunk trying to get some rest while the crew was loading iron ore on the car deck below. They were in Manistique, and it was Sunday night, May 29, 1909, a date she would not soon forget. Suddenly she was thrown from her bed and landed on the floor with a thud—a floor that was tilting. It took no time for her to realize that there was something very wrong. She dressed hurriedly while the floor tipped even more, then rushed out the cabin door, across the slanting deck to the ladder (stairway) that led down to the car deck, and off the boat. Once away from the boat and on level ground, she watched the *No. 4* roll completely on her side and sink in twenty feet of water.

The accident, the worst to date in the Ann Arbor's history, took place in a matter of minutes. The entire crew got off safely, but hardly anyone escaped with more than the clothes on his or her back. That night the company put them up in the Hiawatha Hotel, and the following day they returned to the boat to retrieve their belongings. The crew members with cabins on the starboard side of the boat were able to climb aboard and remove some of their things, but those whose cabins were on the port side—the mates and engineers—were not so fortunate. Their cabin entries were completely submerged.[1]

The capsizing occurred due to a serious error by the loading crew. Car ferries were designed to be quite stable, but in the loading and unloading process they were subjected to some instability by the very fact that it was impossible to load both sides of a boat at once. The Ann Ar-

After the *Ann Arbor No. 4* capsized at Manistique, the company had to remove plates on the starboard side and take off several railcars before she could be righted and pumped out. *(Photo from the A. C. Frederickson Collection.)*

bor had adopted guidelines that, had they been followed, would have prevented the accident. The *No. 4* (and all other Ann Arbor car ferries) was designed with four tracks running the length of the boat. The two inside tracks could hold eight cars each; the outer tracks four cars each. The normal procedure was to load half of one inside track first (four cars); followed by all of the other inside track (eight cars), then complete loading the first track (four more cars). In that way there was never a disparity of more than half of one track's capacity at any one time. The outside tracks were loaded the same way. One outside track received two cars, the other outside track four cars, and then the final two cars were loaded on the first track. Whenever the railroad crew pushed cars onto the boat, they placed idler cars (unloaded flatcars) between the locomotive and the cars to be left on the boat on each pass. Never were they to put more loaded cars on a track than would remain there, and never was the locomotive to be placed on either the boat or the apron.

When loading the *No. 4* that night, the crew properly loaded the two inside tracks; but then, for whatever reason (probably to save time), they ran an entire string of eight railcars filled with iron ore onto the port outside track. Later the railroad engineer said he had intended to leave only two of the cars on the track and pull the others off, but the boat imme-

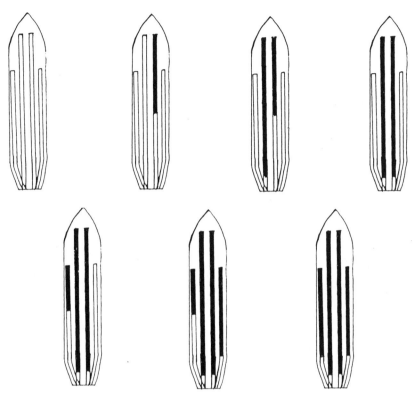

The proper loading sequence (from left to right in the diagram) requires that the imbalance of railcars never be greater than half a track. (*Drawings from the author's collection.*)

diately began to list. Before the loading crew could uncouple the two cars so he could back off, a coupling broke near the engine, making it impossible to remove any of the cars. All the crew could do was get off the boat and watch.[2]

As the boat listed more and more to port, the cars on the starboard side tipped over and crashed against the cars on the port side, crushing stanchions and tearing out the smokestack. The boat went straight to the bottom. The *No. 4* had been secured to the pier with a heavy line, which parted as she rolled over. The sound was heard all the way into downtown Manistique. The rudder and propellers were damaged as the boat was torn from the apron, and the apron itself was destroyed.

Two days after the accident the *No. 3* arrived and took most of the crew back to Frankfort. Six stayed on to help with the salvage. The company rigged a makeshift apron in the upper harbor, allowing the men to load railcars onto its other car ferries, but it was slow work. They had to load one car at a time. The Ann Arbor hired the tug *Favorite* to right the vessel, a task that proved even more difficult than expected. Nothing could be accomplished without first removing some of the railcars. A full twelve hundred tons of iron ore had been loaded. The job took about three weeks. They began by removing a substantial number of plates on the ship's starboard side and then pulled out about half of the cars using a large crane. They couldn't remove the remaining cars without cutting some of the stanchions, which they were hesitant to do because they didn't want to endanger the vessel's structural integrity any further. With as many cars as possible removed, they built a cofferdam—a watertight structure—around the stern and began pumping.

Once the boat was righted and afloat, the damage looked worse than it was, with a gaping hole in her starboard side, a number of bulging plates in her port side, and a slight list due to the imbalance of the cars that remained on the boat. The boilers had been torn from their fastenings, but the engines were intact. Much of the deckhouse would have to be rebuilt or replaced. Fortunately, the hull below the waterline was sound with no leakage. The *Favorite* towed the *No. 4* to Frankfort, where the remaining cars were removed. She was then taken to Milwaukee for major repairs.[3] It was late September before she returned to service.

The accident was expensive: $28,186 to raise the boat and $36,645 for repairs.[4] It is not clear who, if anyone, was held responsible. The railroad engineer who ran the eight loaded cars onto the *Ann Arbor No. 4* obviously made the decision that sank the boat, but the mate was responsible for loading the boat and the captain was responsible for everything. Captain Fred Robertson was called back to Frankfort and made marine superintendent, but shortly thereafter he retired from the Ann Arbor and started a fish business in Northport, Michigan. It may be that he was less forgiving of himself than his superiors.

Less than a year later another Ann Arbor captain, forty-one-year-old B. F. Tulledge, found himself in a potentially career-ending situation. He was in Manitowoc doing something all captains fear—filling out a wreck report. Just four days earlier he had been stuck in windrows near Manistique, and now he was explaining why he no longer had a ship. It began at 4:45 p.m. on Tuesday, March 8, 1910. There was no warning. The *Ann Arbor No. 1* had finished loading at the Chicago and North Western slip

Ann Arbor No. 4 after righting, with *No. 3* alongside. The *No. 4* was towed back to Frankfort and then to Milwaukee for major repairs. *(Photo courtesy of the Benzie Area Historical Museum.)*

in Manitowoc and was ready to get under way. As he was about to give the order to cast off, Captain Tulledge looked down from the bridge and saw smoke coming from the forward part of the ship. He sounded the alarm instead.

By all accounts, the fire took no more than ten minutes, and perhaps as few as five, to envelop the entire ship in flames. The burning wooden hull was filled with railcars full of lumber, sashes and doors, malt, pails, chairs, wagons, cheese, bark, and paper—all flammable—like a fire made entirely of kindling. It was impossible to fight the fire onboard. The crew and the lone passenger simply tried to get off—and that was harrowing for some. The *Pere Marquette No. 17*, which was standing by, passed a ladder between the rails of the two ships, some twenty feet above the water, and most of the crew crawled across to safety. One crew member asked for a line from the *No. 17*, and when he got it, he jumped off the *No. 1* and crashed into the side of the *No. 17*. He was injured but not seriously. Another fell from the ladder into the water and was fished out by the crew of the *No. 17*. The entire crew got off safely. One of the few people to save any belongings was the passenger, William Hern, of Two Rivers, Wisconsin. He salvaged his satchel and trunk. Captain Tulledge lost all of his belongings, including his license, in the inferno.

Ann Arbor No. 1 burning in Manitowoc on March 8, 1910. The *No. 4* is on the left. *(Photo from the A. C. Frederickson Collection.)*

The switch engine that had loaded the ship was still nearby, but there was no chance of pulling the cars off the boat. They had already been secured with jacks, and the crew members could not possibly fight their way into the flames raging on the car deck to loosen them. The Manitowoc Fire Department arrived quickly and put three streams of water on the fire. The *Pere Marquette No. 17* put another stream on the fire, as did the shipyard itself. Before long, the *Ann Arbor No. 4* arrived; the *Pere Marquette No. 17* departed and the *No. 4* took her place. She put another three streams of water on the fire, but it was all in vain. There was no hope of saving the *No. 1*, but there were still some serious concerns— that the boilers might blow up and the fire spread to the nearby coal yards. Neither happened. For about an hour the ship's whistle blasted across the city as a kind of dying last gasp of the vessel. The exhaust pipe had burned and fallen across the whistle cord, activating the whistle and adding to the feeling of helplessness that infused the hundreds of people watching the tragic event. By the end of the evening the *No. 1* had burned to the waterline.

The next morning the *No. 4* towed her out of the slip to a point near the south breakwater, where she sank in fifteen feet of water. Parts of the wreck came within three feet of the surface, but it was thought she would not pose a hazard to navigation because of her location.[5] In the fall, the Ann Arbor attempted to salvage the engines, but the effort was abandoned after a storm interrupted the proceedings. The following May the Coast Guard determined that the submerged hulk was a menace to navigation and ordered it removed. The Smith Wrecking Company raised and towed it to Muskegon, Michigan, where it was sold to the Love Construction Company for use as a sand scow.[6]

The accident dealt a serious blow to the Ann Arbor, but it could have been much worse. Had the ship left port before the fire occurred, it is likely that none of the crew members would have survived. Without time to lower a lifeboat, they would have soon perished in the icy March waters of Lake Michigan. The *No. 1* was insured for $60,000 and valued at $100,000 on the company books. The company took a $40,000 charge against its profit for the year. Coupled with the $64,000 cost of raising and repairing the *No. 4,* the Ann Arbor suffered its greatest losses since the company's inception. Fortunately, they occurred in a very good business year—one in which the company could afford them. In spite of the losses, the company showed a net income of $84,294—a full $66,000 ahead of the previous year.[7]

The cause of the fire was never publicly revealed. Some thought that spontaneous combustion in the car filled with malt may have started the conflagration, but there was no evidence to support that explanation. Captain Tulledge was ordered back to Frankfort, but it does not appear that he was held responsible for the disaster. When the company launched a new car ferry in January of the following year, B. F. Tulledge was her master.

There is an epilogue to the story. Nearly seventy years later, the *Anchor News,* a publication of the Wisconsin Maritime Museum in Manitowoc, printed an article written by Gordon Heffernan, the son of Frank Heffernan, who was chief engineer on the *Ann Arbor No. 1* at the time she burned. The younger Heffernan stated that his father knew who started the fire but didn't tell anyone for fear of losing his job. He laid the responsibility on a young deckhand who had been in the company's employ for about two weeks. Whenever the ship was in port, one of the deckhands was assigned to lubricate the steering engine machinery, which was located in the forward part of the ship beneath the car deck. The space around the machinery was used to store lube oil, grease, kerosene, and waste material. There was no electricity in that part of the ship, so the deckhand usually carried a lantern for illumination. The young man assigned to the job that day had been sloppy in the past, not bothering to take a lantern. Instead, he had carried a torch he had made by wrapping burlap around the end of a sawed off broomstick, dipping it in kerosene, and lighting the end. Since nearly everything in the compartment was highly flammable, it wouldn't have taken much of a slip to start a fire. Several of the crewmen were aware of the young man's practice and had voiced their concerns to the mate.

Years later Chief Engineer Heffernan told his son, "When I returned to the ship after a short visit with my family that afternoon, and just seconds before I was to go down to the engine room, I heard a cry of 'Fire, Fire' up forward on the cardeck and to my surprise, saw huge clouds of black smoke emanating from the access hole of this storage room, followed quickly by this young deckhand with the flaming torch in his hand. Apparently, he had ventured too close to the kerosene drums. The young deckhand, from around the farm area of Okema, Michigan, was never seen again. He just took off."[8]

There was an inquest by the federal inspectors for boilers and hulls, but there is no evidence that any of the crewmen divulged what they knew. Gordon Heffernan stated, "The officials from Milwaukee questioned the crew about the cause of the fire. My father was present at the hearing, but I do not know whether or not he gave this information to the inspectors. I believe he was happy in his $120 a month job as chief engineer and did not want to jeopardize his position by releasing too many details pinpointing the cause of the fire. Other crewmembers at the meeting may have felt the same way."[9]

With the burning of the *No. 1* the Ann Arbor sorely needed another boat—and not just another *Ann Arbor No. 3* or *No. 4*. It needed a larger boat and a better icebreaker. Competitive lines had already built larger, more powerful ships. The Pere Marquette had built three vessels 340 feet in length with capacity for thirty-two railcars, and the Grand Trunk Railroad, operating between Grand Haven and Milwaukee, owned two ships significantly larger and more powerful than the Ann Arbor boats.

While it is not known for certain, the Ann Arbor had probably stuck to the shorter length when building the *No. 3* and *No. 4* because of perceived harbor restrictions. In the early days, the shallow channel into Frankfort Harbor may have discouraged the purchase of a longer, heavier boat, but by 1910 the channel entrance was twenty-two feet deep and the Ann Arbor badly needed a boat that could cross Green Bay to Menominee in winter.

The company turned to Frank E. Kirby, the naval architect who had designed the *No. 1* and *No. 2*, and Kirby delivered. The *Ann Arbor No. 5*

Ann Arbor No. 1 burning in Manitowoc. The young man on the far right of the group of people in the middle is Gordon Heffernan. *(Photo from the A. C. Frederickson Collection.)*

was 360 feet long and 56 feet wide with a capacity for thirty-two railcars—the largest car ferry on the lakes and a superb icebreaker. On her initial voyage to Frankfort from the shipyard in Toledo, where she was built, she plowed through two feet of blue ice without difficulty. Later she would show an ability to go through sheet ice up to three feet thick and at times would force her way through ice fields that extended a full twenty feet to the bottom. Almost immediately upon her arrival in Frankfort, she became known as "The Bull of the Woods."[10]

The ship's two steam engines produced three thousand horsepower, making her not only the best icebreaker but the fastest boat in the Ann Arbor fleet, setting new records to every destination across the lake. The *No. 5* would get stuck in the ice occasionally but not for the prolonged periods of time that had plagued the earlier boats. She was also the first car ferry on the lakes to have a sea gate, a structure that could be lowered at the stern to reduce the danger of taking water over the stern in a major storm. Captain Tulledge had a fine flagship to command.

The *No. 5*'s value was multiplied by the fact that she could be used as an escort for the other Ann Arbor boats, leading the way and breaking them out when they got mired in windrows. In February 1912 the *No. 3*, *No. 4*, and *No. 5* made a round trip from Frankfort to Manistique that

Ann Arbor No. 5 cut a striking figure as she rested in Frankfort Harbor shortly after she was built. *(Photo from the A. C. Frederickson Collection.)*

proved her value. About five miles south of Manistique all three boats became stuck in a windrow that extended for about a mile, blocking their way. The *No. 5* freed herself, skirted the windrow, and entered Manistique. After unloading her cargo and loading for the return trip, she backed out of the harbor and broke the other boats out. The *No. 3* and *No. 4* went into Manistique, unloaded, and loaded for the trip back to Frankfort; then left the harbor to follow the *No. 5* south and west along the Michigan and Wisconsin shore. The going was slow, and the three ships stopped each night, becoming frozen in by morning. They broke themselves out at the start of each day and continued, with the *No. 5* breaking a path through the ice. Finally, they reached a point off the Wisconsin shore where they could cross Lake Michigan to Frankfort in relatively open water. The return trip to Frankfort took five days—the entire round trip nine days—but the three ships completed their assignment successfully. Only a few years earlier the Ann Arbor's smaller boats would have been stuck indefinitely.[11]

Ironically, the *No. 5* did not go to Menominee until the spring of 1912. The slip was too small to accommodate a vessel one hundred feet longer than the earlier boats and had to be rebuilt. Thereafter, the *No. 5* did her job, keeping Green Bay open longer than before, but even she, alone, could not keep a channel open all winter.

Friday evening, January 12, 1912, was clear and cold in Frankfort, with a light east wind. The high school girls played and won a basketball game

Visitors to the Royal Frontenac Hotel arrived by Ann Arbor train and Lake Michigan boats each summer. *(Photo from the A. C. Frederickson Collection.)*

in the Armory building, a dance was held at the Eagle's Club in Elberta (formerly South Frankfort—the name was changed in 1911), and a switch engine was moving railcars around in preparation for loading an Ann Arbor boat. About midnight, with the game over and the dance winding down, the Royal Frontenac Hotel across the harbor in Frankfort caught fire. The hotel was unoccupied and unattended, the company having shut it down each winter since 1907 due to lack of guests. There was no possibility of saving the huge wooden structure. In fact, had there not been the east wind blowing the flames away from the rest of the town, much of Frankfort might have perished with the hotel.

Word of the fire spread quickly, and soon Frankfort residents, many of whom had been asleep, were pouring from their homes to witness the blaze. As the fire raged, Bill Rathburn watched with particular interest. He owned several slot machines that were in the hotel game room for the entertainment of guests in the summer, and he was not about to lose them if he could help it. The fire was still at the other end of the five-hundred-foot-long building, so there was time to get his machines out if he could get inside the building. He tried the door, and it was open. Mr. Rathburn saved his slot machines and by so doing set off a night of looting that was totally out of character for Frankfort residents. Townspeople ran into the building and emerged with chairs, tables, lamps, bedding, paintings—all manner of goods. If it could be carried, someone took it. By the time the fire had spread to the whole building, residents were carrying their new treasures back to their homes.

It is difficult to understand how otherwise honest, hardworking, churchgoing people would do something they obviously knew to be wrong. One possible explanation is that there was no Ann Arbor management presence in town and no individual thought he or she would get caught. A more compelling explanation is that the townspeople knew everything would be burned anyway, so they were not really stealing—the Ann Arbor would lose its chairs, tables, paintings, and other expensive furnishings regardless of what the residents did. Whatever the rationale, it was not a glorious night for the people of Frankfort.

A few days later an Ann Arbor detective and Benzie County sheriff William K. Gates arrived in town. The Ann Arbor official and Sheriff Gates did not buy the proposition that it was acceptable to steal furniture that would have burned up anyway and demanded that the property be returned. It was (and still is) against the law to steal from a burning building. The stolen goods were of uniformly higher quality than the china, glassware, and furniture in most Frankfort homes, and it would not have been difficult to prosecute a case of larceny from a burning building, but the Ann Arbor said it was willing to reduce the charge to petty larceny for anyone who returned the stolen goods. So residents from all across town showed up with beautiful glassware, lamps, and ornate pieces of furniture to accept their punishment—a fine of $9.10 per person. There never was an explanation for the cause of the fire. Many speculated that the Ann Arbor was losing money on the hotel and was glad to see it gone. There was no effort to rebuild the Royal Frontenac Hotel.[12]

SIX ✵ *The Men Who Built It*

The Ann Arbor Railroad progressed northwest through the state of Michigan, crossed the lake to Wisconsin, and became a quality organization due to the efforts of a few uniquely visionary and tenacious people—not the least of whom was James Ashley.

When James Mitchell Ashley died in 1896, a six-paragraph obituary appeared in the *New York Times*.[1] The last sentence of the final paragraph mentioned that he had been president of the Ann Arbor Railroad.[2] Born in Allegheny, Pennsylvania, in 1824, James was raised in the small southern Ohio town of Portsmouth, where his father was a preacher. As he grew up he developed a strong sense of right and wrong, a conviction that became so powerful he broke with his father (and the church) over the issue of slavery. James could not accept the church's willingness to condone the practice in the southern states. He left home at the age of fourteen and worked on various riverboats for two years before returning to his home town of Portsmouth. For the next several years he worked as a printer and editor for several newspapers and studied law under the tutelage of a local lawyer, passing the bar at the age of twenty-five.

Ashley worked with the Underground Railroad from 1839 to 1841 and continued to help slaves escape to the North for the next ten years. In 1851 his activities became public knowledge, and it was time for him to leave Portsmouth for his own safety. He found a job opportunity in Toledo and late in the year returned to Portsmouth to marry Emma J. Smith. The couple settled in Toledo and had four children: James Jr.,

James Mitchell Ashley. *(Photo courtesy of the Library of Congress, Prints and Photographs Division.)*

1854; Henry, 1856; Charles, 1864; and Mary, 1866.[3] Ashley made sure that his daughter attended college, a unique privilege for a woman in those days. James Jr. and Henry became heavily involved with the railroad upon the completion of their schooling.

James Ashley was elected to Congress in 1858 as a representative from Toledo. In Congress, he was a major voice for the abolition of slavery, placing a proviso in the enabling acts for the territories of Nebraska, Colorado, and Nevada requiring the people in each territory to covenant that slavery not be established within its limits without the approval of Congress. In the House of Representatives, he officially took charge of the Thirteenth Amendment, which abolished slavery, and was credited by many for its passage. He was a friend of Abraham Lincoln's and campaigned for him in the presidential elections of 1860 and 1864. He counted many of the leaders of the time as friends, including Charles Sumner and Horace Greeley.[4]

After the Civil War, Ashley was very hard on the South, feeling that Andrew Johnson was much too soft in his reconstruction policies. He

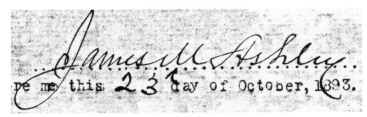

James Ashley's signature on a petition to the U.S. Circuit Court, Northern District of Ohio, Western Division, in the case of the *Craig Shipbuilding Company v. the Toledo, Ann Arbor and North Michigan Railway Company. (Courtesy of the National Archives and Records Administration—Great Lakes Region, Chicago.)*

took part in the effort to impeach Johnson, and when it failed his political career was doomed. He lost his bid for reelection in Ohio, but some of his friends in Washington persuaded President Grant to appoint him governor of the Montana Territory. Ashley accepted the appointment and moved west with his family in 1869, expecting a good reception because of his antislavery policies. What he found were frontiersmen mostly comprised of opposition party members and former Confederate soldiers for whom he represented the enemy. Within a year he was recalled.[5] The end of his political life was a huge blow, but it set the conditions for a new career in railroading upon his return to Toledo and subsequent move to Ann Arbor in 1875.

Ashley's sense of fairness was evident in everything he did. In 1887, he delineated in the annual report of the Toledo, Ann Arbor and North Michigan Railroad (TAA&NM) what may have been the first profit-sharing plan ever devised. The plan stated that whenever a dividend was paid to stockholders each employee with five or more years of service would receive a payment as well based on his or her length of service. Also, upon retirement after at least twenty years of service, each employee would receive stock certificates whose par value equaled the wages paid for the final year of employment.[6] As it turned out, no employee ever received a payment because there were no dividends before the road went into receivership in 1893. Ashley's position on the strike in 1893, which helped bring down the business, was also based on his sense of fairness. He agreed to the wage demands of the workers but was unwilling to force two engineers who had been with the company for eighteen years to join the union against their will. Had he acquiesced, his future might have turned out differently.

With the railroad built and operating in the early 1880s, Ashley began to expand. After some false starts he organized the Toledo, Ann Arbor and North Michigan to extend the line north to Mount Pleasant. Ashley now resided in New York, where he could keep the financial front alive and put twenty-five-year-old James Jr., Big Jim as he was soon known, in charge of construction. While James supplied the direction and sought financial backing for the business, James Jr. made it happen. A large and imposing man, James Jr. used his physical presence and visibly strong will to make James's dreams come true. In the fourteen years during which the railroad expanded north and west from Ann Arbor, Big Jim's reputation grew, bolstered by incidents such as the siege that occurred in January 1886 at Howell.

As James Jr.'s construction crew approached the small town of Howell in late 1885, it was necessary to lay track across the tracks of the Detroit, Lansing and Northern Railroad (DL&N), which ran northwest-southeast, just south of town. The DL&N track was raised on an embankment, so Ashley's men would have to cut a path through the embankment and build a bridge for the DL&N to pass over their tracks. The company had already laid track on either side of the junction, but the DL&N management would not allow Big Jim's men to cross. Ashley wanted to build a wooden trestle, but the DL&N wanted a trestle built of stone. That would take longer to construct and be more expensive.[7] Also there were questions concerning the right of the Toledo, Ann Arbor and North Michigan to cross the opposing track; these would be settled at a later date in the Michigan Supreme Court.[8]

The Ashleys could not wait. They needed to initiate rail service to Howell and north into Gratiot County within a month if they were to cash in on financial commitments from municipalities (estimates range from twenty thousand to two hundred thousand dollars), which they needed to pay their contractors. Big Jim took matters into his own hands on Saturday, January 2, 1886, when he took a special train with about three hundred workers, many armed with muskets and bayonets, from Toledo to the point of the junction. He expected resistance, but the DL&N men were overmatched and retreated. His men blasted a passageway through the embankment with dynamite and began laying track. Overnight his men constructed an eighty-foot wooden bridge to allow the DL&N to pass over the TAA&NM track. By noon on Sunday the work was completed and he retired from the scene with his men. In a few hours the DL&N retaliated. A train filled with workmen arrived with a car full of gravel and immediately began tearing up the TAA&NM track. Then they poured gravel into the gap in the embankment.

When Big Jim learned of the action, he telegraphed his brother Henry in Toledo to bring reinforcements and returned to the crossing. Ashley's men advanced by foot over the snow-covered field to the crossing with muskets at the ready, but the DL&N men fled. Ashley's men tore up some of the DL&N track on each side of the bridge to prevent the railroad from bringing in any more gravel, and the war was on. Big Jim and his men stood guard at the crossing to protect their turf. The Monday DL&N passenger train did not run because of the gaps in the track, but the railroad did not take the matter lying down. Big Jim was served a warrant and taken to Detroit to be arraigned for disrupting the U.S. mail—then released on bail.[9]

On his arrival back at Howell, he was greeted as a hero but was arrested again and taken to Brighton. Once more he posted bail and returned to the crossing. By now the citizens of Howell were solidly in the camp of the TAA&NM. Some had put up money to bring the railroad to town, and all would benefit from a connection to Toledo and the East. A citizens' meeting on January 7 condemned the actions of DL&N and requested that the parties settle their differences in court.[10]

Big Jim and about forty of his men stayed at the crossing in preparation for a prolonged siege. He procured stoves and rations, using freight cars for shelter against the January cold. On Friday, January 8, the first Toledo, Ann Arbor and North Michigan train entered Howell, giving the town access by rail to Toledo and the railroad needed money to meet its obligations. James Jr. and his men remained at the crossing until Tuesday of the following week when the railroad commissioner of Michigan convinced the parties to declare a truce and—as the townspeople had requested—settle the matter in court.[11] Big Jim's reputation soared.

In 1890, James became ill. The following year, James Jr. went to New York to act as the company's financial agent.[12] It was in that capacity that Big Jim and the company met their financial demise. In the fall of 1892 the Ashleys attempted to sell bonds to fund improvements for the company and the building of the ships, but they couldn't get a high enough price. That was understandable considering the company was embarking on a project (the car ferries) that no shippers thought could be successful. Since the company could not raise the needed funds, James Jr. put up 20,000 (possibly 25,000) shares of TAA&NM stock that he and his father owned debt free and some company bonds as collateral on which to borrow several hundred thousand dollars, which he loaned to the company. The loans were predicated on the stock maintaining a value of $38 or above.

In December, someone or some group of investors threw a significant amount of stock on the market, depressing the price. Ashley bought enough stock to cover but when more stock was put on the market in April he did not have enough funds. On Monday, April 24, the stock was $38 1/2 at noon; then 15,000 shares were placed on the market. By 12:30 p.m. the price was down to $27. Ashley's creditors dumped his stock later in the day, and the price went to pieces.[13] In the next few days it got as low as $13. The incident also ruined the company's ability to sell bonds. On April 24 the company's consolidated bonds traded at 88. A few days later the best firm bid was 40.[14]

The company needed more financing to pay the interest due May 1 on $2,120,000 of mortgage bonds and to make a scheduled payment on the ships to the Craig Shipbuilding Company, but there was no way to raise the money. John Craig brought a complaint to the United States Circuit Court, Northern District of Ohio, Western Division, on April 27, and the court appointed Wellington Burt as receiver.[15] James Jr. and his father had taken the business much farther than anyone could have reasonably expected on almost no money of their own, but the string had run out. In 1893 James's health began to deteriorate. He suffered a severe diabetes attack in 1894. In the summer of 1896 he took sick on a fishing trip; was taken to a sanitarium in Ann Arbor, and died of a heart attack on September 16, at the age of seventy-one.[16]

Big Jim was financially ruined by the failure of the railroad, but his reputation in New York City remained largely intact. In September 1899 the *New York Times* printed a long article about his exploits.[17] He kept his head and moved to Georgia, where in five years he became wealthy again, trading in lumber and promoting electric power plants. Following in his father's footsteps, he ran for Congress twice but was defeated—the second time by only a few hundred votes. He returned to Toledo, built two power plants, and ran for Congress in his father's old district, but he was not destined for a career in politics. He died of a heart attack on November 3, 1919.[18]

Wellington R. Burt, born in New York State in 1831, was one of thirteen children in the Burt family, whose ancestors first came to America from England in 1638. Despite the early American heritage, the family

The Honorable Wellington R. Burt.
(Photo courtesy of the Saginaw News.)

was poor and moved to Jackson County, Michigan (eighty miles west of Detroit), in 1838. Wellington attended Jackson County schools, worked on the family farm, and spent two years in college. He liked to read and was very observant, taking in all that happened around him. Those who knew him in later life said he would have been a well-informed man whether or not he ever spent a day in college. At the age of twenty-two he decided to see the world, and he did, shipping off on a freighter to Australia, New Zealand, South America, and Van Dieman's Island. He remained abroad for three years, working as a miner, contractor, and sailor.[19]

On his return to Michigan in 1856 he settled on 320 acres of government land in Gratiot County near the center of the state. At the time, the settlers were so poor that the state had to send them food and other supplies. Burt went to the town of Greenville, fifty miles away, bought wheat, and hauled it back to Gratiot County where he sold (or often simply traded) it to the residents. He had started his first business. A year later he took a job in a lumber camp on the Pine River in the Saginaw Valley for thirteen dollars a month. Within a month, he had doubled his salary and was camp foreman. A year later, in 1858, he started his own business, selling logs and sawing some of them into lumber himself. He was on his way.[20]

Wellington had a good head for business and a penchant for hard work. In 1864 he built a new mill along the Saginaw River. By 1870 he had built a complete town with a mill to saw lumber, a stave and heading mill, a shingle mill, a barrel factory, a saltworks, carpenter and black-smith shops, a gasworks to light the mills and the community, and a fire hydrant system to protect his businesses and the residents from fire. In addition, he built some forty-five family residences, two boardinghouses for single employees, a school, a library, and a store. He employed 230 people. Burt named the town Melbourne after his favorite city in Aus-tralia. Ironically, his town and businesses burned in 1876 in spite of his efforts to protect them from fire.[21] Years later, when he built a railroad that passed though the remnants of the town, he officially listed Mel-bourne as a stop.[22]

As the years passed, Burt became more of an investor than a hands-on operator. Before his death, he had substantial timber holdings in Michi-gan, Minnesota, Alabama, Mississippi, and Louisiana. He held stock in several railroads in addition to bonds of several foreign countries.[23] He owned a large lumber mill in Kentucky. In the late 1890s, Burt was con-vinced that Michigan was running out of white pine, so he sent an agent to Minnesota to procure holdings in that state. The agent returned with deeds to 1,720 acres, complete with mineral rights, which he had pur-chased for under twenty thousand dollars. Burt gave the agent the choice of a flat commission or a percentage of the income from the land. The agent chose the commission, giving away his share of millions of dol-lars derived from what was soon to be the newly discovered iron deposits in the Mesabi Range. By 1919, Burt had received thirteen million dollars from a single mine on the property and the land was still producing.[24] He was active in politics, serving as mayor of East Saginaw for a time. He was elected to the state Senate in 1892 and later ran for governor but was defeated.[25]

In 1887, Burt saw a need for a railroad to connect Saginaw, Bay City, and the intervening towns with larger markets. The best way to do that was to connect with the Toledo, Ann Arbor and North Michigan at the little town of Durand. Burt and his group met with James Ashley Jr., and Burt soon joined the board of the Toledo, Ann Arbor and North Michi-gan. He and his group of investors built the Cincinnati, Saginaw and Mackinaw Railroad, which went to neither Cincinnati nor Mackinaw but did connect Bay City and Saginaw with the Toledo, Ann Arbor and North Michigan.[26] On its completion he immediately sold it to the Grand Trunk Railway System after extracting a promise that it would guarantee the bonds he held.[27]

Burt accepted a receivership of the Toledo, Ann Arbor and North

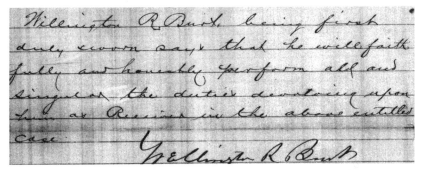

Wellington Burt's signature to a statement that he will perform the duties of receiver of the Toledo, Ann Arbor and North Michigan Railway Company. *(Courtesy of the National Archives and Records Administration—Great Lakes Region, Chicago.)*

Michigan when it failed in 1893 and kept Henry Ashley (James Jr.'s brother and Burt's son-in-law), as general manager. Whether he helped force James Jr. and his father out of the business is unclear. Both were out by mid-1894. In the coming years, James Jr. was known to be extremely upset with his brother. The two men did not speak to each other until 1912, when they shared a carriage to their mother's funeral and set their animosities aside.[28]

Wellington Burt was said to be a hardheaded businessman who could be abrasive and even deceitful—witness his handling of the E. G. Chambers property in South Frankfort (later Elberta). Chambers, a former assistant secretary of war under Edwin Stanton in the Lincoln administration, owned property in South Frankfort that the Toledo, Ann Arbor and North Michigan needed to cross to reach its car ferry dock in 1892. Chief Engineer Henry Riggs secured an injunction to prohibit Chambers from interfering with the construction, and the railroad completed its spur to the dock, but that was not the end of the matter. The company soon commenced condemnation proceedings on the land and discovered that Chambers was a canny opponent. A former lawyer, intelligent, and wealthy, he was not to be run over. He started by saying that since he was a Pennsylvania resident the case could not be tried in a Michigan state court. The court agreed, and two years later the case was heard in a federal court in Grand Rapids, Michigan, which promptly sent the case back to Benzie County. After the hearing, Burt, who was as wealthy as Chambers and did not like to lose, issued an invitation to Chambers to come to Toledo and work out a settlement. When Chambers arrived, they spent most of a day poring over maps and exchanging profanities. Finally, someone suggested a settlement of ten thousand dollars, and Riggs, the chief engineer, was told to draw up a deed, which they would sign the next day. The following morning Riggs and Chambers were in the office when Burt stuck his head in, said there was no way he would ever sign such a deed, and left the premises.

In 1896, after Riggs had left the company, he was brought back to Frankfort to testify in a new condemnation case involving the property. Chambers testified that he had gone to Toledo, met with Burt and Riggs, and they had agreed to a price of ten thousand dollars for the land. Burt testified that he did not recall ever discussing the matter with Chambers and he would never consider paying such an exorbitant price. When Riggs took the stand, the Ann Arbor attorney avoided any mention of the meeting and, amazingly, on cross-examination, Chambers's attorney didn't mention it either. That brought about a very heated discussion between Chambers and his attorney, with the result that Chambers began acting as his own attorney. He immediately asked Riggs about the meeting and the deed. Riggs said he had filed the deed with the county along with other company deeds. Burt's attorney then said he had in his possession the county file of deeds and that the deed for the Chambers land wasn't there. He presented the file to Riggs, who leafed through it, found the "missing" deed, and showed it to the court. The jury found for Chambers, awarding him the ten thousand dollars he thought he had agreed to several years earlier.[29]

Henry Earle Riggs went on to become a prominent civil engineer. Among his accomplishments were a professorship at the University of Michigan and the presidency of the American Society of Civil Engineers.[30] Some forty years later, in writing about his experience as chief engineer for the Toledo, Ann Arbor and North Michigan, Riggs wrote in his understated way that he had a "highly unfavorable opinion of Mr. Burt's memory," though he respected his railroad knowledge.[31]

Despite his questionable "memory," Burt applied his money and considerable business skills to the Ann Arbor throughout the receivership and several years afterward as president. He improved all aspects of the railroad, raising it from a level only slightly above some of the logging railroads to near first-class status. He sold his significant share of the railroad to the Gould interests in 1902 but remained on the board at their request until Eugene Zimmerman and the Detroit, Toledo and Ironton took over in 1905.[32]

Wellington Burt died in 1919, leaving an estate valued between twenty and forty million dollars. He left annuities totaling sixty-eight thousand dollars to his sons and a few servants but stipulated that the rest of his estate could not be divided until twenty-one years after the death of his last grandchild living at the time of his death.[33] His three daughters and one living son immediately contested the will and a few years later obtained distribution of his Mesabi Range holdings. The balance of his estate remains to be distributed despite several attempts to access it over the years.[34]

Biographers of Burt have contrasted him with the Ashleys, writing that the latter were mostly promoters who built the railroad in a slipshod way while Burt turned it into a profitable, quality business. That is true, but it is probably unfair to the Ashleys. James Ashley did not have financial resources of his own (certainly nothing like Wellington Burt's) and was constantly trying to raise money just to keep the business alive. The line was never positioned to become more than marginally profitable until the car ferries began operating. Had he weathered the next few years, he might well have begun plowing money back into the business to upgrade it, as did Burt and those who followed him. Indeed, the level of traffic would have demanded it. Be that as it may, it is a fact that the Ashleys built the line and Burt improved it.

When George Gould became interested in the Ann Arbor and arranged for the election of Joseph Ramsey Jr. to the presidency in 1903, the line became the beneficiary of a first-class railroad mind. Born in Pittsburgh in 1850 and educated as a civil engineer, Ramsey began his railroad career as an engineer at the age of nineteen. For the next twenty-one years he held engineering positions with a number of railroads, including the Pennsylvania.[35] One of his earliest engineering achievements was the construction in 1872 of the Bell's Gap Railroad between the little towns of Bell's Mills and Lloydsville, Pennsylvania. In one nine-mile stretch the grade rose a full twelve hundred feet through mountainous terrain requiring high trestles and a twenty-eight-degree turn (that's a sharp turn!).[36]

In 1890 Ramsey became a railroad president for the first time, and over the next twenty-five years he was president or vice president of eight different railroads. He also became a major player in the financial fights for control of several railroads. He was president of the Ann Arbor from 1903 to 1905, when Eugene Zimmerman and the Detroit, Toledo and Ironton took control of the company. In 1909 he took back control of the Ann Arbor with the help of railroad financier Newman Erb and served a year as vice president, then three years as president with Erb as chairman. Ramsey left the company in 1913 and died in his home at East Orange, New Jersey, in 1916. At the time he was president of yet another railroad.[37]

Eugene Zimmerman, president of the Ann Arbor and the Detroit, Toledo and Ironton Railroad from 1905 through part of 1909, had a plan to make his Detroit, Toledo and Ironton Railroad profitable with the help of the Ann Arbor, but the times and the U.S. government were against him. He had expected to develop coal interests in northern Kentucky that would result in shipments of five million tons a year on his railroad; however, the Hepburn Act forbade a railroad from having an interest in a coal company greater than the amount of coal it needed for its own use. The Detroit, Toledo and Ironton was reduced to relying on normal business traffic, and that was not enough to sustain a profit. In early 1908, the railroad failed to pay the interest on $8,524,000 in mortgage bonds and was thrown into receivership. Since $5,500,000 of the railroad's debt was secured with Ann Arbor stock, a battle ensued for control of both railroads.[38] Zimmerman remained president of the Ann Arbor until 1909, when he lost control of the line to Joseph Ramsey Jr. and Newman Erb.

When sixty-three-year-old Joseph Ramsey Jr. left the Ann Arbor in 1913, Erb assumed the presidency and ran the company for the next eleven years. Born in Breslau, Germany, in 1851, Newman Erb came to the United States at the age of three and was raised in Saint Louis, Missouri. After finishing high school, he got a job as a private secretary and studied accounting at night. He helped form a new accounting firm and began the study of law, passing the bar at the age of twenty-one. He founded a Little Rock, Arkansas, newspaper and another newspaper, the *Arkansas Freie Presse,* the first German-language newspaper in the state. Erb became involved with railroads in 1881 and rose to become a major figure in the railroad business nationwide. In 1885 he organized and ran the Western Telegraph Company, which later was absorbed into Western Union. In 1892 he moved to New York where he broadened his interests. Before long he had gained control of twenty different public service companies scattered around the country. In 1907 he became president of the British Columbia Copper Company. By 1910 he had control of a long list of railroads (including the Ann Arbor and the Pere Marquette) operating in nearly every state in the union.[39]

The Ann Arbor prospered under Erb's leadership. He used its earnings to pay down the debt and invest in new equipment, improving the company's ability to compete each year. In his annual reports, he often acknowledged the forbearance of the stockholders who went year after year without a dividend so the company could become stronger. While at the helm, he phased out the *Ann Arbor No. 2,* bought a new car ferry (the *Ann Arbor No. 6*), and had another on order while more than doubling cross-lake shipments between 1910 and his last year as president, 1924. In early 1925, Newman Erb died in Roosevelt Hospital, New York City, after a prostate operation. He left two daughters but no one to carry on the family name.[40]

SEVEN ✴ *The Winter of 1917*

The arrival of the *Ann Arbor No. 5* in 1911 with her capacity for thirty-two railcars, her power, and her speed, brought the Ann Arbor fleet into the modern era of larger, more powerful ships—an era that would continue until the rebuilding of vessels began in 1958. As an immediate consequence, the old wooden *No. 2* was placed on a part-time basis. She was nineteen years old, and, while wooden hulls were often used for longer periods, many met with unfortunate ends. In 1914 she was sold to the Manistee Iron Works and towed to Manistee where she was dismantled, many of her fittings sold for scrap, and her boilers put in the steamers *Marshal F. Butters* and *Petoskey*. In 1916 she was sold to the Nicholson Transit Company of Detroit, converted into a sand sucker, and renamed the *Whale*.[1] In 1927, after an accident in which she was damaged by the steamer *William E. Corey* in the St. Clair Flats, she was torn apart and abandoned.[2]

The winters were no longer the same. The *No. 5* did not get stuck as often as the smaller boats, and when she did she could usually break herself out in a relatively short period of time. Menominee was still a problem. The Ann Arbor continued to shut down operations there in early January and start up again in April, but day in and day out the *No. 5* pushed her way through heavier ice and lost less time than the *No. 3* and *No. 4*—often improving the performance of the entire fleet by breaking out the smaller boats and leading them through the heaviest ice. Then came the winter of 1917—perhaps the worst ever—the winter that put an end to the invincibility of the *No. 5*.

Ann Arbor No. 6 entering Frankfort Harbor on a windy day. *(Photo from the A. C. Frederick-son Collection.)*

In a sense, it began in the summer of 1916. That year the Ann Arbor had more traffic than it could handle, so it chartered the car ferry *Maitland No. 1* from the Toronto, Hamilton and Buffalo Navigation Company, which planned to operate her on Lake Erie.[3] The Ann Arbor was pleased with her performance over the three-month charter, and when the management heard there was a sister ship under construction at the Great Lakes Engineering Works in Ecorse, Michigan (near Detroit), it decided to buy her. The new vessel, the *Ann Arbor No. 6,* was twenty-two feet shorter than the *No. 5* with less capacity and less power. She differed from earlier Ann Arbor boats in that she did not have the swept back bow for ice breaking.[4] Nevertheless, she was expected to be a good ice-breaker, far superior to the *No. 3* and *No. 4*.

When the *No. 6* was completed and ready for service in early January 1917, the Detroit River and Lake St. Clair were already frozen solid. Conditions were bad enough that the Ann Arbor management seriously considered leaving the boat in Ecorse until spring, but the company badly needed the extra capacity the *No. 6* would provide and decided to take the risk of bringing her to Frankfort. Captain Alexander Larson was sent with a crew from Frankfort to bring her back.

At 3:05 p.m. on January 15, the *No. 6* left Ecorse, and by 6:20 she was stuck in the Detroit River. Captain Larson radioed for a tug, which broke

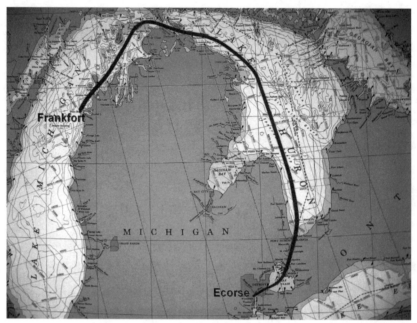

The route of the *Ann Arbor No. 6* from Ecorse, Michigan, to Frankfort. *(Photo of U.S. Government chart by the author.)*

her out in about twenty minutes the following morning. After minor repairs in Detroit, the *No. 6* spent the rest of the day plowing through the ice-covered Detroit River and across Lake St. Clair. The sheet ice ranged from five inches to two feet in thickness. Twice she got stuck in five-foot windrows. Each time she backed off, got up full power, and plowed through. Late in the day she entered the St. Clair River (which was frozen) but had to stop at about 8:00 p.m. because the officers could not see well enough to navigate. The next morning the *No. 6* pushed her way through twelve to fifteen inches of ice with some windrows on her way to Port Huron, tying up for a short time to make adjustments to her machinery and a few repairs.

At 4:35 p.m. she began the 240-mile trip up the open water of Lake Huron to the Straits of Mackinac. All went smoothly until the following afternoon when a gale force wind with snow began blowing out of the northwest. The *No. 6* was in no danger, but she took a pounding from the high waves as she crossed Thunder Bay near Alpena. She was light, with only six cars of coal onboard, which added to her punishment. When

Captain Larson saw Thunder Bay Island's North Point, he hove to, dropped both anchors, and waited out the storm. The storm blew itself out that night, so at 4:35 a.m. on January 19, he got under way and headed north toward the Straits. The *No. 6* arrived off Old Mackinaw Point about 1:30 p.m. The going was slow with sheet ice about eighteen inches thick and windrows up to fifteen feet deep. Captain Larson forced his way between the windrows, passed through the Straits, and was just past Saint Helena Island when he hit a wall. The log entry explains.

January 19   3:15 p.m.   Stuck in heavy windrows about 25 feet deep. Worked to get loose until 5:00 p.m. Was unable to get loose. Banked the fires for the night.[5]

At 7:00 a.m. on the twentieth, some members of the crew donned their heavy foul weather gear and went out on the ice in near zero degree temperatures, their job to "chisel" the boat loose with spuds, axes, and bars. Meanwhile, the crewmen aboard worked the engines forward and backward and moved the coal-filled cars back and forth to change the weight distribution, trying to break loose. At 3:30 p.m. they succeeded, and, realizing that the *No. 6* could not get through the windrows, Captain Larson turned her around and headed back toward Mackinaw City. While making the turn, the *No. 6* broke two blades off her starboard propeller. She lay overnight in the ice off the Mackinaw City docks and radioed for help from either the *Sainte Marie* or the *Chief Wawatam,* car ferries that operated across the Straits of Mackinac year-round and excellent icebreakers, quite possibly the best in the world.[6]

The next morning, January 21, brought a major snowstorm from the northeast—the most severe in several years. The *Chief Wawatam* and the *Sainte Marie* stayed in port while activity in Saint Ignace and Mackinaw City came to a halt.[7] No freight trains were sent out until noon the next day, and then they needed two engines to push their way through the snow. There was no choice but to wait it out. On that day, lying in the ice with the storm raging, Captain Larson made a decision he would later regret. He ordered the crew to unload the 450 tons of coal from the six railcars into the bunkers of the ship. He doubtless felt he would need the coal to power the ship, but in transferring all of the coal to the bunkers he lost the ability to move weight forward and aft in the ship—an ability he would need before long. Early (6:45) on January 22, the *No. 6* left Mackinaw City to see if the ice conditions had improved. By 8:00 it was

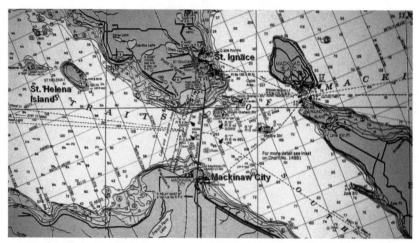

The Straits of Mackinac. Of course, the bridge was not present in 1917. *(Photo of U.S. government chart by the author.)*

clear they had not, so she turned around and headed back to Mackinaw City, but in making the turn disaster struck. The log states:

January 22   While working in heavy ice outside of the city docks we stripped all four blades off the starboard propeller and parts of all four blades off the port wheel. Ice being about 20 feet below the waterline.

The *No. 6* was now immobile.

The *new* plan was for the *Chief Wawatam* to break out the *No. 6* and tow her across the Straits to Saint Ignace where they would work on the propellers—but the *Chief Wawatam* was having troubles of her own. As she approached the *No. 6* she got stuck in the ice and couldn't get loose. At 2:00 p.m. the *No. 6* passed a line to the *Chief Wawatam* so the crew of the *Chief Wawatam* could pull her toward the stationary *No. 6* and hopefully break free. She got loose at 4:40, returned the line to the *No. 6*, moved forward about fifty feet, and got stuck again. At 8:00 she finally broke loose again and returned to Saint Ignace.[8]

Not easily dissuaded, the *Chief Wawatam* returned the next day, January 23, and broke the *No. 6* loose. She began to clear a path through the ice to Saint Ignace, but the *No. 6* was unable to follow. What was left of her propellers could not generate enough power to push her through

Chief Wawatam (left) and *Ann Arbor No. 6* at the Straits of Mackinac in 1917. *(Photo from the collection of Michael Leon.)*

the ice-filled water, so the *No. 6* returned to the city dock at Mackinaw City and the *Chief Wawatam* went back to Saint Ignace. On the morning of the twenty-fourth, the *Sainte Marie* arrived and towed her across the Straits to Saint Ignace. By now the Ann Arbor management was plenty worried about its new flagship. Mr. A. W. Towsley, the vice president and general manager from Toledo, arrived at the Straits (by rail) and made an excursion into the Straits on the *Sainte Marie* to see conditions for himself. He would have to decide whether to continue the effort to bring the *No. 6* to Frankfort or leave her at the Straits for the winter.

Captain Larson's decision to unload the coal cars came back to haunt him. To work on the propellers, it was necessary to lift the stern out of the water so the men could lay planks across the ice to make their repairs. That was normally done by moving several loaded freight cars all the way forward, filling the forward ballast tanks with water, and pumping any water out of the aft ballast tanks. Without any loaded freight cars onboard, he did not have enough weight to tip the boat. He would have liked to have exchanged the six empty cars for six full ones at the ferry dock, but the *No. 6* didn't fit. The ferries at the Straits loaded and unloaded at the bow rather than the stern, and, since bows were typically narrower than sterns, the *No. 6* could not fit between the pilings on either side of the slip.

Fortunately, the Ann Arbor had experience transferring cars directly

The Ann Arbor learned to transfer cars between vessels when one got stuck on a sandbar or in the mud and could not be pulled off. In this photo, the *No. 3* is lightening the *No. 1*. The knowledge was most helpful when the *No. 6* needed to trade cars with the *Sainte Marie* at the Straits of Mackinac in 1917. *(Photo from the A. C. Frederickson Collection.)*

from one boat to another. It had done so a number of times when one of its boats ran aground and had to be lightened before it could be pulled off the bottom. So, at 11:00 a.m., January 25, the *Sainte Marie* placed her bow against the stern of the *No. 6*. The two crews lashed the boats together, adjusted the ballast so the rails lined up, and pulled the six empty cars across to the *Sainte Marie* one at a time. The *Sainte Marie* went to the car ferry dock, exchanged the empties for full cars, returned to the *No. 6*, and repeated the procedure. The whole job was accomplished by 4:00 p.m.

Once the boats were disengaged, the crew of the *No. 6* pulled the cars forward and began filling the forward ballast tanks. Then began the job of replacing four propeller blades on the starboard side and two on the port side. Conditions were all but unbearable. In the next two days, the daily high temperatures were eleven to fifteen degrees, the lows minus five and minus twelve.[9] But the crew members knew their responsibility and stayed at their task. They finished at 8:00 a.m., January 27, then waited for the decision to lay up for the winter or attempt the trip to Frankfort. Local marine people were dubious that the *No. 6* could get

The crew changing propellers on the *Ann Arbor No. 3*, much as the crew of the *No. 6* did in 1917. *(Photo courtesy of Kelene Luedtke.)*

through the windrows near Saint Helena Island even with the help of the *Sainte Marie*, reasoning that the *No. 6* was light (with only six loaded cars), underpowered compared to the car ferries operating at the Straits, and without a bow propeller.[10] Also the Mackinac Transportation Company let it be known that it would not provide further assistance from the *Sainte Marie* unless the Ann Arbor provided the necessary coal. Coal was a scarce resource at the Straits in winter, and it was not going to waste it on a goodwill venture, even though it would be compensated financially.

The decision came back to go for it; so at 6:00 a.m., January 30, the *No. 6* left the lumber dock and followed the *Sainte Marie* into the Straits. As the two ships neared Saint Helena Island, they "ran into heavy ice about fifteen inches thick and windrows about twenty feet deep. Made headway of about three miles this afternoon."[11]

At 6:00 p.m. the *No. 6* damaged her starboard propeller and stopped for the night. Early the next morning, she started up again, following the *Sainte Marie*. She worked her way through about a quarter mile of heavy ice when suddenly conditions improved. With an ice thickness of only

Sainte Marie, quite possibly the best icebreaker in the world in 1917. Note that she loads and unloads at the bow. *(Photo courtesy of the Historical Collections of the Great Lakes, Bowling Green State University.)*

about eight inches, she stopped, loaded some provisions from the *Sainte Marie,* blew her a salute, and continued on alone. By 9:45 a.m. she was in open water, but it didn't last—nor did the relatively good weather. In the early afternoon, off Beaver Island, gale force winds hit from the northeast with snow. The waves built quickly, and visibility dropped to near zero. At 4:15 p.m. Captain Larson changed course to head into the gale and an hour later found what he no doubt was looking for—ice. With the high winds and inability to see more than a few hundred feet, the ice was suddenly his friend (no waves). The *No. 6* "laid in the ice all night waiting for the weather to change."[12]

The *No. 6* left the ice at 5:45 a.m. and headed south toward Frankfort. The wind had moderated, and visibility was relatively good with only a few snow flurries. She passed Point Betsie at 8:50 and arrived in Frankfort at 9:15, February 1, 1917, some seventeen days after her departure from the Great Lakes Engineering Works in Ecorse.[13] Captain Larson had brought her home. She spent the next two days in Frankfort with the crew working on the propellers and making minor adjustments to improve her fit to the slips before beginning cross-lake service between Frankfort and Kewaunee.

While the *No. 6* was lying in the ice off Mackinaw City waiting out the January 21 blizzard, the *Ann Arbor No. 5* was waiting out the same storm in Manitowoc. She had lost her port propeller and shaft in Manistique a few days earlier and had been in the Manitowoc dry dock for four days awaiting repairs. Another ten days passed before she was ready to face Lake Michigan, partly due to the storm and partly due to temperatures of fifteen below zero, which shut down outside work in the yard for five days. She left Manitowoc with the work completed on February 1, the day the *No. 6* arrived in Frankfort. In ten days both vessels would be stuck fast in the ice off Frankfort in an epic struggle to enter the harbor.

The battle began with the *No. 6* returning from a regular Kewaunee trip on the afternoon of February 10. For the last twenty-four hours northwest winds had been piling up a huge ice field against the Michigan shore and the winds were still pushing. Captain Larson took his ship into the ice field and plowed ahead as far as he could, but he was stopped cold by a large windrow about five miles out of Frankfort. The *No. 5*, under the command of B. F. Tulledge, left Manitowoc that evening and ran into sheet ice about an hour and a half out. She continued making her way through the ice until she found the *No. 6* about 2:30 a.m. on the eleventh. Under a cloudy sky with light snow falling and the temperature barely above zero, the *No. 5* proceeded to get stuck alongside her.

The two captains had known each other for years and brought a wealth of experience to the situation. Each had been stuck off Two Rivers Point, Wisconsin, in 1904, and each had made harrowing trips across Green Bay to end navigation on the bay in winter and start it again in the spring. The two ships did not want for knowledge or skill, but they were facing elements they could not master.

After the experience of the *No. 6* at the Straits it was clear that the *No. 5* was the better icebreaker. Indeed, she was a unique vessel among others of her size and power. Decades later Arthur Frederickson described her as follows.

Ann Arbor No. 6 (*left*) and *Ann Arbor No. 5* working together in ice. (*Photo courtesy of Roger Griner.*)

The tapering fore and aft of her hull and her powerful engines gave her a two foot rise and fall of her stern from full ahead to full astern. Her very sharp, well cut away stern which slowly widened to the width of her high, full, graceful bow, which with a slight tumblehome, her hull gradually and gracefully tapered aft through her waist and rounded sharply the slender hips of her blunted stern. While underway, she makes less disturbance in the water than any other ship of her class today.[14]

So the "Bull of the Woods" would lead the way to Frankfort. Captain Tulledge immediately gave orders to fire up the fourth boiler to give her maximum power. That took about four and a half hours. Once she had reached full power, she began working her engines back and forth, much as one "rocks" a car stuck in the snow.[15] After an hour and a half of no success, Captain Tulledge ordered the filling and emptying of her forward (nos. 1 and 2) and aft (no. 7) holds with water, trying to change the weight distribution of the vessel. A sample of her log entries gives some idea of his battle plan.

February 11 6:50 a.m.   Started working (with fourth boiler cut in).
                           Filled No. 7 tank and moved S. C. and S. W. (rail-cars) back 25 feet.

9:15 a.m.	Started pumping out No. 7 and letting water in forward tanks.
11:00 a.m.	12 feet in No. 1 and 10 feet in No. 2. Our headline and cable on No. 6 and the No. 6 cable on us trying to pull us loose while working engines.
11:45 a.m.	Finished pumping out tanks
1:00 p.m.	Changed the No. 6 cable from our bow to our stern. Both 5 and 6 crew worked spudding ice trying to get boat 5 loose.
6:00 p.m.	Put 14 feet in No. 1 and 2 holds and water level with chain locker floor
9:00 p.m.	Started to pump out
10:40 p.m.	Pumped out forward and started filling No. 7 tank
11:00 p.m.	No. 7 filled
11:30 p.m.	Working engine 11:00 p.m. to 11:30 p.m. and did not budge her, so started pumping No. 7 and filling No. 1 and 2 again.[16]

While Captain Tulledge was fighting to break the *No. 5* loose earlier in the day, the *No. 3* arrived from Manistique on her way to Frankfort. She forced her way to within a few boat lengths of the *No. 6*—then got stuck herself. Early the next morning (2:00 a.m.) the wind switched to the east, which should have helped the *No. 5* and *No. 6*, but it didn't; however, it did allow the *No. 3* to break loose about 9:15 a.m. and approach the two boats. Just after noon, she broke out the *No. 5*, and she, in turn, broke out the *No. 6*. Within a couple hours, the Bull of the Woods was leading the way to Frankfort with the *No. 6* directly behind and the *No. 3* trailing; but the wind had switched south and was increasing—not a good omen.

About three-quarters of a mile outside the Frankfort piers, Captain Tulledge saw a very large windrow ahead, totally blocking the way. Knowing he had to get through it to reach Frankfort, he ordered full power and met it head-on. The *No. 5* went as far as she could, stopped, and was unable to back off. By now, a twenty-mile-per-hour south wind was blowing the ice in behind her and the two-degree temperature all but guaranteed that she would not get loose soon. Captain Larson and the *No. 6* ground to a halt right behind her, and the *No. 3* met the same fate a few boat lengths back.

Getting off and on the ship near the bow was not for the faint of heart. *(Photo from the A. C. Frederickson Collection.)*

The next several days had to be a huge frustration to the captains, the crew, and the Ann Arbor management. The wind direction stayed on-shore, ranging from south to northwest and pinning the boats down, while temperatures were exceedingly cold, ranging from well below zero to the teens. On the thirteenth, four men from the *No. 6* and the forward watch from the *No. 5* took a bobsled ashore and returned with provisions after "having to chop a road through the windrows."[17] On the four-teenth, the *No. 4*, under the command of Charles Frederickson, arrived from Manistique and got stuck about two miles southwest of the three ships. *Now all four ships of the Ann Arbor Fleet were stranded in the ice off Frank-fort.* For a railroad that carried 37 percent of its total freight tonnage across the lake this was a catastrophe. The Ann Arbor management knew it had to do something, and did its best. At 7:15 a.m. it sent men from Frankfort with dynamite in an attempt to blast the *No. 5* loose. The men set off the explosives at 12:45 p.m. and blew some holes in the ice, but with no effect on the *No. 5*.

On February 15 the dynamite men returned; the crew rigged up a "snatch block" three hundred feet from the *No. 5* and began pulling the loose chunks of ice away from the boat, using the forward diesel winch for power.[18] More men were hired from shore to cut the ice around the *No. 5*, and some of the *No. 6* crewmen helped pull the ice away. Hot water hoses were run on the port side of the *No. 5* all day. The sixteenth was more of the same—all efforts directed toward freeing the *No. 5*. At 8:00 p.m., the wind began to blow hard from the southwest, again ending any realistic chance of breaking the boats loose.

Early on February 17, a few crew members left for shore and returned about noon with supplies on a sleigh they had rented from a livery barn in town. Meanwhile the dynamite men, the ice cutters, the men working the hot water hoses, and those pulling ice away from the ship labored on. By 2:00 p.m. the sun was shining brilliantly on a beautiful clear day with twenty-five degree temperatures and a thirty-knot wind from the north—picturesque but not helpful to the embattled crews off Frankfort.

While a good idea in theory, the use of dynamite only seemed to complicate matters. On the afternoon of the seventeenth, one blast sent large chunks of ice flying over the *No. 5*, some of which crashed through the roof of the aft pilothouse and the main cabin. Soon men were climbing on top of the cabin roofs to patch the holes, and the further use of dynamite was abandoned. In addition to the damage to the roofs, the explosions managed to damage the compass, which had to be replaced.

Sunday, February 18, brought more efforts to free the ship—but no progress. Some "officials came out for a consultation with the Masters [captains]."[19] Also, many of the crew members walked the three-quarters of a mile to shore to attend church in Frankfort, an opportunity to leave the boats and, for some, to be with their families for a short time. At 6:30 p.m. the wind shifted to the east, giving the boats a fighting chance for the first time. Captain Frederickson on the *No. 4* (the farthest offshore) broke loose first. By 9:15 a.m. on the nineteenth he had freed the *No. 3*, and by noon all the boats were loose. The *No. 5* led the way into Frankfort, getting stuck in another large windrow just outside the piers, but the *No. 3* and *No. 4* were able to break up enough ice around her for her to continue. By midafternoon the wind had increased to thirty knots, the temperature was dropping through the teens, and it was snowing—but the four Ann Arbor boats were safely in Frankfort Harbor.[20]

The remainder of the winter was difficult but nothing like those nine days in February. The *No. 6* continued to experience trouble with her propeller blades, breaking a grand total of thirty-three by early spring.

Three Ann Arbor ships stranded off Frankfort in 1917. The *Ann Arbor No. 5* is in the foreground with the *No. 6* close behind and the *No. 3* a few boat lengths astern. The presence of women may indicate that the picture was taken on Sunday, February 18, and that the passage from shore was relatively routine by that time. *(Photo from the A. C. Frederickson Collection.)*

One day in April the crew replaced all eight propeller blades in twenty-five hours and twenty-five minutes, which was said to be an all-time record. The Ann Arbor management knew something had to be done and found a source of stronger propeller blades for the *No. 6*. From that time on, she experienced no more or less difficulty than the other boats.[21]

The winter of 1917 came to a close with the opening of Green Bay to navigation on April 24. The *No. 4* did the honors, crashing her way across the bay with little difficulty, while the *No. 5* was in the Manitowoc shipyard with another broken propeller. The following winter, 1918, was colder but did not wreak anything like the havoc of 1917. Sixty years would pass before the Ann Arbor would be denied entrance to Frankfort Harbor for so long a period, and it was clear to anyone who followed the winter's events that even the Bull of the Woods had its limitations.

EIGHT ✺ *The Voyage of the* No. 4

All Great Lakes sailors and most people who live near the lakes know that November is the month when most severe storms occur. Cold arctic air pushing south from Canada against relatively warm air from the plains of the Midwest creates low-pressure storm centers with counterclockwise winds that increase in velocity as they pass over the warm water of the Great Lakes. A typical November will bring several gales (defined as weather events with winds blowing thirty-nine to fifty-four miles per hour) and more than a few storms (events with winds blowing fifty-five miles per hour or more). In tropical waters, a storm with winds over seventy-three miles per hour would be called a hurricane, but in the Midwest there is no such category. In the Midwest some storms simply have hurricane force winds.[1]

Charles Frederickson, the master of the *Ann Arbor No. 4* and a captain for nearly twenty years, knew all of this and therefore can be forgiven for not predicting what would happen to him on the night of February 13, 1923. It was a quiet winter night in Elberta with light snow falling. The harbor was frozen across except where the car ferries operated, and ice cutters had begun cutting blocks of ice out of the bay to be stored belowground and sold the following summer. The night was so still that his twenty-one-year-old son Arthur, a wheelsman for his father, could hear the pins being knocked over in the bowling alley across the harbor in Frankfort.[2]

The *No. 4* left Frankfort Harbor at 8:20 p.m. and steadied on her course for Kewaunee with seventeen cars of coal, one of automobiles,

Ann Arbor No. 4 entering Frankfort Harbor. By 1923 the *No. 4* was the smallest and least powerful ship in the Ann Arbor fleet. Ironically, she was the one that would face hurricane force winds in midwinter. *(Photo from the A. C. Frederickson Collection.)*

and one of chlorine. Swells began developing from the west around 9:30, and crew members in the pilothouse could feel the effects of a falling barometer—a change in pressure on their eardrums that made their voices seem to echo inside their heads. Captain Frederickson knew a storm was coming. At 10:00 the wind hit with tremendous power from the west and the temperature began rapidly falling.[3] The wind speed increased to eighty miles per hour, and the temperature continued dropping until it reached twenty degrees below zero.

Gales and storms on the Great Lakes are known to create waves that, though not as high as those produced on the ocean by winds of equal force, are deadly in other ways. The distance between waves (crest-to-crest and trough-to-trough) is shorter, making them steeper than their ocean counterparts and affording a ship less time to recover from one wave to the next. Also they reach their maximum height more rapidly, turning a relatively flat lake into a treacherous sea in a very short time. Gales often produce waves in the eight- to twelve-foot range, and storms are known to produce waves twenty to thirty feet in height—ample to put an underpowered (by today's standards) 260-foot car ferry in a threatening situation.[4] Captain Frederickson found himself in the fight of his life.

A car off its tracks on the *Ann Arbor No. 3* gives some idea of the size of the cars compared to the size of the men in the confined space belowdecks. Four cars abreast on a rolling ship could be most intimidating. *(Photo from the author's collection.)*

Despite the building waves and high winds, Captain Frederickson thought he could take the *No. 4* across the lake to the lee of the Wisconsin shore before the wind and waves overpowered him. He continued on his course for Kewaunee, which effectively headed him into the wind, plowing through ever-increasing seas for the next six and a half hours. By early morning the waves were twenty to thirty feet high and the ship was taking a terrible beating.

The fight for survival occurred belowdecks, where, as the seas increased, the railcars began to break loose. Captain Frederickson left the pilothouse in the hands of his first mate (his younger brother Axel Frederickson) and spent most of his time helping the men secure the cars as best they could. He was a big man, very strong—a natural leader with the trust of his crew. At 1:00 a.m. a carload of Buicks rolled off the stern into Lake Michigan, taking the wooden sea gate with it. Two more cars filled with coal rolled to the stern and hung on the edge. With the sea gate gone, the ship was taking water over the stern. To keep more cars from rolling off the boat, crew members dumped the coal from four cars onto the car deck. They were very concerned that the loss of more cars would create a weight imbalance that could capsize the ship.

The coal helped, but there was still a line of cars on the port-center track running back and forth from the forward bumping post to the derailed cars aft. Arthur Frederickson and Orastus Kinney, a lookout, decided to take matters into their own hands. Their plan was to put end jacks on one car as it hit the forward bumping post. The plan worked for all of a few seconds while the car leaned heavily to the side, immersing Frederickson in coal before the jacks blew apart. Kinney wound up with a broken thumb and Frederickson with a smashed hand. While having his hand tended to, Frederickson looked up to see his father, Captain Frederickson, striding from atop one coal car to another with a seventy-five-pound car jack in each hand. The captain's personal fight to save the ship had a profound influence on the crew and, although no one will ever know for sure, probably affected the outcome. At one point during the night, he found a few men who had gone to the galley for a short rest (by now there was no such thing as being off duty). He told them he had always brought them home safely in the past but he needed their help this time and led them all back to the car deck.

While the situation belowdecks was grim, the view from the pilot-house was not good either. Waves were crashing over the bow and rolling all the way to the stern—on a ship whose cabin deck was twenty feet above her waterline. Ice was building on the cabin deck and the entire superstructure—added weight above the center of gravity that made her pitching and rolling all the more dangerous—and she was taking water over the stern.[5]

By 4:00 a.m., Captain Frederickson knew he could no longer keep his boat headed on course into the wind. She was not powerful enough to fight the wind and huge waves.[6] He had to turn and run with the wind even though he knew that would have dire consequences. If he could get turned around, he couldn't possibly outrun the waves, so he would continually take water over the stern. He did not know where he was—he'd been in hurricane force winds for six and a half hours with only a magnetic compass to help him navigate—and if he found Frankfort he would have to thread a needle two hundred feet wide to enter the harbor. No captain believed that was possible in eighty-mile-per-hour winds and twenty- to thirty-foot waves. South Manitou Island was a possible shelter, and he later stated that he intended to try for it, but the island was twenty miles north of Frankfort and he might not have reached it even if he had known where it was. Assuming he made good on his course across the lake toward Kewaunee, he would have had to steer nearly forty-five degrees off downwind to reach South Manitou, and that might have caused more rolling and yawing than the ship could stand.

So he took matters one at a time, beginning with the turn—the most dangerous act of ship handling he would ever perform as a captain. Ships caught in the open lake ride out storms in one of two ways: They head into the waves if they have the power or run with the waves at their stern. Either way a ship has a fighting chance to survive. When ships remain crosswise to the wind in the trough of the waves, they roll through ever-increasing angles until they capsize and sink. No captain puts his ship crosswise to the wind in a major storm unless forced to do so. The only reasons for ever doing so are when approaching a downwind shore with no place to go (running out of lake) or when the boat does not have the power to stay headed into the wind (as in the case of the *No. 4*). The captain then puts his ship into a turn and prays it will make it through without capsizing and sinking.

The turn took twenty minutes and nearly destroyed the ship. In the words of Arthur Frederickson:

> During this time all anyone could do was hang on with a prayer and watch things smash to pieces, tearing all her side center stanchions loose, causing her upper deck to raise and fall with the sea which caused the steam pipe to the big whistle to break off flush with the deck. The chief engineer crawled on top of the boilers, which was a very dangerous place to be, and shut off the valve, thus saving escaping steam which was so vital to No. 4.
>
> After she came around things went much better as she did not roll so deep. But it was very heartrending to watch the big seas, that often came aboard her open stern and to know that water was slowly gaining on her pumps, thus realizing it was only a matter of time for us all.[7]

Captain Frederickson had much to be thankful for as the *No. 4* steadied on her course toward the Michigan shore—and in later years he had a right to claim credit for an acknowledged feat of seamanship. But he was still in extreme danger with waves rolling over the stern and across the car deck. The two cars of coal hanging on the stern actually helped by forming a barrier, or "breakwater," to the waves, but it was not enough. In time the *No. 4* would sink. At 4:50 a.m. Purser Ferris McKesson sent an SOS message and received a reply from C. O. Slyfield,

The Ann Arbor radio station overlooking the Coast Guard Station and the entrance to Frankfort Harbor. From the radio station C. O. Slyfield maintained contact with the *No. 4* on February 14, 1923. *(Photo courtesy of Roger Griner.)*

who manned the Ann Arbor's Elberta radio station. Slyfield had already received word that the *No. 5* and *No. 6* were safe in Manitowoc and the *No. 3* in Manistique. He had been calling the *No. 4* off and on all night and had about decided she must have made the Wisconsin shore when the message he had feared arrived. Slyfield sent more messages but did not hear from the ship again until 6:00, when he was told that the boat was riding better. The crew did not know its position but hoped to find out at daybreak. Slyfield had been working on a radio compass, a forerunner of the direction finder, and tried to get it into operation, but he had not used it in some time and it did not work. However, when McKesson called again at 6:45 the signal was much stronger and he told McKesson that the *No. 4* could not be more than fifteen minutes out of Frankfort. McKesson immediately went to the pilothouse and informed Captain Frederickson.[8]

In the pilothouse, the captain, a mate, and a crew member had been trying to figure out where they were. They had hoped to be able to see better at daybreak, but visibility was still only a few hundred feet due to steam rising off the water as a result of the very cold air passing over the relatively warm water, so there was no chance of spotting landmarks or lighthouses. One crewman thought they were near Point Betsie, another south of Frankfort. Captain Frederickson listened and then told his wheelsman to continue on his course. When Purser McKesson relayed the message from Slyfield, Captain Frederickson began listening for the Frankfort foghorn in earnest. At 7:35 he picked up the sound off the starboard bow. He ordered a course change to due east and in three minutes could see the Frankfort lighthouse on the north pier. Incredibly, he was only a few hundred feet from the entrance, on course to enter the center of the channel.[9]

By now the *No. 4* had taken an immense amount of water and was riding about five feet low near the stern. Just outside the harbor entrance three large waves crashed into her, first lifting her and then slamming her into the sandbar that extended off the harbor entrance. She lost all headway and tore off the port propeller and shaft. With only her starboard engine operating and the boat filling with water, Captain Frederickson gave full power to his remaining engine and put the helm to port as the waves smashed her against the south pier. The engine room crewmen stayed on duty, working in terribly cold water up to their waists, which gave Captain Frederickson time to bring the *No. 4* entirely inside the harbor entrance before she sank.

By some miracle Captain Frederickson had found his way back to Frankfort Harbor before sinking, but he and his crew were far from safe. Over the years, hundreds of men have lost their lives to the icy waters of the Great Lakes—in sight of shore. Although the upper decks were above water and the engine room crewmen had escaped before being inundated, it was much too cold to remain onboard. They would surely freeze.

The men on duty at the Frankfort Coast Guard Station had been active since receiving a phone call at 5:30 a.m. from C. O. Slyfield explaining the seriousness of the *No. 4*'s condition. At 7:15 they were informed that the *No. 4* was riding well and would be coming into the harbor shortly. In the high wind and blinding snow no one could see the harbor entrance, but they knew how difficult it would be for any ship to make the harbor in those conditions, so they took the breeches buoy to the beach in case she missed the harbor.[10] Then they got a message that the *No. 4* had hit the south pier. Believing they would be needed to take the men off the *No. 4*, they went back to the station and attempted to launch the surfboat, but the slush ice in the harbor was so heavy they could not make any progress. They attempted to get one of the fish tugs to take them to open water, but the tug could not break away from the dock because of the heavy ice. Since they could not reach the *No. 4* by water, they took the breeches buoy out along the north pier, but as they neared a point opposite the boat Captain Frederickson waved them off. He would not allow any of his crew to risk crossing the two-hundred-foot channel on a breeches buoy in the high wind and extremely low temperature (the Coast Guard Station log showed zero degrees with a wind speed of Force 9 on the Beaufort scale [forty-seven to fifty-one miles per hour]).[11]

About 10:30 the sea moderated, so they made an attempt to get the men off the *No. 4*. Three coastguardsmen carrying a long line, wearing ice spurs, and with the aid of ice picks, started out along the ice-covered south pier, crawling over the mounds of ice and eventually reaching the *No. 4*. There they relayed orders from Marine Superintendent R. H. Reynolds that the crew must be evacuated. There was an initial delay because Captain Frederickson said he wouldn't go. He wanted to remain onboard for awhile to see how the ship rode, but when he realized that the crew wouldn't leave without him he gave in. The crewmen placed a ladder from the boat to the pier and left in three groups, each tied together with heaving lines so that should one man slip the others in his group could pull him to safety. Captain Frederickson was the last man off the boat. With the waves still crashing against the pier, sending spray twenty-five to thirty feet in the air, and the entire pier coated with wet ice, the three groups crawled toward shore. That they reached the beach without anyone being washed off the pier into the icy water can easily be thought of as the second miracle of the day.

On shore, Marine Superintendent Reynolds told those of the crew who did not have homes nearby to go to Pratt's Hotel. Five crew members who lived in Manitowoc, along with John Webber, who lived in Wallin, about twenty miles southeast of Frankfort, did just that. The next morning Webber attempted to go home by taking an Ann Arbor train to Thompsonville, but the train got stuck in the snow. He helped the section crew shovel snow to get through. After the men had worked all night the train reached Thompsonville in the early morning, where Webber caught a Pere Marquette train north to Wallin. Exhausted and in the dirty, ill-fitting clothes he had borrowed before leaving the ship, he walked into the general store run by his wife and members of her family. More than a little surprised, his wife immediately chastised him for his appearance, but he remained silent until later in the morning when the Grand Rapids

Ann Arbor No. 4 resting against the south pier after her heroic fight with Lake Michigan. The men crawled off the ship on a ladder and made their way to shore and safety. *(Photo from the A. C. Frederickson Collection.)*

newspaper arrived with the story of the *No. 4*'s battle and eventual sinking—and his wife realized how fortunate she was to have a husband.[12]

The rest of the crew members went to their respective homes. Emil Johnson, a deckhand, walked seven miles down the beach to his home in Arcadia. Captain Frederickson and his son returned to their home in Frankfort. Once home, the captain took off his heavy coat, picked up his accordion, and began playing Norsk sea tunes—his way of unwinding. Nearly everyone had some degree of frostbite, and there were some injuries, but nothing life threatening. Captain Frederickson was proclaimed a hero, as he deserved, and all members of the crew knew they were more than lucky to be alive.

Fortunately for the Ann Arbor, the *No. 4* lay close enough to the south pier that the other car ferries could get in and out of the harbor. The company hired the Reid Wrecking Company of Port Huron to raise her. Work began with the *No. 5* removing the two railcars at the stern using a crane mounted on her car deck. Then divers began construction of a cofferdam at the stern and plugging a six-foot hole in the *No. 4*'s starboard side where she had come up against the riprap alongside the pier.[13] The cofferdam was washed out by a storm on March 16. From

Although one might not know it from the picture, the *Ann Arbor No. 4* was close enough to the south pier that other car ferries could continue entering and leaving the harbor. *(Photo from the A. C. Frederickson Collection.)*

March 22 until April 6 the railroad was shut down between Frankfort and Cadillac due to heavy snowstorms, which made travel impossible. Frankfort became filled with eastbound cars, and there was no choice but to shut the car ferry operations down. The boat crews were pressed into service shoveling snow in attempts to open the way to Cadillac.

The *No. 4* was finally raised on May 21 and towed to the Manitowoc shipyard on May 26 by the *No. 5* and the tug *Arctic*. It was October before she returned, completely rebuilt, with new steel cabins and much improved passenger accommodations. The sinking of the *No. 4* took a financial toll on the Ann Arbor, but, as with the capsizing of the *No. 4* in 1909, the disaster occurred in a year when the company could afford it. The *No. 4* was insured for $245,000. After rebuilding she was valued at $459,000. The company lost $350,000 in revenue due to the loss of the *No. 4*, the remarkably bad weather early in the year, and the less than optimum condition of its locomotives due to a strike the previous year. In spite of the negative factors, the Ann Arbor showed a net income of $80,000 for 1923, up $34,000 from the previous year.[14]

Of all the Ann Arbor boats, the *No. 4* appears to have been the hard-luck boat of the fleet, with three major accidents and a number of groundings, far exceeding those of the other boats. In addition to cap-

While the Ann Arbor crews helped clear the way to Cadillac, the *Ann Arbor No. 4* gathered more and more ice. *(Photo from the A. C. Frederickson Collection.)*

The damage on the car deck was extreme, with bent stanchions and derailed cars. *(Photo from the A. C. Frederickson Collection.)*

The work crew used a crane at the stern of the *Ann Arbor No. 5* to remove the rail-cars before building a cofferdam at the stern of the *No. 4* and pumping her out. *(Photo courtesy of Roger Griner.)*

The *Ann Arbor No. 5* and the tug *Arctic* towed the *No. 4* to Manitowoc for major repairs. *(Photo from the A. C. Frederickson Collection.)*

sizing in 1909 and her heroic voyage in 1923, she settled to the bottom at the Goodrich dock in Manitowoc Harbor after striking a boulder outside the harbor in 1920. She was pumped out and her cargo removed, then towed up the river to the dry dock, where several plates were replaced. The entire list of her mishaps is impressive, if not reassuring.

January 24, 1909	Grounded at Point aux Barques; released herself.
May 29, 1909	Capsized at Manistique.
December 29, 1910	Ashore at Death's Door.
January 12, 1911	Tore off propeller and shaft on rocks entering Manistique Harbor.
October 14, 1911	Grounded on rocks in Rock Island Passage.
February 21, 1912	Grounded one mile north of Manitowoc. Nearly sank while being unloaded.
September 18, 1913	Grounded near Green Island in Green Bay.
February 25, 1917	Lost port wheel and shaft in Manitowoc Harbor.
March 24, 1920	Hit a boulder in the fog outside Manitowoc. Tug *Arctic* helped the ship to the Goodrich dock where she sank in twenty feet of water.
February 22, 1922	Lost a spar in heavy seas.
May 10, 1922	Grounded on Green Island in Green Bay.
February 14, 1923	Sank at Frankfort Harbor entrance.
November 28, 1924	Grounded north of Kewaunee.
February 13, 1925	Grounded north of Kewaunee. Transferred eight cars to the *No. 3* before being pulled off. The *No. 4* was in dry dock in Manitowoc until April 5, 1925.[15]

Hindsight is 20/20, and it now appears that the *No. 4* might have been better off to have turned and run for Frankfort or South Manitou Island when the storm first hit. No one ever criticized Captain Frederickson's judgment in the matter. He later said he knew there were indications of a storm—a light east wind, a falling barometer, and swells from the west—but he made a conscious decision to cross the lake, believing he could reach the lee of the Wisconsin shore before the storm overpowered him. Though he did not say, it is highly unlikely that he ever imagined a February storm could produce hurricane force winds.

NINE ✱ New Ships "Conquer" Green Bay: The Ann Arbor No. 4 Is Retired

In 1922 the *Ann Arbor No. 3* was sent to the Manitowoc shipyard for re-building. Her length was increased by 48 feet, bringing her to 306.9 feet, and her engines, from the old *No. 1* and *No. 2*, were replaced with two triple-expansion steam engines developing 1,400 horsepower. Her capacity was increased to twenty railcars (cars were now longer than when the *No. 3* was built in 1898), and her speed rose to thirteen miles per hour, slower than the other ships but an improvement.[1]

A year later, in the last annual report before his death, Newman Erb explained that the Ann Arbor had increased its cross-lake traffic dramat-ically and the management was considering the purchase of another car ferry. Indeed, even with the sinking and subsequent unavailability of the *No. 4* for seven months, the Ann Arbor ferried 62,031 railcars across the lake in 1923 compared to 32,297 in 1910. In his straightforward way, Erb stated, "The trans-lake Car Ferry movement has shown a progressive increase during the past ten years, due to the expedited service given. The saving of time made against freight car movement through con-gested gateways has been so great as to attract attention to this service."[2]

In June 1924, the Ann Arbor placed an order for a new car ferry, the *Ann Arbor No. 7*, with the Manitowoc Shipbuilding Company. Erb didn't live to see the new ship begin service, but he would have been pleased. She was a beauty—349 feet long, 52 feet wide, and 19 feet deep—pow-

Ann Arbor No. 7 with her raised pilothouse and striking silhouette. *(Photo courtesy of Roger Griner.)*

ered with two triple-expansion steam engines (four scotch boilers) developing 2,700 horsepower. Her silhouette was particularly attractive with a high superstructure (her pilothouse was a level above that on the *No. 6*) and a clean, uncluttered look. She was well designed for passengers with twelve staterooms, a large main cabin, an observation and smoking room, and an attractive oak-paneled dining room that seated thirty-five. In the summer she was able to carry up to 375 passengers, though with limited dining and sleeping privileges. She could carry thirty railcars or a lesser number with automobiles. Cruising speed was fourteen miles per hour, about the same as that of the *No. 5* and *No. 6*.[3]

The *No. 7* made her first trip on February 22, 1925, and her presence made a difference. The Ann Arbor ferried 80,272 cars across the lake that year, a new record. Many Ann Arbor sailors and captains said she was the best boat in the fleet, even after the building of the *Wabash* in 1927, but she was a disappointment in one important respect: the Ann Arbor had expected her to be an outstanding icebreaker—in a class with the *No. 5*.[4] That was particularly important because the Ann Arbor had developed significant business through the port of Menominee—almost as much as through Manitowoc, its largest trading partner on the Wisconsin side. But the ice on Green Bay still shut down shipping for at least two months each year.[5]

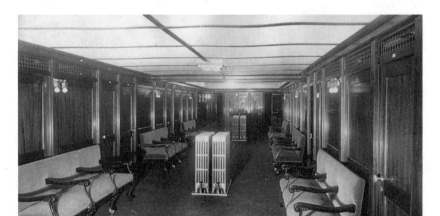

Main cabin of the *Ann Arbor No. 7*. Passengers did not suffer for lack of steam heat. *(Photo courtesy of the Benzie Area Historical Museum.)*

In early March 1924, the *No. 5*, with the *No. 4* lashed to her stern, broke a path across the ice on Green Bay from Sturgeon Bay to Menominee. It took two days and seven hours to cross the sixteen-mile bay with the *No. 5* plowing into the ice at full power (and the *No. 4* pushing from behind), riding up on the ice until she stopped, then backing off and doing it again.[6] Marine Superintendent R. H. Reynolds was onboard the *No. 5* to get a firsthand view of what it took to open Green Bay in winter. Captain B. F. Tulledge was only too happy to oblige. Townspeople from Sturgeon Bay, Menominee, and Marinette walked out on the ice (some drove their automobiles) to witness the spectacle. The *Door County Advocate* proclaimed, "Ann Arbor Carferries Open Navigation on Green Bay Earliest Date on Record."[7]

But it was difficult keeping the ice channel open. Later in the month the *No. 6* entered the bay from the Sturgeon Bay Ship Canal to find the channel gone. With the *No. 4* following behind, she fought her way across to Green Island, a few miles off Menominee; then stripped all the blades off her port propeller. The *No. 4* tried to render assistance, but she was not powerful enough. One of the vessels sent a wireless message describing the crippled condition of the *No. 6*, which the *No. 5*, the "Bull of the Woods," intercepted in midlake on her way to Kewaunee. She al-

Ann Arbor No. 5 with the *No. 4* close behind, breaking her way across Green Bay in 1924. On his arrival, Captain B. F. Tulledge told a newspaper that he was upset with the driver of a Model T Ford who left his car in the path of the *No. 5*, forcing him to stop. The captain said it was very difficult to get his ship under way again in the heavy ice. *(Photo from the A. C. Frederickson Collection.)*

tered course for the ship canal and before long was breaking out the *No. 6*. She towed her into Menominee so she could discharge her cargo, then towed her to Manitowoc for repairs.[8]

The ease with which the *No. 5* forced her way across the bay with the *No. 6* in tow stood in stark contrast to the struggles of the *No. 4* and *No. 6*. A second Bull of the Woods would greatly enhance the company's chances of keeping the ice channel open all winter with a resulting increase in business and profits. Though not the champion they had hoped for, the *No. 7* proved to be a good icebreaker. With the help of the *No. 5* (and later the *Wabash*) the Ann Arbor kept Menominee open in all but a few exceptionally severe winters.

Later in 1925 the Ann Arbor, which had operated as an independent company since 1910, allowed itself to be acquired by the Wabash Railroad. By the end of the year the Wabash owned 66 percent of the Ann Arbor stock. The logic was just about the same as when George Gould gained control for the Wabash in the early 1900s. The Wabash wanted a route to the northwest, and the Ann Arbor needed to increase its westbound traffic. In 1924 the Ann Arbor ferried only two cars west for every three cars east, an obvious waste of westbound capacity. The disparity was somewhat countered by shipping more empties west, but empties hardly represented lucrative trade. In spite of its new ties to the Wabash, the ratio did not significantly improve and in some years it got worse. In 1934 the Ann Arbor ferried twice as many loaded cars eastbound as westbound.[9]

With traffic across the lake increasing (to 88,780 cars in 1926) the Wabash Railroad contracted with the Toledo Shipbuilding Company to construct a new car ferry, which it leased to the Ann Arbor. On June 25, 1927, the *Wabash* began service. She was the largest car ferry on the lakes—366 feet long, 58 feet wide, and 19 feet deep—and would remain so until the Pere Marquette built the *City of Midland* in 1941. The *Wabash* was the most passenger friendly of the Ann Arbor boats with attractive wood-paneled staterooms and a spacious main cabin with an observation area that housed a readout of the ship's gyrocompass, the first on an Ann Arbor boat. The cabin deck was reinforced so it could hold automobiles, and thereby attract more passenger business, but that feature was never used. With the pilothouse on a level below that of the *No. 7*, she did not have the same striking silhouette, but she was pleasing to the eye. She was powered by two triple-expansion steam engines (four scotch boilers) developing 2,700 horsepower with a cruising speed of fourteen miles per hour.[10] She could hold a maximum of thirty-two freight cars or some combination of railcars and automobiles.

Like the *No. 7*, she was somewhat of a disappointment as an icebreaker—good but not up to the level of the Bull of the Woods. She was built with ballast tanks fore and aft that could be filled with water and pumped out to change the weight distribution of the ship and break up ice close to the hull, but the process took well over an hour and was not effective in practice.

The addition of the *Ann Arbor No. 7* and the *Wabash* gave the Ann Arbor four modern, powerful ships plus the 306.9-foot *No. 3* and the 259-foot *No. 4*. As the smallest and least powerful ship, the *No. 4* was marginalized—used only when absolutely needed. With traffic declining during the Depression of the 1930s, that was not very often. In 1937 she was sold to the state of Michigan for use as an auto ferry at the Straits of Mackinac. Rechristened the *City of Cheboygan*, she served for many years and in 1948 was altered so she could load autos at the bow and the stern. On completion of the Mackinac Bridge in 1958 she was sold to Edward Anderson, who had her engines removed and converted her to a barge

The *Wabash* leaving Manitowoc Harbor. Note that the cabins extend almost all the way to the stern. *(Photo from the A. C. Frederickson Collection.)*

Main cabin of the *Wabash*. The observation area with the gyrocompass readout is at the far end. *(Photo from the A. C. Frederickson Collection.)*

for the storage and processing of potatoes at Washington Island. She was renamed the *Edward H. Anderson*. In 1961 she was towed to Benton Harbor, Michigan, where she was used for the same purpose. In September 1973, she was towed through the Great Lakes and the Welland Canal to

The observation room on the *Wabash* with a repeater of the gyrocompass on the left. *(Photo from the A. C. Frederickson Collection.)*

Quebec, where she was picked up by the German tug *Seetrans 1* and towed across the Atlantic. The remains of the proud *No. 4*, which had survived capsizing, sinking in Frankfort Harbor, and any number of groundings and mishaps, passed Gibraltar on November 3, 1973, on her way to Genoa, Italy, where she was cut down for scrap.[11]

The late 1920s represented a zenith for Ann Arbor cross-lake service. In 1929 the company ferried 105,006 railcars across the lake and reported a net income of $628,811—but it was not to last.[12] The Great Depression decimated railroads nationally and had a profound effect on the Ann Arbor. In 1931 traffic was off by 25 percent from its 1929 high; the company was $404,883 in the red and in a receivership that would last until 1943.[13] Only one year in the 1930s resulted in a profit. While traffic was down, there was enough activity to keep the larger boats running most of the time. Most car ferry employees and the city of Frankfort did not feel the effects of the Depression as much as other parts of the country.

Shortly after the sinking of the *No. 4* in February 1923, Marine Superintendent Reynolds attended a conference in Madison, Wisconsin. He told those assembled that the *No. 4*'s sinking would not have occurred were it not for the low level of Lake Michigan. At the time many Lake Michigan ports were concerned over the withdrawal of water from the lake through the Chicago Drainage Canal.[14] He did not state—but could have—that modern arrowhead breakwaters such as those at Ludington and Manitowoc would also have saved the *No. 4*.

The Ann Arbor had been trying to secure a safer harbor entrance at Frankfort since 1916. In that year House of Representatives Document no. 1089 outlined a very satisfactory arrowhead breakwater project, but it contained a proviso that the city of Frankfort must put up 50 percent of the funding, an amount the city could not possibly raise. In November 1922 the U.S. Corps of Engineers held a hearing on the need for a safer harbor entrance to Frankfort, but it had not issued a ruling by the time the *No. 4* sank. Whether or not it was swayed by the sinking is uncertain, but it ruled favorably on the project in 1923.[15]

Congressman J. C. McLaughlin, whose district included Frankfort, made a case that Frankfort should not be expected to put up any of the money for new breakwaters because 99 percent of the tonnage was merely shipped *through* it. The real beneficiaries of a safer harbor entrance would be shippers and consumers in the rest of Michigan, Ohio, Wisconsin, and Minnesota. He was successful.[16] Congress passed and the president signed a Rivers and Harbors bill in 1925 authorizing the construction of the breakwaters. Funding was slow and delays frustrating, but when the project was completed in 1932 the harbor entrance was vastly improved. The breakwaters extended 2,000 feet offshore, about twice the distance of the old piers. The opening between the breakwaters was 450 feet (over twice the distance between the old piers) with the channel dredged to 20 feet at the opening. Gone were the days of waiting for the wind to shift before entering the harbor and the risk of running aground on the sandbars in a storm. The harbor entrance was much safer under all conditions.

The original piers, still two hundred feet apart, were shortened and before long became known as the stub piers. The lighthouse at the end of the north pier was removed and placed on a twenty-foot base at the end of the north breakwater. It was felt that the increase in height was necessary because there had been times when spray sent high into the air by waves crashing against the pier had frozen against the light, dimming its brightness and occasionally blocking it altogether.[17]

The combination of improved harbors, improved aids to navigation, and larger, more powerful boats brought a period of relative safety crossing the lake that never really ended. In 1929 the *No. 7* was fitted with a direction finder. That year the *No. 7* entered Manistique Harbor, a particularly challenging harbor to enter in poor visibility because of rocks on either side of the channel, in a fog with the use of the direction finder and *without* a man forward with a lead line. Soon all the boats in the fleet were similarly equipped.

The gyrocompass, which was installed on the *Wabash* when she was built, was a big advancement, though it was surprisingly many years before most of the fleet was so equipped. The *No. 5* got one twenty-one years later, in 1948, and the *No. 7* in 1949. The *No. 3* and *No. 6* waited even longer. The advantage of the gyro was that it pointed to true north and was not subject to the variation and deviation present with a magnetic compass. Variation (the difference between magnetic north and true north) was not a big factor on Lake Michigan because magnetic north is very close to true north there, and it does not significantly change in the sixty-odd miles across Lake Michigan. Deviation, the difference between magnetic north and where the compass actually points, was a significant problem because the placement of iron and steel, which affected the compass reading, changed every time the car ferry loaded and unloaded. When the Ann Arbor chartered the *City of Milwaukee* in 1979, she arrived without a gyro. The Ann Arbor had one installed.

Car ferries without gyros had a compass in the crow's nest, which, because of its height above the ship, gave an accurate magnetic reading. The crow's nest was equipped with a speaking tube so the mate (a nonlicensed officer was not entrusted with this responsibility) could read the compass and immediately report the reading to the pilothouse. Since communication was difficult, particularly in bad weather, it was a practice on some ships to release some steam from the ship's whistle (not actually blowing the whistle) so the mate would know his message had been received and he could climb down. The crew in the pilothouse could then alter the ship's heading accordingly. Another method captains used to obtain correct deviation numbers was to take a compass bearing on a known object such as a lighthouse or pier of known bearing from the ship after loading but before leaving the slip. Some also took a bearing at a known point from between the piers when leaving the harbor. That helped, but the effect of metal on the compass changed with the ship's heading and there was no good way to know for certain what those changes would be.[18]

In the 1940s radar was installed on the ships, greatly reducing the danger in fog and other low visibility situations. In 1950 the old wireless was scrapped and the entire fleet was equipped with radiotelephones. Weather information improved in the 1930s and the decades that followed, but car ferry captains were not impressed. Retired captains today point out that the Ann Arbor recorded weather information on their crossings and relayed it to the Weather Bureau, but they felt they needed to base their own decisions on their experience—and, of course, they could telephone across the lake to hear firsthand what the weather was like on the other side.

Although larger, more powerful ships, better aids to navigation, better communications, and improved harbor facilities greatly reduced the danger to ships navigating the Great Lakes, Lake Michigan could still be very treacherous. On November 7, 1940, a low-pressure center 150 miles west of Washington State began its path eastward in what would become one of the worst storms in Great Lakes history—the Armistice Day storm of 1940. The storm began by destroying the new Tacoma Narrows Bridge. It then continued east, crossing the Rockies on November 9; bringing winds up to sixty-six miles per hour to Amarillo, Texas, on the tenth; and moving into the Great Lakes region on the eleventh. That day the temperature in Chicago dropped from sixty-three degrees to twenty. The storm took 157 lives, 59 of which belonged to crew members on Great Lakes vessels.[19]

The storm on Lake Michigan began on the morning of the eleventh with strong southeast winds and rain, which changed to southwest hurricane force winds and driving snow. Various ports reported winds of 60 to 80 miles per hour (and 126 miles per hour at the Lansing Shoals Lighthouse at the north end of Lake Michigan).[20] Before it was over, Lake Michigan would claim the 420-foot *William B. Davock* and the 380-foot *Anna C. Minch.* Both sank with all hands near Pentwater, Michigan. The Canadian vessel *Novadac,* 253 feet in length, was stranded in shallow water in the same area, and but for the heroic behavior of two local fishermen the crew might have met the same fate. All but two were saved.[21] The Pere Marquette car ferry *City of Flint* (about the size of the *Ann Arbor No. 7*) approached Ludington Harbor in winds up to seventy-five miles per hour. Unable to make the entrance, she landed on the beach outside the harbor where the captain ordered her scuttled. The Coast Guard removed the passengers on an 800-foot breeches buoy while the crew remained onboard. The captain's action saved the ship. After the storm she was pumped out with relatively little damage.[22]

The *Wabash* departed Frankfort for Manitowoc at 9:08 a.m. on the eleventh. The wind switched to southwest at 1:00, which actually helped the *Wabash* get into Manitowoc, as its direction was now offshore. The ship remained in Manitowoc for the next thirty-four hours. The *Ann Arbor No. 7* left Kewaunee at 10:55 a.m. in a strong east-southeast wind with rain. Although the wind direction changed to southwest en route, she was able to get into Frankfort at 4:50 without any appreciable difficulty.

The *No. 7* stayed at the slip for the remainder of the storm, though she was not unscathed. At 7:30 p.m. on the eleventh, the *No. 5*, which had been out of service and was tied up between the slips, broke loose and crashed into the *No. 7*, breaking her loose from the apron and parting her mooring lines. She spent the remainder of the storm backing her engines at half speed with two anchors out to keep from being blown across the harbor. Meanwhile the *No. 5* drifted across to the Frankfort side of the harbor, ending up lodged against the Olsen fish docks. The *No. 3*, which had been tied up at the other slip, broke loose and drifted to the Frankfort side, landing opposite Mineral Springs Park. The boats remained in that condition until the morning of the thirteenth when the winds subsided. The *No. 7* pulled both boats off the mud and returned them to their moorings before loading and resuming her normal schedule.[23]

The only Ann Arbor boat caught in the open lake was the *Ann Arbor No. 6* with Captain Anton B. Jacobsen in command. At 11:12 a.m. on the eleventh, she left Manitowoc for Frankfort in the same southeast gale the *Wabash* and the *No. 7* encountered, but she was not as well positioned. When the wind turned southwest at 1:00 and increased to hurricane force, Captain Jacobsen knew he would not be able to get into Frankfort. The huge waves, building all the way from Chicago with winds behind them blowing at seventy miles per hour, made the 450-foot opening between the breakwaters seem exceedingly small. Neither Captain Jacobsen nor anyone else onboard had ever seen waves as big as those that afternoon and, just like Captain Frederickson on the *No. 4* in 1923, he had no desire to put his ship in the trough of the waves by turning her around. Fortunately he had another option, South Manitou Island, and he took it—as Captain Dority of the *No. 1* had done back in 1894.

At 1:10 he headed his ship north toward the island. At 5:30 he came abreast of Point Betsie and it started to snow. What he did not need while bringing his ship between South Manitou Island and the mainland was poor visibility, but fortunately he was able to keep the island in sight as he passed to the east side and entered the lee of the land. At 7:40 he put the bow on the beach at South Manitou Harbor with both engines going

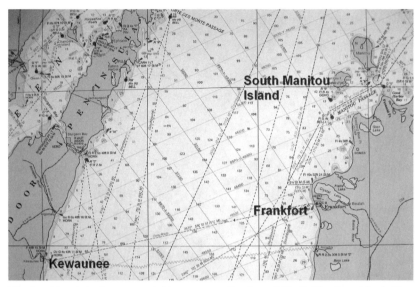

The two islands in the upper right corner are South and North Manitou. The half-moon indentation in South Manitou is the "harbor" where the *No. 6* spent one day and twenty-two hours with her bow pressed against the beach. *(Photo of U.S. government chart by the author.)*

forward at full speed to keep the wind from blowing the stern onto the beach. There was forty feet of water under the stern. She remained in that posture for nearly twelve hours while the storm raged; at 7:30 a.m. on the twelfth the wind moderated and he was able to reduce the engines to half speed.

The *No. 6* remained against the beach all of the twelfth, but the wind was moderating more. At 1:55 a.m. on the thirteenth, Captain Jacobsen reduced the speed to slow, and at 5:00 he began attempting to back off the beach. That was easier said than done. He put water in the aft holds and moved the freight cars aft, trying to lift the bow and depress the stern, but it didn't work. Captain Jacobsen had no choice but to send a wireless message to Frankfort requesting help. Twelve hours later, at 5:45 p.m., the *No. 3* arrived, and in just over an hour the *No. 6* broke loose. The *No. 3* went on to Manistique, and the *No. 6* completed her trip to Frankfort, two days and six hours late—but alive and well.[24]

TEN ✳ *The Winter of 1936: The Great Depression*

The Great Depression of the 1930s was very hard on railroads nationwide. Freight revenues in 1932 were slightly over half of those in 1930; even by 1940 they were 10 percent below the 1930 level.[1] The Ann Arbor went into receivership on December 31, 1930. Its parent, the Wabash Railroad, followed a year later, and its parent, the Pennsylvania Railroad, narrowly avoided a similar fate. Walter S. Franklin and Frank Nicodemus were named coreceivers for the Ann Arbor, with Franklin as president. Franklin, a former Pennsylvania Railroad employee, was already president of the Detroit, Toledo and Ironton Railroad, which was controlled by Pennroad, the holding company made up of large Pennsylvania Railroad stockholders. When the Wabash went bankrupt at the end of 1931, he resigned his position with the Detroit, Toledo and Ironton to become a coreceiver and president of the Wabash (and the Ann Arbor) with Frank Nicodemus. In 1933 Franklin resigned both jobs to return to the Pennsylvania Railroad. Norman. S. Pitcairn was named coreceiver and president of the Ann Arbor and the Wabash.

Born on November 8, 1881, in Harrisburg, Pennsylvania, Pitcairn was educated at Princeton University, graduating in 1903 with a degree in civil engineering. He began his career as a rodman for the Pennsylvania Railroad. By 1928 he had become General Superintendent of the Eastern Ohio Division, an important job. In 1931 he was nominated by Walter Franklin to take his place as president of the Detroit, Toledo and

Ironton Railroad and then as receiver for the Wabash and the Ann Arbor when Franklin moved on to the Pennsylvania Railroad in 1933.[2] Pitcairn was not generally liked—a receiver who must make draconian changes to restore a company to solvency is not likely to win a popularity contest—and his background as a Pennsylvania Railroad man probably didn't help.[3] Pitcairn and Nicodemus, who was general counsel, ran the company throughout the Depression years.

The severe drop in business activity across the country brought about a like drop in the shipments of raw materials and finished goods—a destructive factor no amount of cutbacks could overcome. The *No. 4* was taken permanently out of service and sold to the state of Michigan in 1937. Other boats were laid off from time to time, but throughout the Depression the majority of the Ann Arbor car ferry employees were relatively secure in their jobs. The *No. 4* was out of service most of the time, but other boats ran regularly with one ship occasionally laid off. With the *No. 5*, *No. 6*, *No. 7*, and the *Wabash*, the Ann Arbor had four powerful ships with which to fight the winters. Only the *No. 3* was suspect due to her smaller size and significantly less power. The boats handled most winters well, even keeping Menominee open, but 1936 was a significant exception.

Statisticians do not place the winter of 1936 among the twenty coldest on the Great Lakes, but residents of Wisconsin and Michigan, and car ferry employees, might beg to differ.[4] While it was cold it was very cold, and storms could be more dangerous than ice. By mid-January the inner portion of Frankfort Harbor was frozen. On January 16 the *Benzie County Patriot* printed an article stating that the Coast Guard had marked a path across Betsie Bay from Frankfort to Elberta and requested that anyone drilling holes to catch minnows do so far enough away from the path so as not to be a hazard.[5] The car ferries were suffering some delays getting into the slips due to ice but otherwise encountered no significant problems.

Then it got cold! From January 21 through February 18 there were only seven nights when the low temperature in Manitowoc was above zero. The warmest night was 7 degrees above; the average 7.83 below.[6] The Michigan side of the lake was warmer but not much. Not only was it cold but a series of blizzards hit the Midwest. On January 22 fishermen abandoned their trucks (they now used trucks and autos rather than horses and sleighs) and hiked their way off Green Bay to safety. The drifts were so high and the snow so blinding that they didn't dare risk driving their vehicles. It was 22 below in Menominee.[7]

Left to right: Ann Arbor No. 6, No. 5, and *No. 7* attempting to force their way through the stub piers into the Frankfort inner harbor in 1936. *(Photo courtesy of Roger Griner.)*

Green Bay was frozen, but the car ferries had established an ice channel and were making their trips to Menominee, though with some delays.[8] A greater problem was brought about by westerly winds shoving slush ice into the basin between the breakwaters at Frankfort. On January 27 at 1:30 a.m. the *No. 6* left the slip but could not fight her way through the basin to get out of the harbor. She returned to the slip and departed at 6:30 after the *No. 5* broke a path through the ice.[9]

On February 3 and 4 another blizzard hit the Midwest, burying Manitowoc, Kewaunee, and Menominee in snow. High winds, intense cold, and drifting snow shut down highways and rail traffic throughout most of Wisconsin. Kewaunee was literally cut off for five days: no mail, no trucks or busses. The only communication was by telephone and telegraph. Plows were called back after the first day because they had no hope of clearing the roads. That night the temperature plunged to twenty-four below zero, and the next day much of the equipment was frozen.[10] On the eastern side of the lake, Frankfort was enveloped in snow. Schools were closed, roads were covered with drifted snow, and commerce was brought to a standstill. The temperature was fourteen below zero.

Just before the storm began on February 3, the *Ann Arbor No. 3* was activated after ninety-one days out of service. She crossed the lake to Man-

Ann Arbor No. 3 entering Kewaunee on a winter day. *(Photo from the A. C. Frederickson Collection.)*

itowoc that night and started back toward Frankfort on the fourth. By then the blizzard was in full force—powerful winds out of the northeast switching to the northwest and heavy snow. In a little less than three hours the seas were so high that she turned back to the Wisconsin shore. She entered Kewaunee and remained there almost two full days while the storm blew itself out. The *No. 3,* only 306.9 feet long and 1,400 horsepower, was much smaller and less powerful than the newer Ann Arbor boats and more vulnerable to winter storms. On the same day the *No. 3* succumbed to the storm, the *No. 6* crossed the lake to Kewaunee, returned to Frankfort, and recrossed to the Wisconsin side. She recorded delays due to the bad weather but felt no need to remain in port.[11]

The storms and high westerly winds aggravated the recurring problem on the Michigan side of the lake—slush ice shoved into the basin between the Frankfort breakwaters. When the *No. 6* returned to Frankfort on February 5 the seas were again raging and the basin was filled with ice. She fought her way past the breakwaters but soon was stuck in the slush ice filling the basin. She lay all night in the ice (perhaps safer than being out in the lake) and finally reached the inner harbor and slip at 11:50 the following morning, February 6. She recorded over a full day of delays; ten hours, five minutes due to the stormy seas and fourteen hours, forty-five minutes while she was stuck between the breakwaters.

At 3:45 a.m., February 3 (the day the *No. 3* was activated), the *Wabash* left Frankfort for Menominee. The night was clear and cold with a light east wind and no hint of what was to come. She easily crossed the lake, arriving at the Sturgeon Bay Ship Canal at 7:30. By 7:50 she had reached the west end of the canal, and by 8:05 she was stuck in the channel of Sturgeon Bay. Thus began forty-one hours—almost two full days—of battling her way across the twenty miles from the town of Sturgeon Bay to Menominee. Captain Bernard Tulledge used the methods at his command to break through. He ordered water pumped into the forward holds to change the weight distribution, then had it pumped out. He worked the engines forward and astern, much as one "rocks" a car in the snow. Of course, he didn't control the engines himself—the system of relaying commands to the engine room via Chadburns was too cumbersome—so he turned over the operation of the engines to the engine room. An engineer (usually the chief engineer) worked the throttles, giving full power ahead until there was no forward progress and then astern.

The ship broke free at 2:10 p.m., but the going was very slow. Six hours later she was opposite Sherwood Point and a half hour after that she was stuck again. She broke loose at 10:45 but one hour later was stuck about two miles northwest of Sherwood Point. The last log entry for the day read, "NNW gale and snow."[12] Captain Tulledge and the *Wabash* were in the teeth of the storm that shut down Manitowoc, Kewaunee, and Menominee.

That night Captain Tulledge continued to work his boat as long as he could. He pumped water into the forward holds; then pumped it out. By the time the water was out the blinding snow brought his visibility to zero. He stopped all activity and waited for dawn. At 7:20 a.m. on the fourth, he began to work the engines. By then the ship was out of the ice channel. He turned her around and attempted to back into the ice channel, but he was not successful. At 10:50 he turned around again and began the arduous task of breaking a new ice channel. The going was excruciatingly slow, but he made progress. The last log entry of February 4 read, "Green Island at 8:55 p.m. making 1 mile per hour."

The *Wabash* reached the slip in Menominee at 1:38 a.m., February 5.

The *Wabash* passes through the bridge at the Sturgeon Bay Ship Canal. *(Original photography by W. C. Schroeder. Photo courtesy of Roger Schroeder.)*

The *Wabash* following the ice channel across Green Bay. *(Photo from the A. C. Frederickson Collection.)*

Pilothouse of the *Wabash,* from which so many battles across the bay were fought.
(Photo courtesy of the Benzie Area Historical Museum.)

Once there, Captain Tulledge may have wondered why he made such an effort, because the railroad yard was empty—completely shut down by the storm. The temperature dropped to twenty-four below zero before morning; then rose to minus ten at noon. Eleven and a half hours passed before the yard was cleared and a switch engine began unloading and loading the ship.

The *Wabash* left Menominee at 7:17 p.m. By 9:20 she had reached Sherwood Point but soon after became stuck off Quarry Point. The temperature was fourteen below. This time the *Wabash* had help from Captain Frederickson and the *No. 5.* The "Bull of the Woods" broke her out at 12:20 a.m. on February 6. She got stuck again near the bridge at 6:00, and again the *No. 5* came to the rescue. This time the *No. 5* passed her and led the way through the canal and into the lake. The *Wabash* reached Frankfort at 1:55, having lost twelve hours, five minutes fighting the ice on Green Bay. The February 3–6 trip to Menominee was the last for the *Wabash* until late March, but the *No. 5* continued crossing Green Bay throughout the month of February. Ironically, the ice channel carved out by the *Wabash* and the *No. 5* held up for the next three weeks.

The storms kept coming, and the weather stayed cold. On February 8

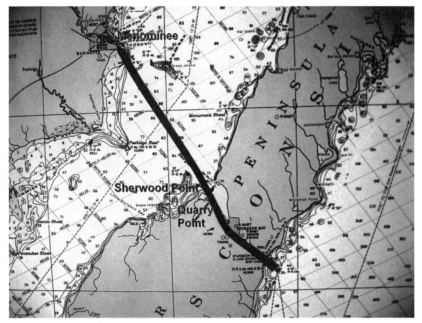

The sometimes tortuous route through the Sturgeon Bay Ship Canal and across Green Bay to Menominee. *(Photo of U.S. government chart by the author.)*

and 9 a northeast blizzard crossed the lake. The storm stranded three fishermen on Green Bay seven miles from Menominee. The snowdrifts were so high that the men couldn't possibly drive their car and the visibility so poor that they didn't dare walk. They built a fire, burning fish boxes and the sides of their portable shanty to keep warm until the storm partially let up about 3:00 a.m. With better visibility they began hiking toward shore, arriving home in the early morning. All three men claimed they were not unduly cold, and two of them returned to the bay that day to retrieve their car. That night the chief of police of Menominee left spotlights burning on the city hall all night to act as a beacon for others who were out on the bay and attempting to reach shore.[13]

The same storm buried Frankfort and Benzie County in snow. Cars were covered with drifted snow and abandoned on highways while their drivers sought shelter. The plows could not keep up and at one time had difficulty even returning to their base in the town of Honor. Some area schools were closed for a week because of the inability of school busses to pick up their students.[14]

Frankfort suffered under an immense amount of snow in 1936. *(Photo courtesy of Robert McCall.)*

The *Ann Arbor No. 3* left Frankfort at 3:45 p.m. on the eighth in a gale force east wind that shifted to southeast and then the southwest. By 5:45 she was back in Frankfort to wait out the storm with the *Wabash;* the *No. 5, No. 6,* and *No. 7* remained on the west shore of Lake Michigan. The storm raged through the night and into the next day, driving more and more ice into Frankfort Harbor.

When the winds moderated on the afternoon of the ninth, the harbor was jammed with ice—much as James Ashley had feared back in the 1890s. The *Wabash* took three hours and twenty-five minutes to fight her way from the slip into the lake (which was also filled with ice). By then the *No. 6* had arrived from Kewaunee and was stuck by the lighthouse at the end of the north breakwater. She needed three hours fifty-five minutes to force her way through the basin and between the piers to the slip. While she was fighting her way in, the *No. 3* was trying to get out. Her log read, "Three hours fifteen minutes delay leaving the harbor account of other ferries making their way in through the piers"—though one has to believe the delay was due to more than "other ferries." A day later she took seven hours and twenty minutes to get out of Frankfort.

The storms continued to roll across the lake. On the night of February 13, the *No. 3* sought the shelter of North Manitou Island for six and a half hours in a strong northeast wind with snow (blizzard). The *Wabash*

Although it was taken in January 1943, the photo records a scene similar to what often occurred in 1936—car ferries stuck inside the basin while a storm from the west shoved more and more ice between the breakwaters. Here the *Ann Arbor No. 7, No. 3,* and *No. 6* are stuck in the basin while the *Wabash* rides out the storm in the lake. The boats were broken out (in 1943) by the *Ann Arbor No. 5* when the storm subsided. *(Photo from the A. C. Frederickson Collection.)*

wasn't so bothered by the storm but became stuck for two and a half hours in the ice about a mile off Kewaunee. She was released by the *No. 7,* but when she got into Kewaunee it took over five hours for crews to clear the yard of snow so a switch engine could unload and load her.

And so it went: delays getting in and out of harbors because of the ice, storms, even getting stuck in ice well out in the lake. On the night of the eighteenth the *No. 3* became stuck in a windrow fifteen miles off the Michigan shore. She spent the night and much of the next day frozen tight in the middle of the lake, finally breaking out on her own after seventeen hours. On February 23 the *No. 6* became stuck in a large windrow on her way to Manistique. The radio log, written by Carl G. Frederickson, gives a poignant picture of her struggle.

February 23   3:37 p.m.   Called Manistique. Stopped 3:30 p.m. in windrow one and one-half-hour from Manistique and working to free ourselves.

   8:00 p.m.   Called Manistique. Still stuck fast and going to take another crack at her. Just cleaned fires.

	9:07 p.m.	Still stuck fast. Only a change in wind will let us free account of pressure.
February 24	8:22 a.m.	We are still stuck and ice is pushing bad. Unable to get loose until pressure stops.
	9:07 a.m.	Same Position.
	10:00 a.m.	Went down on ice and took five pictures of the boat and fellows spudding the ice from along her port side. Ice was packed 25 ft. deep and on the level it was three to four feet thick. One windrow was 10 ft. 7 inches high and about 50 feet wide. No one of the crew has ever experienced a vision of ice in such form in the middle of Lake Michigan. Ice on all sides and when it snows we will be encrusted with ice of all kinds.
	11:01 a.m.	Broke loose and trying to back away from this big field of windrows. Looks pretty bad on all sides now.
	1:00 p.m.	Arrived Manistique.[15]

Through it all the *No. 5* kept going to Menominee. The ice channel across Green Bay carved out by the *Wabash* and the *No. 5* held up, and Captain Frederickson made most of his trips in near normal time. Of course, he had to wait at the yard in Menominee for crews to clear the tracks so the switch engine could unload and load the boat. On February 22 Captain Frederickson announced that he had crossed the lake from Frankfort to Menominee and had been in ice all the way— the lake was frozen over. Similar statements appeared in newspapers on both sides of the lake. The captain and his chief engineer, Sam Arnerson (the crewman credited with saving the *No. 2* in 1907 when one of her engines jammed in a heavy sea), stated that Green Bay was frozen up to thirty-six inches thick in spots with four to five foot windrows, but in Lake Michigan some windrows had thirty feet of ice beneath them.[16]

On February 27 the Ann Arbor began ferrying railcars meant for the Pere Marquette boats. Ludington was even more blocked by ice than Frankfort, and the car ferries were not able to keep up. On the same day the *Wabash* became stuck in the ice a half mile outside Frankfort in a northeast gale with snow (another blizzard). It took her four hours and

Ann Arbor No. 6 had much more difficulty with ice than other ships of her size in the Ann Arbor fleet. *(Photo from the A. C. Frederickson Collection.)*

Ann Arbor No. 5 in Menominee Harbor. *(Photo from the A. C. Frederickson Collection.)*

fifteen minutes to reach the breakwater and another hour and fifty minutes to make the slip. Unlike many of her visits to the west shore, the switch engine was ready to unload. The blizzard did its usual damage on both sides of the lake but the *No. 5* went on to Menominee. This time,

Ann Arbor No. 5 passes through the Sturgeon Bay Ship Canal as skaters take a close look. *(Original photography by W. C. Schroeder. Photo courtesy of Roger Schroeder.)*

The intrepid *Ann Arbor No.* 5 passed through the Sturgeon Bay Ship Canal and across Green Bay throughout the entire winter of 1936. *(Original photography by W. C. Schroeder. Photo courtesy of Roger Schroeder.)*

however, the ice channel had moved and she was obliged to plow out a new one. It took her eleven hours to cross the bay.

The month of February was devastating from a business standpoint with huge, costly delays. Both the *Wabash* and the *No. 6* lost five full days due to weather and ice. Though the lost time was nearly identical, the *Wabash* established a much better record. More than two of her five lost days came from one round-trip to Menominee. The Ann Arbor would not have chanced sending the *No. 6* on such a mission. The *No. 3*, underpowered by the standards of the day, had by far the worst record: eleven days, twenty-two hours lost—over 42 percent of the month due to weather and ice delays.[17] The month of February 1936 was easily the worst for the Ann Arbor since February 1917, when the *No. 3, No. 4, No. 5,* and *No. 6* were kept out of Frankfort for nine days. While they did not lose as much time, the loss was more devastating. In 1917 the company could withstand some financial reverses. It had ample business with the transportation needs of World War I, but in 1936 the losses simply weakened an already weak financial statement.

Though the winter of 1936 did not rate in the top twenty on the Great Lakes, it did its damage. Twenty-seven years would pass before Lake Michigan again froze shore-to-shore.

ELEVEN ✳ *Prosperity and Improvement*

The Ann Arbor's fortunes began to improve in 1940 when it registered a positive net income, and in 1941 the company was solidly in the black.[1] The federal government's massive transportation needs during World War II virtually assured profitability. On January 1, 1942, the Wabash came out of receivership, and on the last day of the same year control of the Ann Arbor was returned to its Board of Directors. The two railroads elected former coreceivers Norman Pitcairn president and Frank Nicodemus general counsel, evidence of the trust both boards of directors had in the abilities of the two men. Pitcairn remained president of the Ann Arbor until May 1947, a month after he resigned his presidency of the Wabash. He died in early 1948.

Pitcairn was replaced by Arthur K. Atkinson, who also became president of the Wabash. Atkinson, who was born in Denver in 1891, rose through the ranks without the pedigree of a college education. He attended Denver's School of Commerce and Accounts before launching his career with the Denver and Rio Grande Railroad as an errand boy in the Auditing Department in 1909. He held a number of clerical positions, becoming a statistician, bookkeeper, traveling accountant, and special accountant. In 1920 he left the railroad to join the U.S. Railroad Commission as a field accountant, and in 1922 he took a job with the Wabash as an assistant auditor. Ten years later he became secretary treasurer of the Wabash, treasurer of the Ann Arbor, and a director of both.

Atkinson, as president, was not said to have been particularly well liked by his subordinates. He was often said to be in a bad mood, which could not have made it easy for those he supervised. He liked to smoke, play poker, and associate with other corporate executives. His substantial ego (he kept scrapbooks of all his accomplishments) set him apart from other officers in the company, but he did enjoy talking with "average workers" and did so often. He had a great facility for remembering names, which helped him with the rank and file. Although his relations with his immediate subordinates left much to be desired, he was acknowledged inside and outside the Ann Arbor and the Wabash to be extremely knowledgeable about the railroad industry and a constant source of energy.[2] Atkinson remained president until mid-1959, when he stepped down (or up) to become chairman of the board. His time in office was a prosperous one for the Ann Arbor.

In 1954 the Ann Arbor expected to build a new car ferry similar to the Chesapeake and Ohio's *City of Midland,* a 389-foot vessel built in 1941 and very successful.[3] The company had a hull tested at the University of Michigan and was delighted to learn that the new ship would be 29 percent more efficient than its present ships. There was much discussion about the name for the new ship with the city of Kewaunee making a strong case for recognition as the original trading partner with Frankfort, but when the bids came in at about six million dollars the company had to abandon the idea. The cost was prohibitive—more than its entire net earnings since World War II.[4]

In 1958 the company began a modernization program; a ship could be substantially improved and repowered for about 40 to 50 percent of the cost of a new vessel. The *No. 3* was considered too small and old for further investment and the *No. 5* was considered too old, so the *No. 6* was selected. She was sent to the Manitowoc Shipbuilding Company in Manitowoc, where she underwent an ambitious modernization process. First she was split in two and thirty-four feet added to her length; then she was cut horizontally around the entire hull a few feet above the car deck, and the upper section was raised two feet to provide eighteen feet of clearance between the car deck and the main deck. The extra clearance was necessary to provide room for the new triple-deck railcars used by the auto industry and for piggyback trailers.[5] The old steam engines were removed and replaced with two 2,750 horsepower nonreversing Nordberg diesel engines, making her the first diesel-powered car ferry on the lakes. The engines powered two propeller shafts with variable pitch propellers, which could be adjusted to push the vessel forward or astern.

The *No. 6* emerged in March 1959 as a new vessel, complete with

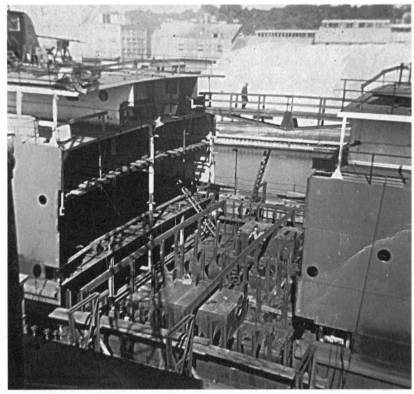

Ann Arbor No. 6 as she appeared when she was cut in two at the Manitowoc shipyard. Thirty-four feet were added to her length. *(Photo from the A. C. Frederickson Collection.)*

The *Arthur K. Atkinson* shortly after she was rebuilt. *(Photo from the A. C. Frederickson Collection.)*

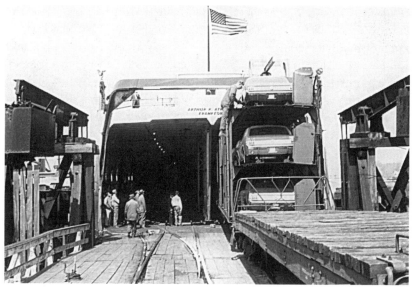

The *Arthur K. Atkinson* (and later the *Wabash* and *Viking*) could carry triple-deck rail-cars after she was rebuilt. *(Photo from the A. C. Frederickson Collection.)*

modern pilothouses fore and aft, a single stack, and a new name—the *Arthur K. Atkinson*—in honor of the president of the Ann Arbor and Wabash railroads. With her increased length she could hold four more railcars, and her higher cruising speed (seventeen miles per hour) materially increased the number of crossings she could make each year. The winter of 1959 was a difficult one because of heavy ice, with the Ann Arbor dropping the Menominee route for three weeks, the first time it had done so in many years; but the *Atkinson* arrived too late in the spring to prove her mettle as an icebreaker. As it later turned out, she was a disappointment—plenty of power to break ice but not enough to back off. The variable pitch propellers were designed to give full power forward but only 80 percent power in reverse, so the *No. 6*, even after becoming the *Atkinson*, never did shake her reputation as a poor icebreaker.

In 1960 the Pennsylvania Railroad worked out an arrangement whereby the Norfolk and Western Railroad combined with the New York, Chicago, and St. Louis Railroad (better known as the Nickel Plate Road) and leased the Wabash (from the Pennsylvania) to form a "new" route to the East Coast.[6] That left the Pennsylvania free to merge with the New York Central. Since the Norfolk and Western saw no value in the Ann Arbor route, the railroad was suddenly up for sale. Fortunately the

Detroit, Toledo and Ironton Railroad, still under the control of the Pennsylvania, saw some of the same value in the Ann Arbor that Eugene Zimmerman had seen in 1905 (an east-west route to Minneapolis and Saint Paul) and petitioned the Interstate Commerce Commission to approve its purchase of the railroad for three million dollars. The purchase took almost three years to receive approval and clear exceptions filed by the Railroad Labor Executives Association, whose concern was the loss of jobs on the Wabash, but in late August 1963 the Ann Arbor became a wholly owned subsidiary of the Detroit, Toledo and Ironton Railroad under a single management team.[7]

David Smucker, president of the Detroit, Toledo and Ironton (and now the Ann Arbor as well) was enthusiastic about the prospects for the Ann Arbor. He believed the car ferries could generate traffic that would benefit both lines and was willing to invest resources to make that happen. In late 1962, well before the sale of the Ann Arbor was consummated, the Detroit, Toledo and Ironton invested in the remodeling of the *Wabash*. She was sent to the Manitowoc Shipbuilding Company, where, like the *No. 6*, she was cut horizontally above the car deck and her clearance (car deck to cabin deck) increased by two feet. Rather than repower her, the company opted to convert her from coal-fired to oil-fired steam. Thus she was still a steamboat but would not pose a pollution problem. Her cabins were modernized, and she was given a single stack—all for about half a million dollars. Shortly after the sale of the Ann Arbor was completed in August 1963, the name was changed to the *City of Green Bay* in recognition of the city that was the final destination for much of the tonnage carried on the Ann Arbor boats. In addition to the work on the *Wabash*, the Detroit, Toledo and Ironton invested in modern dockage facilities, purchased diesel locomotives, and moved the home office from Owosso, Michigan, to Frankfort.[8]

In 1964 the *Ann Arbor No. 7* was sent to the Fraser-Nelson Shipbuilding and Dry-Dock Company in Superior, Wisconsin (near Duluth), for a major rebuilding. Like the *Atkinson* and *Wabash*, she was split apart horizontally and her cabin deck raised nearly four feet to accommodate the new triple-deck railcars. She was repowered with four 1,760 horsepower General Motors diesel engines, which ran generators producing electric power to operate two electric engines rated at 1,530 horsepower for each shaft—a total output of 6,120 horsepower. Thus she was the first diesel-electric car ferry on the Great Lakes. The remodeled *No. 7*, christened the *Viking* to embody the spirit of one of the Ann Arbor's major destina-

The *Wabash* was a handsome ship after she was remodeled. *(Photo from the A. C. Frederickson Collection.)*

tions, Saint Paul, also was given a bow thruster to speed up the docking process. The bow thruster consisted of a cylindrical hole five feet in diameter across the fore and aft axis of the ship near the bow with a reversible propeller in the middle. Powered by a 500 horsepower engine, the propeller could shove the bow to either side, greatly adding to the ease (and speed) of docking.[9] The combination of diesel-electric power and the bow thruster made a tremendous difference in the handling of the ship. No longer did a captain need to signal the engine room through a Chadburn and wait for his order to take effect. He had direct control from the pilothouse and from the aft pilothouse when docking.

Another design advance was the addition of a flume type stabilization system, the first on a Great Lakes vessel, to reduce rolling in a heavy sea. The system was made up of holds on each side of the ship that contained water and were joined in the middle. The holds were designed with openings that allowed some but not all of the water to pass through to the other side of the ship. When the ship rolled to starboard, some water passed to that side but not enough to increase the roll. When it began to roll back to port, the excess weight on the starboard side slowed the roll to port. Water would find its way to the port side before the roll was completed, and the process would begin again.[10] It was thought that the system would allow the car ferry to save time by taking a more direct route across the lake in a crosswind and would require less gear (and time) to secure the cars.

Ann Arbor No. 7 after she was split horizontally around her entire hull. Her cabin deck was raised two feet to allow clearance for piggyback and triple-deck railcars. *(Photo from the A. C. Frederickson Collection.)*

The Ann Arbor management was very proud of the *Viking* and with good reason. She was easy to handle, fast (a cruising speed of eighteen miles per hour and top speed of twenty-one miles per hour), and a very good icebreaker. Captains stated that she could plow through four feet of solid sheet ice. One could easily make the case that she was the most modern car ferry on the lakes, but she did have one drawback. Unlike the *Atkinson*, which retained two boilers, all of her boilers were removed. In summer that made no difference, but in winter she did not have the availability of steam and hot water to heat the cabins, clear ice off the decks, and to some extent heat the car deck. The *Viking* was entirely heated by electricity and was known to be cold in winter, but, on the other hand, it cost money to keep boilers operating. The *Viking* was cost effective.

The higher speeds of the *Viking* and the *Atkinson* greatly increased the demands on their captains. A captain was responsible for everything that occurred aboard ship, but he obviously could not do everything himself. In practice the chief engineer took responsibility for all things mechanical and electrical, and the mates ran the ship, including loading and unloading when in port and piloting when en route across the lake. Three

The *Viking* turning in Frankfort Harbor in the mid-1970s. *(Photo courtesy of Jonathan Hawley.)*

mates stood six four-hour watches every twenty-four hours. The captain was responsible for bringing the boat into and out of port. Entering port and docking required the most skill, for that was when there was the greatest chance of a mishap. When the runs were five to seven hours across the lake a captain could take the boat out of port, turn the vessel over to the mate on watch, retire to his cabin and do some paperwork, or, at night, go to sleep. The *Viking* and the *Atkinson* now crossed the lake to Kewaunee and the Sturgeon Bay Ship Canal in four hours, and it was only five hours to Manitowoc. There simply was not time for a captain to get enough rest. He might be able to survive for a few days, but twenty straight days, which was the Ann Arbor system, was more than anyone should be required to endure. The Ann Arbor recognized the problem and changed the system to eight days on, four days off (with pay), eight more days on, and eight days off (without pay).[11] While the captain was off, the senior mate with a master's license assumed command.

The decisions to improve the *No. 6*, the *No. 7*, and the *Wabash* essentially ended the careers of the *No. 3* and *No. 5*. In early 1962 the *No. 3*, which had been idle for over a year, was sold to the Bultema Dredge and Dock Company in Manistee. She was towed from Frankfort Harbor in May and cut down to be used as a barge. Oddly, the company left her rail tracks in place, and that brought her back to gainful employment as a car

Ann Arbor No. 3, cut down and renamed the *Manistee*, as she appeared at Saint Ignace in 1965. *(Photo from the A. C. Frederickson Collection.)*

Ann Arbor No. 5 tied up in Frankfort in 1965. *(Photo from the A. C. Frederickson Collection.)*

Ann Arbor No. 5 cut down to a barge and used as a barrier off South Haven, Michigan, during a construction project by the Bultema Dredge and Dock Company. *(Photo courtesy of Valerie van Heest with the permission of the Saint Joseph Herald Palladium.)*

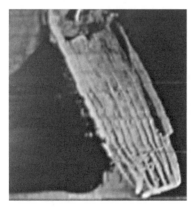

Sonar image of the *Ann Arbor No. 5* as she rests 160 feet beneath the surface of Lake Michigan. *(Photo by Diversified Wiboats, Inc., courtesy of Valerie van Heest.)*

ferry at the Straits of Mackinac in 1967. While the *Chief Wawatam*, which operated across the Straits, was being repaired, the *No. 3*, now named the *Manistee*, was pushed back and forth across the straits hauling railcars, much as she had in the past. When her work was done, she was towed back to Manistee, but she was again pressed into service in 1968.[12]

The proud *Ann Arbor No. 5*, the "Bull of the Woods" and "Winter Flagship," as Charles Frederickson characterized her, was sold to Bulk Food Carriers of San Francisco in April 1966, then to Hudson Waterways Corporation, the U.S. Maritime Commission, and in the fall of 1967 to Bultema Dredge and Dock of Manistee.[13] Past and present crew members watched her depart with reverence, though in her final years she had become a shell of her former self. In 1948 she received a thorough remodeling, including a new cabin deck, cabins, and new car deck, along with wiring, a sanitary system, heat, laundry space, and clothes dryers. She also received a new Sperry Gyro Compass; but when she returned to Frankfort she was not as fast or as good in ice.[14] There was speculation as to what had happened, but the company never did explain. Some captains said the company had changed to a different propeller to speed her up and it didn't work.[15] Whatever the reason, she was no better as an icebreaker than the other ships, and as the newer vessels were rebuilt she became inferior.[16]

The Bultema Dredge and Dock Company cut her down to be used as a barge and in 1969 towed her to a location near South Haven, Michigan, where the company was working on a project. She was sunk to act as a breakwater while the work was being done. The project was expected to be completed before winter but ran behind schedule, so the *No. 5* spent the winter resting on the bottom of Lake Michigan. By spring 1970 her keel had been broken in two places by the action of wind, water, and ice. The Bultema Company literally scrapped the forward two-thirds of the ship under water but felt they could pump out and float the stern section (about 160 feet long). They were successful in raising the section and began towing it farther into Lake Michigan so that if something went wrong it would sink in deep water. Then they headed north, intending to take it to Holland or Muskegon, but one of the pumps failed and it was soon evident that the remainder of the *No. 5* would sink. The men did their best to recover their pumps as she settled to her final resting place in 160 feet of water.[17]

TWELVE ※ *A Profound Influence*

When control of the Ann Arbor was returned to the Board of Directors in 1942, the railroad had been shipping cars across the lake for fifty years. The car ferries had a profound influence on the Frankfort/Elberta community and, to a lesser extent, on Kewaunee and the other destinations across the lake. Most Frankfort/Elberta residents had never seen either town without the boats, and there was every indication that they would continue forever. The Ann Arbor was the area's largest employer with the best-paying jobs. Young men could leave high school with no particular training and find jobs on the boats that paid good wages. Those who possessed that unique combination of intelligence and drive required to reach the top could rise to become captains with no other formal education. Indeed, nearly all the Ann Arbor captains began their careers as deckhands and chief engineers as coal passers.

Frankfort residents knew who commanded each ship and usually had opinions about who was the best captain—and every high school boy knew which ship was entering or leaving the harbor by the sound of its whistle. A common practice for Frankfort/Elberta residents was to drive to the harbor entrance and watch the car ferries pass between the breakwaters and through the stub piers during a blow. Residents knew it required considerable skill to bring one of the big ships into the harbor in a high wind. A captain might have entered the harbor hundreds of times, but previous success didn't count for much. There was a very real danger that the wind might slam the ship into one of the piers, and the local residents understood the drama.

A common practice of Frankfort/Elberta residents was to watch the ships enter and leave the harbor from the vantage point of the Elberta Bluffs just south of the harbor entrance. *(Photo from the A. C. Frederickson Collection.)*

From the first trip in 1892 car ferry crews were expected to work thirty straight days to accumulate two days off. Most crewmen didn't actually take two days off at the end of thirty days; they simply accumulated them for times when the ship was laid up. That might not happen for the better part of a year. Descendants of crew members say that they often did not get all of their time off even then. Crewmen had very little time off that they could use to build a normal life. A wiper or coal passer might have sixteen hours off duty each day, but he usually could not get off the boat. If he could, he might be in a town not his own. In his home port his free time might consist of an hour or so sitting in a car at the dock with his wife or girlfriend. Indeed, it would seem a miracle that he could find an opportunity to see a girlfriend, let alone get married. But many of the men were married and had stable home lives.

That so many crew members supported families was a tribute to their basic work ethic and their values. A significant number were Scandinavian (the Trinity Lutheran Church in Frankfort conducted services in English and Norwegian into the 1940s) and brought with them a culture that placed a high value on reputation and a relatively low value on the display of wealth. An orderly home, clean, neat clothes, and a re-

Not all crossings involved ice and storms. Crew members were often treated to breathtaking sunrises, sunsets, and scenes whose beauty defied words. *(Photo from the A. C. Frederickson Collection.)*

spectable job were most important. Captains and other officers were respected as might be bank presidents, lawyers, and other professional people. Car ferry crews, officers and men, were well compensated in relation to others in their community but not compared to laboring and professional workers in large cities. As more than one of their children remarked in later years, "we didn't have much but we didn't know it—and we were happy."[1]

In October 1949 the Ann Arbor changed the work rules to twenty days on, eight days off.[2] The change made a very real difference to the crew members and their loved ones. Fathers had much more time to be with their families, and they also had an opportunity to take short vacations. As railroad employees with a given number of years service, they could obtain free passes. Other railroads generally honored the passes, allowing them to travel anywhere in the country. The time off and the ability to travel were advantages, but the men were still gone from their homes about three weeks out of every month.

While the car ferries were operating, the only practical time for a crew member to see his family was when the boat was in port. If he was off watch, he could leave the boat while it was unloading and loading, a period of about an hour and forty-five minutes. Sometimes crew members who lived in Manitowoc traded watches with Frankfort men so they would have time off when in port. The Frankfort men did the same when the vessel was in Manitowoc. The crew always hoped for full loads. A smaller load meant less time in port. A captain or mate might go home for part of that time while an unlicensed crew member was more likely to have his wife, and perhaps their children, come to him. The captain was never really off, even when he went home. He was quite likely to be called by the Ann Arbor with some kind of problem requiring a decision. These short visits, which occurred two or three times a week, did much to keep a presence of the father in the family. The wife, out of necessity, made most of the everyday household decisions, but the father could still be the disciplinarian and the head of the house. Children knew their fathers were aware of what they were doing.

Most car ferry families did not view the time their men spent working on the boats as a hardship despite the time away from home. Car ferry jobs were respected and paid well compared to other local options. Most men began work on the ferries for the money but came to love the boats. For the families, there were some obvious hardships—the boats ran on holidays and often fathers were not able to see their children perform in school plays, or sporting events, but there were some perks. Fathers sometimes took their children aboard the boats and allowed them to make crossings, eat with the crew, stand on the bridge, and watch as the ships entered and left port. These were big experiences. Joan Olsen, whose father was Captain Carl Jacobsen, vividly recalls her experiences as a young girl on the docks at night with her mother, watching the huge freight cars looming out of the darkness and rolling onto the ship. The magnitude and power of the scene have never left her.

While Barbara Johnson was in high school, she and a few of her friends rode the car ferry with her father, Captain Edward Ericksen, across the lake to Manitowoc each August to buy school clothes. They always left Frankfort at night so they could spend the entire next day in Manitowoc and return on the night boat to Frankfort. Sons and daugh-

While the boats unloaded and loaded, crew members off watch could have a brief time together with their loved ones. *(Photo from the A. C. Frederickson Collection.)*

ters of other car ferry employees did the same. All were impressed with the food. Ann Arbor employees ate steak and roast beef while their families ate chicken. Captain Ericksen often brought home items he had purchased in Manitowoc (cheese, bratwurst, or articles of clothing) that could not be obtained in Frankfort.

Crossing the lake was a thrilling experience for the children of car ferry employees, but it did not always go as planned. Take the case of Jack Thomas Carter, first cook on one of the Ann Arbor boats. Jack's wife, Virginia, was ill just before Thanksgiving so he decided to help out by taking his three daughters across the lake on the car ferry. He always fixed an outstanding dinner for the crew with turkey, ham, and other enticing selections topped off with pies and cakes. The girls were thrilled, but when the ship left port it immediately started to roll in the heavy seas of Lake Michigan brought on by a November storm. Jack served the meals but only to two of his daughters. His oldest child, fifteen-year-old Dolores, was seasick in his cabin the entire way across the lake. While the adventure did not go as planned, none of the girls ever forgot it.[3]

By and large, there was little thought given to the safety of the crews. Most children did not think of the safety of their fathers but did recall their mothers talking on the phone to other wives during a storm. They could call the Ann Arbor office but didn't feel they got much information. They might be told a boat was going to return to Manitowoc or take shelter at South Manitou Island, but they would not know where the boat actually was or whether it was in trouble. The wives talked to each other and worried.[4]

Of course, not all men were married and not all went home when their ships were in port. Three watering holes were frequented by the crews: Peasoup's in Elberta and Baker's Bar and the Villa Marine in Frankfort. A passerby might do a double take as he peered into one of the bars at 9:00 a.m. and saw a few men inside drinking beer, but the men were not hopeless derelicts, just car ferry men who had come off duty at 8:00. They would be off duty again at 8:00 p.m. when they might or might not have an opportunity to leave the ship. In Manitowoc there were similar bars (the Foam Tavern being preferred) where the off-duty men could drink at a more civilized hour in the evening. The ship usually had a three-hour layover in the evening while it awaited cargo—time for a leisurely drink and a stroll back to the boat. Barkeeps say the men were never rowdy—they simply wanted a quiet drink and a place to talk.[5]

With the number of men leaving the ship in Frankfort and Manitowoc, it was important to make sure they returned in time for the ship's departure. A ship always blew one long and one short blast of its whistle half an hour before sailing, but the company went a step further. When a crew member left the ship he signed a list giving his location and phone number. When the whistle blew, the wheelsman on duty called every number on the list plus the local bars. There were three cab companies in Frankfort to provide transportation.[6]

Given the regimen of shipboard life, it was natural that some men rebelled, trying to establish their independence in their own way. One such crew member was a watchman (who shall remain nameless) on one of the boats. At night the watchman's job was to go to various locations in the ship every half hour and insert a key in a clock at each location to show that he had been there. It was essentially a fire watch and could be completed in about twenty minutes, leaving the watchman about ten minutes to spare. One night when the ship was scheduled to remain in Frankfort the watchman decided to go to Peasoup's, so on one of his rounds he collected all of the clocks and took them with him to the bar. There, while enjoying a leisurely drink with some friends, he dutifully inserted the key in each of the clocks every half hour until he returned to

In the early years, crewmen had to walk about two miles around the harbor and across a bridge to the business district of Kewaunee. Occasionally Coast Guard personnel ferried the men directly across for a visit to a hotel or watering hole. *(Photo from the A. C. Frederickson Collection.)*

the ship. It was an imaginative ploy, but it did not fool the watch officer. The crewman was caught and disciplined, though, amazingly, he did not lose his job.[7]

Manitowoc and Frankfort were the only ports where the men left the ships with any regularity. In other ports, conditions were not right. In Kewaunee, for example, there was a two-mile walk around the harbor from the docks to the downtown area. Cabs were not an option because until later years there was no road for most of the way.

The car ferries were as much a fixture to the summer residents of Frankfort and the surrounding area as to the year-round residents. During World War II many Frankfort and Benzie County summer residents from Chicago and northern Illinois reached their summer homes by driving to Manitowoc and taking the Ann Arbor car ferry across the lake to Frankfort. The drive to Manitowoc was about 130 miles compared to well over 300 to drive around the south end of the lake and north to Frankfort. In a time of gas rationing that made a big difference. After the war and through the 1950s and 1960s many continued to use the boats. A breadwinner could leave his or her family at its summer residence for a month, or even all summer, and commute back and forth on the week-

The car ferries were popular with residents of Chicago and Milwaukee who had summer cottages in the Benzie area. *(Photo from the A. C. Frederickson Collection.)*

ends. Most took the Friday night boat from Manitowoc to Frankfort, arriving early Saturday morning, and the night boat back to Manitowoc on Sunday, arriving early enough to drive to Chicago and be there in time to start the day on Monday. A commuter could get a few hours sleep each way by renting a stateroom. The trips were taxing but less so than driving, which could take up to eleven hours. Also there was a special thrill to standing on the foredeck of one of the ships as it entered Frankfort or Manitowoc Harbor. In the late 1960s, as the roads were improved, the advantage decreased, but many still took the boats regularly.

The big ships continued to operate without much fanfare. There were occasional bouts with ice, particularly in 1959 and 1963, but by and large they ran regularly and without mishap. From time to time there were incidents that created a stir, such as the time in July 1955 when part of the parking lot caved in at Elberta. Four automobiles sank into the bay when the retaining wall was breached by the water. Imagine the surprise of the crew member owners when they returned to find their cars *gone*. The Luedtke Engineering Company brought a derrick to extract the cars, but it could only pull one out of the water and sand. The others

Four crew members suffered a nasty surprise when they found the seawall and their automobiles destroyed on returning to Elberta from across the lake. *(Photo from the A. C. Frederickson Collection.)*

came up in pieces. The railroad repaired the retaining wall and filled the gap with crushed stone, leaving the remnants of the cars buried.[8]

In 1965 the Ann Arbor began helping the U.S. Fish and Wildlife Service plant lake trout in Lake Michigan. A car ferry would carry one or two trucks, each containing twenty-five thousand small lake trout, and when it reached the appointed location slow down almost to a halt, lift the sea gate, and pump the small fish into the lake. They also unloaded small salmon in Platte Bay.[9]

Relations between the Ann Arbor and the city of Frankfort were generally good—each needed and supported the other—but in 1951 they became strained over a condition that had been building for the past few years. Local housewives found that they could not dry clothes outside when the ships were in port—more accurately, when they were leaving port. Black smoke and soot from the ships' stacks drifted across the harbor and landed on everything outdoors. Whether Frankfort or Elberta was most affected depended on the wind direction. Wisconsin ports were

having similar difficulties and not just with the Ann Arbor. The Chesapeake and Ohio boats (formerly the Pere Marquette) were guilty as well.
There was speculation that the Ann Arbor was burning poorer quality
coal than in the past, but no one really knew.[10]

In April 1951 the *Benzie County Patriot* published two pictures of
Frankfort Harbor on a bright, clear day. In one the harbor entrance and
Coast Guard Station were clearly visible. In the other, taken while the *No.
7* was leaving port, the Coast Guard Station was completely obliterated by
smoke from the vessel. A number of articles appeared in the spring and
early summer. Then, on July 30, P. C. McNulty wrote a letter to the mayor
of Frankfort in which he explained that he had recently brought his boat
into Frankfort Harbor and was appalled by the soot that accumulated on
it overnight as a result of the smoke belching from the Ann Arbor car ferries. He wrote that Frankfort was an ideal port for yachtsmen but the soot
was a real concern, and he offered to write a letter of protest to the Ann
Arbor in his capacity as commodore of the Great Lakes Cruising Club.[11]

Commodore McNulty's letter brought the city nearer a showdown
with the Ann Arbor. By then the city of Frankfort had passed an ordi-
nance making it illegal to produce excessive smoke. The city council
could now ask a judge for an injunction to make the Ann Arbor com-
ply.[12] The "showdown" occurred on August 13 when the city council and
representatives from the Ann Arbor met in Frankfort. The meeting was
conciliatory. The Ann Arbor people acknowledged the problem, volun-
teered that they faced similar problems in other locations, and said they
would make an effort to alleviate the nuisance.[13]

The basic cause of the problem (aside from what kind of coal the
ships burned) was the need for additional steam pressure to power the
engines when the ships got under way. When they tied up, the firemen
let the fires in the furnaces die down by cutting the airflow to a level that
would keep them burning but at a slow rate. The steam pressure would
drop accordingly. Sometime before the boat was ready to leave, they
would add coal and increase the airflow. The fresh coal increased the
heat and provided the steam pressure the ship needed to get under way,
but it also produced heavy black smoke.

To alleviate the problem, the firemen began banking the fires when
the ships docked. To do this, they added fresh coal, then cut the airflow
down so it would burn very slowly and turn into coke. When it was time
to leave, they broke up the piles of coke and turned up the airflow. That
increased the heat (and steam pressure), giving the ship the needed

The smoke problem was not limited to Frankfort/Elberta. Manitowoc residents were no happier with the smoke from the *Ann Arbor No. 5* as she passed through the Tenth Street Bridge than were their counterparts across the lake. *(Photo courtesy of the Manitowoc Times Herald.)*

power, and the coke burned more cleanly than fresh coal. Once the ship cleared the harbor, the firemen added fresh coal. The crews also found that they could leave the harbor with less than their normal running steam pressure. The only exception was on particularly windy days when a prudent captain wanted full power available.[14]

The following spring (1952) the Ann Arbor installed a smoke abatement system that the Wabash Railroad had been using on its car ferries at Detroit.[15] The system was first installed on the *No. 3* and made a considerable difference. The Ann Arbor then made arrangements to equip the entire fleet.[16]

Later in the same year (August 1952) Barbara Ericksen was eating perch for dinner with her family. She liked perch but was growing tired of it, having eaten it nearly every night for the last seven weeks. Perch was cheap—it could be caught in many of the lakes near Frankfort at almost no expense. Her father, Captain Edward Ericksen, was on strike along with the other licensed officers of the Ann Arbor, Wabash, Chesapeake and Ohio, and Grand Trunk car ferries. The strike began July 3 and continued through August with no significant progress. The Great Lakes Li-

Except during the strike, all the Ann Arbor boats were seldom in Frankfort Harbor at one time, as in this picture, taken in 1960. *(Photo from the A. C. Frederickson Collection.)*

censed Officers Organization was asking for a wage increase of twelve dollars a day, and the company was offering fifty-seven cents.[17]

For many, the strike was a chance to spend time with their families and enjoy the warm weather. Some found summer jobs, which were available during the resort season, but all had to watch their expenses. By September the summer jobs had evaporated, the children were back in school, and it was time to go to work. With the resort season at an end, the local merchants felt the financial pinch as well, and several were heard saying that perhaps the hated smoke from the boats hadn't been so bad.

The Ann Arbor officers (captains, mates, and engineers) wanted the dispute to go to arbitration because that would allow them to go back to work immediately, but the officers of the Chesapeake and Ohio and Grand Trunk were not so inclined. Both railroads had actually fired their licensed officers, and the men were not willing to enter arbitration without a guarantee that they would get their jobs back. The Ann Arbor and Wabash officers finally agreed to arbitration after obtaining approval from the strikers at the Grand Trunk and Chesapeake and Ohio. The logic was that with the Ann Arbor operating, the Chesapeake and Ohio and Grand Trunk would be more likely to settle than watch their business go to a direct competitor.[18]

So the strike came to a close and the boats began running on September 20, seventy-eight days after it began. The Grand Trunk settled in mid-October and the Chesapeake and Ohio near the end of the month. Both rehired their licensed officers. In February 1953 the arbitration board reached a decision on the Ann Arbor. The officers received a net salary increase of two dollars and ten cents a day, nowhere near what they had asked but more than the officers of the Grand Trunk and the Chesapeake and Ohio received.[19]

THIRTEEN ✺ *The Men Who Built It—Continued*

The early entrepreneurs and businessmen—the Ashleys, Wellington Burt, Joseph Ramsey, Newman Erb—all had a great influence on the Ann Arbor and helped make it a quality organization. Another group of men was equally important throughout the life of the company—the men who sailed the boats, especially the captains. Ashley's boats were useless without captains to make critical decisions, usually without all the facts: cross the lake in a storm or stay in port, enter a harbor in a fog or wait for the weather to clear, fight mountainous waves in a storm or run for the shelter of South Manitou Island, enter Green Bay in the spring through the canal or Death's Door—or turn back?

Captains became excellent weather forecasters. They had to because the information they got from the weather service was not specific enough. A good captain could simply look at the lake and have a reasonable idea of what to expect for the next several hours. Often a captain left Frankfort in a southwest gale knowing full well that it would switch to northwest before he reached the Wisconsin shore, allowing him to enter the harbor with safety.

Captains were expected to be excellent ship handlers. Car ferries differed from bulk freighters in that they entered and left a harbor at least twice a day and usually more. A good captain had to dock his ship quickly and be capable of entering a harbor in a strong wind or with poor visibility. Captains developed a method of dropping an anchor at exactly the right spot as they approached the dock and using it as a pivot point to bring the boat into position to back into the apron.

Often a captain was a better wheelsman than any of his crewmen. Once Bruce Jewell, who later became a fine captain, was wheeling for Captain Duane Bishop on a winter day as they were approaching Frankfort. There was a strong southwest wind blowing, and ice extended several miles from the shore into the lake. Captain Bishop told Bruce to head for a point about one mile south of the harbor. Bruce did not see the point but did what he was told. The ice pushed them north as they approached the shore, placing them right in front of the harbor entrance as they reached the breakwaters.

Skill was important. If a captain was heading downwind in a big sea and found it necessary to turn around into the wind (perhaps thinking that he could not thread the needle of the harbor entrance) he could not just have the wheelsman turn the ship around. A good captain called the engine room about fifteen minutes before he expected to make the turn so the engineer could get up as much steam pressure as possible. Just before starting the turn, he rang the Chadburns for full power, and on completion of the turn he rang again to reduce the power to normal. When a captain failed to round at full power he subjected the boat to unmerciful rolling, endangering his ship and his crew.[1]

The early captains were pioneers. When Captain Kelly turned the *No. 1* around in 1892 and returned to Kewaunee because she was rolling heavily, he didn't *know* how much rolling she could endure without capsizing and he didn't know how well the gear that held the railcars in place would do its job. When he crossed the lake in a blinding snowstorm, fighting huge waves and high winds, trying to find Kewaunee with only a magnetic compass to guide him, he had little, if any, experience to rely on. Only a few package steamers and Goodrich passenger vessels operated at all in the winter, and none was as aggressive as the ships of the Toledo, Ann Arbor and North Michigan.

When Captain Butler got stuck for the winter in Green Bay in 1900 he was engaged in a battle that wouldn't be won until 1925 when the *No. 5* and the *No. 7* began keeping the channel to Menominee open all year. Captain Larson, then a mate, discovered that ice could be treacherous on both sides of the lake in 1904 when he became stuck off Kewaunee for a month. And captains developed techniques for breaking ice. Although the bow propellers didn't work, backing and using the wash from the propellers brought about a similar effect. They developed the method of "bucking" the ice in which they ran into the ice at full power until the boat stopped, then backed off and tried again. If they could not back off, they filled the forward holds with water to make the bow heavier and crash through the ice. Then they could back off and run into the ice again at full power. They became adept at breaking each other out, either by backing and using the wash of the propellers to break up the ice or by running alongside the stranded vessel.

Most early captains (and crew members) began their careers working on sailing vessels as young men, often at the age of fourteen, and switched to steam vessels as they became more prevalent. Many were Norwegian and gathered their first shipboard experiences on the ocean, later settling in Frankfort because of the town's natural beauty, surrounded by hills on three sides, and its resemblance to their homes abroad. None had education beyond high school, but all had the necessary intelligence and drive.

Unaccountably, Captain Edward "Tim" Kelly, who made so many initial decisions when the boats began operating in 1892 and led the way for others to follow as the first captain of the *Ann Arbor No. 1,* appears to have dropped out of sight. His name is not listed in census records in the Great Lakes States, nor does it appear in personnel records. We know he existed because he appears quite distinctly in Kewaunee newspaper articles in late 1892 and early 1893, but I have not been able to find a record thereafter. That is unfortunate because he played such a prominent part in the development of the boats—first to cross the lake with loaded freight cars, first to fully test the equipment for securing the cars in stormy conditions, first to take a car ferry across the lake in a winter storm, and first to test the ability of the boats in ice. By the time he left the Ann Arbor in February of 1893 the boats were being hailed as champions, able to handle the dangerous winter storms and break heavy ice. He demonstrated to the world that Ashley's ideas would work.

Frank A. Dority, who brought the *Ann Arbor No. 2* from Toledo to Frankfort in 1892 and commanded her for three years, faced and conquered the same unknowns. Born in 1861 in Hammond, New York, Frank began sailing at the age of sixteen with his father, a captain. In the following years he shipped out on a number of vessels, sail and steam, and was master of the *Osceola,* the package freighter under contract to the Toledo, Ann Arbor and North Michigan, when the *No. 1* and *No. 2* were under construction.

Frank went through the same learning process as Captain Kelly as he crossed and recrossed the lake during the winter of 1893. Also he led the way for others, such as Captain Alexander Larson, who in 1940 wrote of his early trips across the lake with Captain Dority. Frank married Maud E. Lee of Frankfort on December 16, 1892, but a change in his career took the couple away from the Michigan town. He left the Toledo, Ann Arbor and North Michigan at the end of 1894 and in 1895 brought out the *Shenango I* and *Shenango II,* the car ferries designed by Frank Kirby that operated on Lake Erie. Later he commanded the *Eastland,* said to have been the fastest ship on the lakes at the time. He left the *Eastland* in 1908, seven years before she capsized in Chicago Harbor, taking 835 lives in the worst tragedy ever on the lakes.

Captain Dority sailed the ocean as well as the lakes. In 1909 he took the *Chippewa,* a relatively unseaworthy, two-hundred-foot passenger vessel resembling a riverboat, from Lake Michigan around the horn of South America and up the Pacific Ocean to Seattle. In 1920 he returned to Seattle to pick up the *Iroquois,* a slightly more seaworthy vessel of about the same size, and bring her to Chicago. Captain Dority commanded the Steamer *Missouri,* a training ship, during the World War I with six hundred men under instruction. In 1927 he left his active life on the lakes to become marine superintendent for the Wisconsin Michigan Transportation Company, which operated the *Milwaukee Clipper* between Milwaukee and Muskegon. He retired in 1934. Maud died in 1928, but Frank lived until 1953, passing away at the age of ninety-one.[2]

Frank Eugene Butler had been an Ann Arbor captain for only two years when he spent sixty-three days marooned in the ice of Green Bay in 1900. Born in Sheboygan, Wisconsin, in 1867, he grew up in Frankfort, where his father operated a harbor tug. Tugs where in constant demand because sailing vessels and most steamships could not enter a harbor and dock safely without assistance. (Car ferries, with their twin propellers, were an exception.) When Frank reached the age of sixteen he began working on a harbor tug in Manistee as a fireman during the summer months, continuing his schooling in Frankfort in the winters. After three years he shipped out on the *Mineral State,* a sailing schooner operating between Wisconsin ports and Cleveland. His next ship was a steamboat, carrying ore from Escanaba, Michigan, to Port Huron, Michigan, and coal on the return trip. He achieved his master's license in 1888 at the age of twenty-one.

In 1896 he joined the Ann Arbor as a second mate and a year later married Eliza Belonga of Frankfort. The couple had four children. In

Captain Frank E. Butler.
(Photo courtesy of Barbara J. Butler.)

1898 he became captain of the *Ann Arbor No. 1*. Captain Butler did not stay with the Ann Arbor after his long winter in Green Bay. In July he left to become first mate on the Pere Marquette steamer *Pere Marquette*, though he soon returned to his roots, operating a harbor tug in Ludington. He worked for a Chicago company that owned several tugs and contracted with the Pere Marquette to keep the harbor open in winter. In the summers he took his tug to Chicago, where he towed steam vessels up and down the Chicago River. Captain Butler remained with the company, becoming its senior captain, and retired in 1941 at the age of seventy-four. He lived to be ninety-five, passing away in 1962.[3]

Captain Alexander Linus Larson, who brought the *Ann Arbor No. 6* to Frankfort on an epic seventeen-day voyage in 1917, left his home in Halse, Norway, at the age of fourteen in 1889. He boarded a vessel bound for China and didn't see land again for the next three and a half months. Alex worked on ships out of Norway and England for three years, then came to the United States in 1892. He soon found his way to Frankfort, where his mother and two of his brothers had resided since 1883. He immediately found employment on Lake Michigan schooners and on January 10, 1893, began working for the Toledo, Ann Arbor and North Michigan as a deckhand on the *Ann Arbor No. 1*.[4] Two days later the *No. 1* left Frankfort and crossed the lake in a blow, ending up in Manitowoc though she was originally headed for Kewaunee. Several men left the ship and the lakes for good because of the beating they took in the storm. Alex, perhaps due to his experience on the ocean, stuck it out. On April 10, 1900, he became first mate under Captain Fred Robertson, and on April 1, 1904, shortly after having been stuck in the ice off Kewaunee for a month, he was made captain of the *Ann Arbor No. 2*.

Captain Alexander L. Larson.
(Photo courtesy of Fran Larson.)

Alexander married Kristine Glarum in 1902. Kristine was also from Norway, but they met in Frankfort, where they lived all of their married lives. The couple had three children; a daughter, Elsie, who died of typhoid fever at age four; a son who died in infancy; and a daughter, Agnes. In his forty-seven years with the Ann Arbor, Captain Larson commanded all eight Ann Arbor ships, retiring in 1940. At the time of his retirement he left an invaluable legacy in a letter he wrote to the railroad describing the car ferry operations in the early days of 1893—a poignant picture of the times that would otherwise have been lost forever. Soon after his retirement, Alexander and Kristine built a cottage on Crystal Lake, a few miles north of Frankfort, in which they spent their summers. In 1943 Alexander was elected mayor of the city. The couple celebrated their fiftieth wedding anniversary in 1952. He died in 1953 at the age of seventy-eight.[5]

Charles Olaf Frederickson was born Karl Olaf Andaerson, the son of Anderess Frederick and Oliana Andaerson, in Fredrickstadt, Norway, in 1873. He left home in 1887, after his confirmation in the Lutheran Church at age fourteen, to sail the high seas, shipping out on sailing ships and steamboats for the next seven years. In 1894 he sailed from Glasgow to Montreal, then worked his way up the Saint Lawrence River

Captain Charles O. Frederickson.
(Photo courtesy of Daisy Butler.)

and across the Great Lakes to Frankfort, arriving in July 1895. On his arrival in the United States he took his father's name, Frederick, adding
the *son* to denote his lineage. Before long his younger brother Axel arrived and, following his lead, adopted the Frederickson surname.
Charles began working in the sawmills around Frankfort but soon signed
on with the *Ann Arbor No. 1* as a wheelsman. He rose quickly, becoming a
mate in 1900 and a captain in 1904.

Charles was tall and lean, about six feet four, and very strong, even in
later life. He wore size thirteen and a half Florsheim shoes that he
bought through a mail-order catalog. Although he didn't need to, he
could easily handle the seventy-five-pound jacks used to keep the railcars
in place as the boat rolled. Like many men with great physical strength,
he seldom used it. His soft manner and the respect in which his subordinates held him were sufficient to command attention. Charles married
Gertrude Carlson in 1898. Gertrude, also Norwegian, arrived in the
United States in 1888. The couple had seven children. Sadly, Gertrude
contracted pulmonary tuberculosis and passed away in 1915. Charles
married again, Emily Simmons; the couple had two children, but the
marriage did not last. In 1924 he married Agatha Brokstad, who, like

Charles, was born in Norway. Although they had no children, they remained married for the rest of their lives.

Captain Frederickson was credited with saving the *No. 4* and her crew in the famous 1923 storm that ended with the sinking of the ship in Frankfort Harbor. He spent much of that turbulent night belowdecks with the crew while his brother Axel ran the pilothouse.[6] He continued as captain of the *No. 4* until 1925, when he took charge of the *No. 5*, which he commanded for over ten years. In the brutal winter of 1936, when the *No. 5* was the only ship the Ann Arbor trusted to keep the port of Menominee open, he proclaimed her the company's "Winter Flagship." He retired in 1938.

Two of his sons, Arthur and Carl, worked on the car ferries, but only Arthur remained with the boats, rising to the rank of captain himself. Although Charles adjusted well to life in the United States, he never lost his ties to Norway. On his retirement, he and Agatha visited their native Norway. He subscribed to a weekly Norwegian-language newspaper, which he enjoyed reading to his grandchildren in his native language. Charles passed away from a stroke in 1951, a few months after Agatha's death. He was seventy-eight years old.[7]

Sam Arnerson, the assistant engineer who played such a huge role in saving the *Ann Arbor No. 2* when her port engine jammed in 1907, was born in Denver, Colorado, in 1878. He began sailing on Great Lakes lumber hookers at the age of fourteen and joined the Ann Arbor as a fireman in 1896. He was twenty-nine years old when he performed his heroics, freeing the port engine, which gave Captain Frederickson the power he needed to run the pumps and bring his ship into the shelter of Onekama. Sam rose to become a chief engineer, serving in that capacity on the *No. 4*, *No. 5*, and *No. 6*. Sam and his wife Lidia lived in Frankfort and had two children, neither of whom followed him to a career on the boats. Sam retired in 1948 after fifty-two years of service with the Ann Arbor. He died in 1956 at the age of seventy-seven.[8]

Bernard "Barney" Fabian Tulledge was born of English parents in Marilla, Manistee County, Michigan, in 1868 and began working for the Ann Arbor in 1898 as an officer. In the same year he married Ella Bluswick, also from Manistee. The couple moved to Frankfort, where they remained throughout their married life, raising two children, Florence, and William. In 1902 he became master of the *Ann Arbor No. 2* and was captain of the *No. 1* when she burned in 1910. Also he commanded the *No. 5* on her historic trip to Menominee in March 1924—the trip that convinced the Ann Arbor that it was possible to keep Menominee open all winter with newer, more powerful ships. Captain Tulledge commanded every ship in the Ann Arbor fleet over the course of his career, which spanned thirty-five years. He retired in 1937. Bernard was highly respected in Frankfort and became a director of the local bank. He and Ella celebrated their forty-ninth wedding anniversary on January 4, 1947. He passed away later the same year.[9]

Anton Berner Jacobsen, the captain who took the *No. 6* to the shelter of South Manitou Island in the Armistice Day storm of 1940, left his home in Boda, Norway, in 1887 at the age of fourteen to sail the ocean. His first voyages were on sailing ships; later he turned to steam. He came to the United States and across the Great Lakes to Minnesota, where he married Petrine Amalie Larsen. Petrine had emigrated from Norway to the United States through the sponsorship of a Minnesota farmer and was working off her passage when she met Anton. The couple moved to Chicago and then to Ludington, where they had two children, Carl and Alfred. Anton first worked on the bulk freighters for the Pittsburgh Steel Trust Company; then for twenty years on the Pere Marquette ships out of Ludington before moving to Frankfort and becoming a captain for the Ann Arbor in 1924. Captain Jacobsen served on the Ann Arbor boats until his retirement in 1943. He passed away twelve years later, in 1955, at the age of eighty-two—front-page news, as were the deaths of all Ann Arbor captains.[10]

Captain Jacobsen's oldest son, Carl Melward Jacobsen, grew up in Ludington. On graduation from high school he moved to Frankfort where, at the age of eighteen, he shipped out as a fireman on one of the Ann Arbor boats in 1925. Like his father, he rose through the ranks to become a mate and then a captain. Six feet tall and always well dressed, Carl loved the boats from the beginning. As captain, he ran a clean, orderly ship and kept his own stateroom, which had a bunk bed with drawers under it, in the same fashion. Reading was one of his pleasures.

Captain Jacobsen was conservative, watchful of the weather and unlikely to take unnecessary chances, but his tonnage figures rivaled those of more aggressive captains. Although he did not take as many risks, he did not have as many mishaps. He avoided approaching the dock too fast and causing damage, going out on days that turned out to be unsafe, or attempting to run in fog when it was prudent to slow down or stop. In the early 1960s when an October storm decimated a fleet of amateur salmon fishermen in Platte Bay, north of Frankfort, he kept his ship in port.

Captain Anton B. Jacobsen.
(Photo courtesy of Joan Olsen.)

Captain Carl M. Jacobsen.
(Photo courtesy of Joan Olsen.)

In 1932 Carl married Lila Charity Gorivan, the daughter of a former logger who became a butcher and farmer in Benzie County. The couple raised a family of two daughters, Joan and Jean. When Carl retired in 1973 he said he was happy he no longer had to put up with ice on the decks and ladders in winter. He was ready for another life, but his thoughts never left the boats entirely. When he and Lila decided to remodel their home he suggested a bunk bed with drawers under it, but he was outvoted.[11]

When Edward C. Ericksen graduated from school in Norway, his schoolmaster suggested he go on to higher education, but that was not possible. Instead he migrated to the United States in 1926, working for a short time in Seattle and then in Alaska. He was eighteen years old. Edward found the English language difficult at first, but within a couple years he mastered it, except for the brogue that stayed with him for the rest of his life. In 1928 he moved to Frankfort where his father was employed as an oiler on the *Ann Arbor No. 5*. Edward did not particularly want to work on the boats, but there were no other good-paying jobs available and the work was steady. He signed on as a seaman on the *No. 7*. In 1933 he married Cecelia Anderson, the daughter of Charles Anderson, a lake boat captain and farmer. She and her family had lived on South Manitou Island from 1913 to 1927 before moving to Frankfort. The Ericksens had three children, all girls.

Once Edward realized he was on the boats to stay he decided to make something of himself. In 1937 he earned his mate's papers and in 1948 his master's papers. Edward was considered tough but fair by his crew, and his competence was acknowledged by all who knew him. While working his way up the ladder, he held various deck jobs, spudding ice in the cold of winter when necessary. He never really warmed up to that procedure—always a little concerned that if he actually opened a crack in the ice he might slip and fall in the water.

Captain Ericksen fashioned a fine career with little formal education, but he made sure his daughters had a better start. There was never a question of whether the girls would go to college. All three did. Edward enjoyed being a captain but said that it was a lonely job. He would have liked to have fraternized more with his crew but felt (correctly) that a captain should keep some distance. He served the Ann Arbor for forty-five years, retiring in 1973 at the age of sixty-five. Edward and Cecelia remained in their home in Frankfort. He died in 2007 at the age of ninety-eight.[12]

Captain Edward C. Ericksen.
(Photo courtesy of Barbara Johnson.)

Arthur Carl Frederickson, the son of Captain Charles Frederickson and his wife Gertrude, was born in Frankfort in 1902. He started work on the car ferries at the age of fourteen with a grade school education and two years later left to fight in World War I in the navy. When the navy learned his true age he was mustered out with an honorable discharge. He returned to Frankfort and a year later was again working on the Ann Arbor car ferries. After eleven months, he began shipping out on other lake vessels, filling in on the Ann Arbor boats in the winter when the other ships were laid up. He was a wheelsman for his father on the night the *No. 4* sank in Frankfort Harbor in February 1923. On the day following the sinking he returned to the south pier of Frankfort to take some pictures and there met his future wife, Lucy Ferris. They were married in April 1925.

In 1926 Arthur left the Ann Arbor and Frankfort. He achieved his master's license by 1927 and worked for about six years on the Pere Marquette boats out of Ludington as master and mate, then on bulk freighters. He returned to the Ann Arbor in 1945 and moved his family to Frankfort in 1948. At the time of his return there were no openings for a captain, so he shipped on as a mate, filling in for captains when they were off the ship. That was not unusual. Seldom was there an actual opening for a captain when a mate achieved his master's papers, and,

Captain Arthur C. Frederickson.
(Photo courtesy of Daisy Butler.)

though Arthur had received them years earlier, he did not have seniority with the Ann Arbor.

Arthur was tall and strong, like his father, though in later life he was not as thin. He was also quite gregarious and enjoyed conversing with members of the crew and the passengers. He was known as a fun-loving person who enjoyed pulling a practical joke. As a mate, and later a captain, he began following a lifelong interest in history, obtaining car ferry logbooks dating back to the early 1890s from the company and roughing out a history of the Ann Arbor boats. He also tracked down newspaper articles, talked to as many "old timers" as he could find, and put together an outstanding collection of photographs of the ships and the Frankfort area. In 1949 he and Lucy published their first book, *The Early History of the Ann Arbor Carferries*. The couple published another book on the Ann Arbor boats, a book on the Chesapeake and Ohio car ferries, and two more about shipwrecks near Door County, Wisconsin.[13] He also began writing a weekly column in the *Benzie County Patriot,* "Harbor Notes," in which he passed on news of the boats and their crews. In a sense, his columns performed the function of an employee newsletter except that it was published for all to read and learn more about the boats.

Captain Frederickson pursued his historical interest throughout his time with the Ann Arbor. He passed away of a heart attack in 1966 at sixty-four years of age.[14] Much of his collection of historical materials is held in the Historical Collections of the Great Lakes at Bowling Green State University, Bowling Green, Ohio.

William C. Bacon grew up in Frankfort. His father, Glenn D. Bacon, was an engineer on the car ferries, and Bill knew at an early age that he wanted to work on the boats. He worked weekends during high school. At the age of sixteen the only job he could get was in the galley, but at eighteen he began work in the Engine Department as a wiper and coal passer. In two years he transferred to the Deck Department, and in five years he had his pilot's license.

Bill missed two years on the boats during the Korean War, but when he returned he began studying for his master's license, which he obtained in 1959. Four years later, in 1963, he was selected by the Ann Arbor to be port captain, a position he held until his retirement in 1981.

Bruce K. Jewell commanded the last Ann Arbor ship to operate across the lake. An Elberta native, the son of Frank and Bertha Jewell, he liked sports, especially baseball, but while still in high school began working on the car ferries in the summer of 1944. When he graduated in 1946 he joined the army paratroopers, serving for three years. Back in Elberta in 1949, he didn't want to return to the boats. He was accepted at Michigan State College of Agriculture and Applied Science (now Michigan State University), but when he got to East Lansing the students looked so young that he didn't think he would have the patience to fit in. He returned to Elberta and tried a number of jobs over the next three years. In 1952 he married Beverly Johnson and, with more responsibility, turned back to the boats, signing on as a seaman.

Once he knew his future was with the car ferries Bruce began to learn all he could about the boats and their operation. In 1960 the Ann Arbor gave him six weeks off (without pay) to attend a course that would earn him his mate's papers at the Burns School of Navigation in Rochester, New York. He was so well grounded in the basics that he completed the course in two weeks, but instead of returning to Elberta he spent the next four weeks learning the ins and outs of radar operation. The Ann

Captain Bruce K. Jewell. *(Photo courtesy of Bruce K. Jewell.)*

Arbor had recently equipped all of its ships with radar, but few mates were proficient at interpreting what they saw. On his return Bruce was suddenly invaluable. His captain, C. D. Bishop, made use of him to the fullest, running when there was poor visibility (fog, snow, rain), which otherwise would have forced him to slow down or stop. More than once Bruce awoke in his stateroom to an order that he come to the bridge even though he was off watch. He obtained his master's papers in 1967 and became a captain four years later.

Bruce and Beverly had three children, two girls and a boy. Their son Jack followed in his father's footsteps, signing on the *Viking* in 1978. His career was cut short when the line failed in 1982. Captain Jewell remained with the company until it shut down. He was the last captain to command the *Viking*.[15]

FOURTEEN ✺ *The Decline*

When the Detroit, Toledo and Ironton Railroad took over the Ann Arbor in late 1963, the management had every intention of improving car ferry service to the benefit of both railroads. The *Viking* was the showpiece of those intentions, but the railroad also invested in new locomotives, railcars, track, and various upgrades. John E. Chubb, who replaced David Smucker as president of the Ann Arbor and the Detroit, Toledo and Ironton in late September 1963, felt that the merger would benefit both railroads. He expected to invest considerable money for capital improvements, believing there would be a payback for the Detroit, Toledo and Ironton and its owner, the Pennsylvania Railroad.

His plan was to modernize equipment, put the car ferries on a regular schedule to attract passenger business, and aggressively seek new business. He felt that the passenger business was an important opportunity because it was in a sense "free." The ships had to run anyway. He also believed, and earlier studies supported him, that the Ann Arbor offered an opportunity for east-west business for the Detroit, Toledo and Ironton and that the merged companies could earn more on the same business than they could separately. Also he believed there were economies to be had in a single management of the two railroads.

In 1964 the company published a passenger schedule and increased its passenger revenue by 50 percent to almost $140,000. By the end of 1968 passenger revenue reached $250,000, the highest ever. In 1965 the company entered into a contract with the Ford Motor Company Steel Division to haul taconite, originating in the Humboldt Mine in the Upper

Peninsula, to the company's Rouge Plant in Dearborn, Michigan. The taconite was shipped from Humboldt via the Soo Line to Dotty, Michigan, where it was turned over to the Manistique and Lake Superior Railroad, the Ann Arbor's tiny subsidiary. The Manistique and Lake Superior hauled it forty miles to Manistique, where it was loaded onto the Ann Arbor car ferries and taken across the lake to Frankfort. The Ann Arbor Railroad hauled it to a connection with the Detroit, Toledo and Ironton, which delivered the ore to Dearborn. The Ann Arbor could not compete for the business on cost—Ford shipped the ore in its own ships from Lake Superior—but the company could operate throughout the winter months when the locks at Sault Sainte Marie were closed.[1]

Taconite is a very hard, low-grade iron ore (20 to 30 percent iron) that was originally ignored in Minnesota because of the abundance of high-grade (60 to 70 percent) ore. In the 1940s, a method was developed to extract the iron from taconite as the presence of higher grade ore decreased. The taconite rock was first crushed and then ground into a fine powder with water and separated by a flotation system whereby the iron powder floated to the top and was skimmed off. It was then combined with clay to form marble-sized pellets and heated to over 2,200 degrees Fahrenheit. The taconite pellets were finally shipped to steel mills in bulk freighters.

There were numerous technical problems. A major concern was that moisture in the clay (the loaded railcars were subject to rain and snow) might freeze in transit, resulting in a huge ball of iron and clay that would be impossible to handle on arrival. For its first shipment, the Ann Arbor placed tarpaulins over the cars and company executives supervised the recording of temperatures across the lake and at Dearborn. Speed was of the essence. The taconite arrived at seventy-five degrees thirty-six hours after leaving the mine in Humboldt.

Another problem was the sheer weight of the cars filled with taconite. When the *Atkinson* was first loaded at Manistique she struck bottom with just fourteen cars. The Army Corps of Engineers deepened the harbor by two feet, which translated into three more cars. The weight was also a problem for the railroad. The ore required special cars with small wheels to lower the center of gravity. The small wheels concentrated the weight over a smaller area of track, increasing the wear and tear on the track and necessitating a slower than normal speed.[2] In 1965 the Ann Arbor handled 50,000 tons and in 1966 contracted for 250,000, about 4,500 carloads; but the business was short-lived. Neither the Ann Arbor nor

Ford found it profitable. The relationship ended in the spring of that year.

In 1967 the company initiated tractor-trailer service to Menominee and in 1968 began similar service to Kewaunee aboard the *City of Green Bay*.[3] The Ann Arbor also began piggyback service from Frankfort to a number of eastern cities.[4]

The management was doing its best to innovate and attract new business, but the profits were not forthcoming. The Ann Arbor lost $357,330 in 1963. The Detroit, Toledo and Ironton took over late in the year and had little influence on the financial results.[5] The following two years were better, with deficits of around $50,000 each year. In both years, had events turned out a little differently, the company would have shown a small profit. John Chubb explained that in 1964 the company had paid $124,800 in wage increases, which, while justified, were enough to keep the company in the red. In 1965 the company paid $52,874 in severance pay to crew members on the *Viking* who no longer had jobs when the ship went diesel. Again there was no question of the justification of the payments, but they kept the company from showing a profit.[6]

Other problems did not help. In November 1965 the *City of Green Bay* struck a rock outside Manistique, tearing a hole in her no. 4 hold, damaging thirty-seven plates, and bending one frame. The Coast Guard judged the vessel safe to proceed on her own power to the Manitowoc shipyard for repairs. The estimated cost of repairs was two hundred thousand dollars. The Army Corps of Engineers was unable to find the rock.[7]

A more far reaching problem stemmed from a structural change in the railroad industry that occurred in the 1960s and cost the Ann Arbor much of its time advantage over railcars shipped through Chicago. The Chicago gateway (a gateway is an interchange where two or more railroads exchange railcars) was actually a series of gateways as cars had to pass through several yards to clear the city and progress on their way to their western destinations. Each yard handled every car separately, causing delays that could accumulate into several days.

In the 1960s, railroads began adopting the use of unit trains (cars all shipped from one origin to one destination) and run-through trains (trains that do not give up or receive cars en route to their destinations). These trains were handled as individual units at the yards, greatly reducing the transit time. Unit and run-through trains were needed innovations for railroads but worked against the Ann Arbor.

The wake-up call came in 1966 when the Ann Arbor posted a deficit of $756,170. Despite the operation of three modern ships, the oil-fired *City of Green Bay,* the diesel-powered *Arthur K. Atkinson,* and the diesel-electric *Viking,* which could cross the lake to Kewaunee in four hours, the company was losing money. John Chubb attributed the disastrous performance to higher wages and payroll taxes, the higher cost of supplies and materials, and a 5.3 percent decline in revenues. He made no statement of his confidence in the future as he had done in previous annual reports.[8]

In early 1967 John Chubb moved on to the Pennsylvania Railroad, becoming a vice president. Charles Towle, a former vice president of the Detroit, Toledo and Ironton and director of industrial engineering of the Pennsylvania Railroad, became president of the Ann Arbor and the Detroit, Toledo and Ironton. Towle continued the policies of John Chubb. In May the company filed with the Interstate Commerce Commission (ICC) to abandon Manistique and the Manistique and Lake Superior Railroad, a move Chubb had advocated before leaving the Ann Arbor. Without the taconite business, there wasn't enough traffic to justify maintaining the port facilities and operating the railroad. The company stated that it had lost $149,026 on visits to the port and operation of the railroad in 1966, which included the taconite business.[9] Traffic was so light without taconite that the town didn't put up much of a fuss. On February 29, 1968, the ICC examiner recommended the abandonment of Manistique and the tiny railroad.

The Ann Arbor got a slight reprieve from its financial difficulties in 1967 with a deficit of $45,125, but in 1968 the problem came back with a vengeance. The deficit increased to $461,870. Charles Towle stated the matter simply: revenues had increased by 5.9 percent but costs by 11.8 percent. The major increases in expenses stemmed from the cost of improving the track from the little town of Diann, Michigan, to Owosso, in order to allow the railroad to haul more coal, and from necessary repairs on the car ferries.[10]

Not only was the company running at a deficit, but it was siphoning cash from the parent railroad. The Detroit, Toledo and Ironton had expected to advance cash to improve parts of the railroad and to finance the remodeling of the *Viking*—which was completed in 1965—but the Ann Arbor required another $320,037 in 1967 and $73,900 in 1968.[11]

In April 1969 the railroad filed with the ICC for abandonment of the Menominee run due to high costs and lack of business.[12] Because of the distance, slowing down for the Sturgeon Bay Ship Canal, and crossing

Green Bay, the cost of a Menominee trip was almost double that of a Kewaunee trip. Towle testified that the Ann Arbor had lost $57,000 in 1968 on 131 trips. Annual carloads had dropped from 7,366 in 1955 to 3,127 in 1968 despite a concerted effort on the part of the Ann Arbor Sales Department to generate more Menominee business. Even that volume would have been marginally profitable if the ships had been more fully loaded, but the boats were only averaging 23.9 cars per round-trip, about half of the boats' capacity. It was possible to make money, but to do so each boat had to be more fully loaded and that was not possible.[13]

The ICC held hearings in September 1969. In late February 1970 Captain Bruce Jewell returned to Frankfort from Menominee with the *Viking* and told Port Captain Bill Bacon that if the Ann Arbor could not send him there more than once a week he shouldn't go. He said he could keep the ice channel open if he went every few days but not when a week passed between trips. He acknowledged that the *Viking* was physically able to make the trips, but the strain on the vessel was excessive. In a sense, the Ann Arbor was way ahead of him. The ICC examiner approved the abandonment in early March. Captain Jewell had made his last trip across Green Bay.

Thus ended seventy-six years of noble effort on the part of Ann Arbor captains and crews. The epic struggles included Captain Frank Butler's sixty-three days in the ice on the *No. 1* in 1900; countless battles through the Sturgeon Bay Ship Canal and Death's Door to open and close navigation on Green Bay; Captain Bernard Tulledge's historic trip across the bay in 1924 to convince the Ann Arbor that larger, more powerful ships could keep Menominee open in winter; and Captain Charles Frederickson's uninterrupted trips across the bay throughout the winter of 1936 when Lake Michigan froze from shore-to-shore. The heroics were not limited to the pioneer captains. Later captains, in the 1940s, 1950s, and 1960s, had their own stories of forty- to fifty-hour battles across the bay complete with heavy ice, windrows, and blizzards. Now only Kewaunee and Manitowoc remained.

The deficits kept increasing. In 1969 the Ann Arbor lost $1,442,976 and required a cash transfer of $1,531,810, principally from the Detroit, Toledo and Ironton, to stay solvent. Various factors contributed to the loss: higher maintenance costs to improve rails for the coal-hauling business, a $500,000 loss in revenue from the cement-hauling business (the plant had a fire and the market was slow), and the loss of 2,200 westbound railcars due to "the shift of auto parts to '69 cars which are not routed by the car ferries." Put another way, the company's revenues increased by a mere $1,600 while operating expenses increased by 8.5 percent.[14]

The Ann Arbor was hardly operating in a vacuum. Mighty Penn Central, the giant combination of the New York Central and the Pennsylvania Railroad and owner of the Ann Arbor and the Detroit, Toledo and Ironton, lost $193,215,000 on its railroad operations in 1969. Its stockholders were unaware of the gravity of the loss because the company posted a small profit of $4,388,000, entirely due to its other businesses and real estate holdings.[15] While the Ann Arbor and Penn Central were vastly different in size, one of their problems was distressingly similar—wages increasing more quickly than freight rates. Worse, rate increases tended to lag behind wage increases by about a year. In a sense, the railroad was always one rate increase behind.[16]

By 1970 the management was deeply concerned. In March Charles Towle told the board, "We have had some force reductions and have minimized boat and train operations, but it is apparent that major surgery will be required on the Ann Arbor if the railroad is to survive unless there is a drastic change in traffic patterns."[17] The Menominee abandonment helped, as did two rate increases, but costs were still rising. The company entered negotiations with the Chesapeake and Ohio, which operated car ferries from Ludington, to make cross-lake traffic more profitable. The Ann Arbor would abandon Manitowoc, leaving all the business to the Chesapeake and Ohio, and the Chesapeake and Ohio would abandon Kewaunee. Both railroads would benefit from the reduced expenses of operating only one port. The railroads filed with the ICC in October 1970.[18]

The Ann Arbor also negotiated to share trackage with the Chesapeake and Ohio from Clare to Thompsonville. The Ann Arbor's track was in poor condition and would require upgrades. It would help to have the Chesapeake and Ohio contribute to the upkeep, but the companies could not reach an agreement.[19] In June, Penn Central filed for bankruptcy under Chapter 77 of the Federal Bankruptcy Code.[20] The company did not have enough cash to pay its obligations.

In December the Ann Arbor suffered a nine-car wreck near Pittsfield. The year-end deficit was $821,079, and the company required $1,829,000 cash from the Detroit, Toledo and Ironton to continue operation.[21] The management forecast a small profit for 1971, and the Sales Department continued to seek out new business. Particularly promising was the possibility of shipping sand from the little town of Yuma, near Thompsonville, to Ford Motor Company casting plants at Cleveland and Flat Rock, Ohio.[22] The business would net the railroad $1.5 million in annual revenues and another .5 million to the Detroit, Toledo and Ironton, but the company could not get agreement from Ford. Meanwhile it was burdened with the cost of a seventeen-car wreck and an accident in December in which the *Atkinson* severely damaged her bow. More ominous, the company faced the probability of upgrading 123 miles of track from Clare to Frankfort. The federal Department of Transportation was expected to come out with new safety standards in October, and no one at the Ann Arbor thought its track would pass inspection. The estimated cost to bring the entire road, including yards, up to standard was $1,130,000—money the company did not have.[23]

In July Towle explained to the board that the management was trying to liquidate all properties held by the company that were not essential to the operation of the railroad or had potential for online industrial development. An Elberta property brought $60,000, and twenty acres in Frankfort brought $15,000. He also told the board that the petition to abandon Manitowoc was being heavily contested by the Green Bay and Western Railroad (which connected at Kewaunee), the Chicago and North Western and the Soo Line (which connected in Manitowoc), and the Michigan Department of Public Service.[24] The ICC was dragging its feet, and it might take years to get a resolution.[25] The deficit rose to $1,665,063, and the Detroit, Toledo and Ironton poured another $2,162,562 cash into the Ann Arbor.[26]

In May 1972 the *City of Green Bay* was taken out of service, leaving only the *Atkinson* and *Viking*. In July the company filed with the ICC to abandon the railroad north and west of Thompsonville and the car ferry service. Towle felt that it was impossible to make money on the car ferries given the current rate structure, the high costs, and the company's inability to increase productivity. Hearings were scheduled for October 5 but were pushed back again and again. The deficit soared to $1,958,226.[27]

In early January 1973 the *Atkinson* burned out a bearing while turning in ice-filled Frankfort Harbor. The company elected not to repair her and discontinued service to Manitowoc. The *Viking* continued to make trips twice daily to Kewaunee. In July the hearings on the abandonment of Thompsonville to Frankfort and the car ferries were delayed indefinitely when an environmental group sued the ICC to prevent it from allowing the abandonment of an eastern railroad. The logic was that railroads were better for the environment than trucks, so allowing the abandonment would damage the environment. In October the Detroit, Toledo and Ironton Board of Directors voted to discontinue cash transfers to the Ann Arbor. The railroad had invested $11,000,000 since the purchase in 1963. On October 15, the Ann Arbor board met and voted to file for bankruptcy in federal court under Chapter 77 of the Bankruptcy Code. The deficit reported to the ICC for 1973 was $2,861,000.[28]

FIFTEEN ✸ *More Winter Ice:*
1959, 1963, 1977

In the "modern" era the Ann Arbor car ferries experienced occasional difficulties with storms and ice but nothing like the constant assault of 1936. Each winter the boats lost some time to ice delays, especially on the Menominee run, with an occasional serious problem. In February 1943, the *No. 6* fought for sixty-five hours to cross the twenty miles from Sturgeon Bay to Menominee.[1] In March 1950, the *No. 7* got caught in a storm that kept her on Lake Michigan for twenty-three hours.[2]

With the infrequency of significant problems, one might assume that the ships had "conquered" the elements, but that proved to be absolutely mistaken in the winters of 1959, 1963, and 1977. Each took its toll, and, ironically, in 1959 and 1963 the company was not as able to fight the ice as it had been in 1936. The *Ann Arbor No. 5*, hero of the 1936 battles, was modernized in 1948 and thereafter was an adequate icebreaker but not the "Bull of the Woods" that had seemed so invincible.

In 1959 the Ann Arbor was kept out of Menominee for over five weeks—the first prolonged period since before the building of the *No. 7* in 1925. In February the *No. 7* made an extremely difficult trip across the bay in which she loosened hundreds of rivets. She was not sent back. The *Wabash* and the *No. 5* kept the ice channel open, but in March the channel was allowed to go unused for five days. Working together, the two ships attempted another crossing on March 10. The going was terribly slow; then the *No. 5* lost her steering gear just north of Sherwood Point.

The *Ann Arbor No. 5*, Captain Frederickson's "Winter Flagship," lost her superior ice-breaking abilities after she was modernized in 1948. *(Photo from the A. C. Frederickson Collection.)*

She was forced to rig an emergency tiller and return to Sturgeon Bay. At the Christy Shipyard, her rudder was lashed amidships. She was towed through the canal into Lake Michigan, and Captain Arthur Frederickson took her to Manitowoc, steering by the engines. At 9:00 p.m. on March 12, two days and nights after she left Frankfort, the *Wabash* was ordered to abort her trip and take the cargo to Manitowoc. Like the *No. 7*, the *Wabash* was found to have loose rivets throughout the ship. No Ann Arbor ship returned to Menominee until April 13.[3]

The winter of 1963 was the fifth coldest on the Great Lakes in the twentieth century. Only the winters of 1904, 1918, 1920, and 1977 (yet to come) were colder.[4] In 1904 and 1977 Lake Michigan froze across. In 1904 the Ann Arbor had three car ferries approximately 260 feet long and 1,200 horsepower with which to fight the ice. Two were built of wood, one of steel. Two of the ships, the *No. 1* and *No. 3*, were imprisoned in the ice off the Wisconsin shore for over thirty days. The third was held in Frankfort when the Ann Arbor suspended cross-lake service for over a month. In

Photo of the *Wabash* taken from the *Ann Arbor No. 5* as the two ships fought their way into Green Bay on their way to Menominee in 1959. The trip was never completed because the *No. 5* damaged her steering gear and had to go to Manitowoc for repairs. The *Wabash* was recalled after two days of almost no progress and sent to Manitowoc. *(Photo from the A. C. Frederickson Collection.)*

1963 the Ann Arbor was much better equipped with the *No. 5* (even with her reduced ice-breaking abilities) the *Atkinson*, the *No. 7*, and the *Wabash*—349- to 370-foot ships with power ranging from 2,750 to 5,500 horsepower. Their size and power made a difference, but they struggled.

Unseasonably cold weather in November and December 1962 set the stage; then in mid-January powerful storms crossed the lake and temperatures plummeted. From January 17 to January 24 Frankfort absorbed twenty inches of snow accompanied by below-zero temperatures. On January 20 winds of forty-five miles per hour drove the snow so that huge drifts accumulated in some spots and others were laid bare. During the night Frankfort was actually cut off from Elberta.[5]

On the Wisconsin side of the lake cold records were being set. The January 24 *Door County Advocate* reported two nights in the previous eight with temperatures of twenty-six degrees below zero. On January 29 the paper reported that fifteen of the last seventeen days had recorded below-zero temperatures.

The *Wabash* passing through the Sturgeon Bay Ship Canal. *(Original photography by W. C. Schroeder. Photo courtesy of Roger Schroeder.)*

Throughout January the car ferries regularly crossed the lake, with the *No. 7* and the *Wabash* keeping Menominee open. One of the vessels visited the port every two or three days. Green Bay was covered with ice, but the boats followed the ice channel and recorded minimal delays until late in the month. The *Wabash* lost over ten hours on each of her last three trips in January; then she took over a day and a half to cross the bay on a particularly arduous trip February 4–6. She called for assistance from the *No. 7* and a Coast Guard cutter while stuck about a mile off Sherwood Point. The *No. 7* arrived, broke her free, and the two ships went on to Menominee, but when they left it was for the winter. No Ann Arbor boat returned to Menominee until April 9.[6]

The storm that cut Frankfort off from Elberta on January 20 blew large quantities of slush ice into the basin between the breakwaters. While that initially was not enough to materially hamper the boats, winds from the west and northwest continued to force ice into the harbor over the next ten days.[7] As the slush ice continued to build in the basin the car ferries had more and more difficulty getting in and out. It became a

The *Arthur K. Atkinson* leaving Frankfort Harbor in 1962. *(Photo from the A. C. Frederickson Collection.)*

The *Arthur K. Atkinson* appears out of the gloom off the stern of another Ann Arbor ship in 1963. *(Photo from the A. C. Frederickson Collection.)*

common sight to see one of the big ships fighting her way into the basin and through the stub piers; plowing into the ice with her engines straining to the limit, then backing off and plowing into the ice again. At times a ship took up to three hours to make good the three-quarter-mile distance from the breakwaters to the slip.

The boats helped each other. When the *Wabash* got stuck outside the stub piers on January 24 the *Atkinson* broke her out. When the *No. 7* got stuck in the basin on January 27 the *Atkinson* broke her out. Then the *Atkinson* got stuck for ten hours entering the harbor on January 28. The *Wabash*, activated to duty at noon that day, left her slip and backed out to the *Atkinson*, releasing her in about an hour.[8]

For the next few weeks the boats continued to fight heavy ice entering and leaving Frankfort Harbor but nothing more serious. Sometime in the third week of February, the lake was reported to be frozen all the way across, even opposite Chicago. Lake Superior was reported to be frozen across for the first time in recorded history. The *Benzie County Patriot* stated:

> With Lake Michigan now completely frozen over the west winds blow across the lake as they do the prairies in the western states and there is no open water to moderate the temperatures. The frozen lake appears now, at least from the shore, like the frozen wastes of the arctic.[9]

The ships established an ice channel from Frankfort to Kewaunee, which they called "Route 66." They could follow the channel to the Wisconsin side then down the shore to Manitowoc. While the winter was hard on the boats and their crews, there were some advantages: no waves and less need to secure the railcars with heavy gear. Most of the time the crew members were comfortable. The ships, even the diesel-powered *Atkinson*, were heated with steam. The men could play cards or watch television in their off-duty hours, though sleep could be difficult at times due to the noise from the straining engines and the ice pushing against the sides of the ship. Deckhands had to go outside with steam hoses and shovels to clean the decks and ladders, but the days of putting the crew on the ice with spuds and axes were long past.

Working in ice was always hard on captains. Most captains wanted to be in the pilothouse whenever the ship was working, which was nearly twenty-four hours a day. A captain might sleep while the fires were being cleaned or if activity was shut down for some other reason such as poor

Leaving Frankfort in midwinter. *(Photo courtesy of John Hunsberger.)*

visibility. Captains varied in their approach. Some were more willing than others to turn the ship over to the mate on watch, particularly if the mate carried a master's license. Also some captains, if the ship was stuck fast, left orders to be awakened if she broke loose. For chief engineers, the situation was almost identical. The chief was responsible for all things mechanical and electrical—and there was plenty that could break down while a ship was straining to the limits of her power against the ice. Like captains, the chief engineers stayed on the job as long as their stamina permitted.

All of the boats suffered some damage. On February 6, while turning around in Green Bay about a mile northwest of Sherwood Point, the *No. 7* damaged her propellers. On her return to Frankfort, she "tipped up" the stern by putting six fuel cars onboard and running them forward while pumping water into the forward holds and out of the aft hold, just as Captain Larson's crew of the *No. 6* had done at Saint Ignace in 1917. Crew members went out on the ice to inspect the damage. Two days later the ship was laid up for the winter at the Manitowoc shipyard.

On February 21, the *Wabash* tipped up in Frankfort. Captain Carl Jacobsen saw that one blade and part of another were broken off. The *Wabash* continued operating across the lake but went into dry dock in Manitowoc three days later. On the day the *Wabash* went into dry dock, the *No. 5* tipped up in Frankfort so the crew could observe the damage that had occurred when she struck a submerged object (possibly ice) while docking in Manistique. The crew worked on the damaged propeller all afternoon and the *No. 5* went back into service, but by February 24 she was headed for the Manitowoc dry dock.[10]

The last few days in February and the first in March were particularly challenging. On February 26 the *Door County Advocate* announced that Sturgeon Bay had endured thirty days with a temperature reading below zero, threatening the record of thirty-six days set in 1936. On that same day, low temperatures on the east side of the lake ranged from minus thirteen to minus twenty-six degrees. In Copemish, about twenty miles inland from Frankfort, the temperature reached forty below.[11]

The boats continued to cross the lake but with great difficulty, often getting stuck near Frankfort Harbor but also several miles into the lake. On March 5 the *No. 5* required just over twenty-four hours to cross the seventy-two miles from Frankfort to Manitowoc. Much of that time was spent stuck in the ice seven to ten miles off Frankfort. Were it not for help from the *Atkinson*, she would have remained icebound much longer. The *Wabash* and the *Atkinson* experienced similar problems. On March 6 the *Atkinson*, which normally crossed the lake in four hours, left Frankfort on what may have been her longest trip to Kewaunee ever. The log tells the story.

March 6   Depart Frankfort 1:20 a.m.

Stuck in windrows at 2:20 a.m. Loose 3:45 a.m. Stuck at 4:20 a.m. Working engines and shifting water in holds, trying to get loose.

Got loose at 12:15 p.m. Got over to Boat 5 and broke her loose at 1:45 p.m.

Broke trail to open water for No. 5. Left her at 2:05 p.m. and turned around heading back for West Shore. Stopped engines at 2:45 p.m. a/c engine trouble.

Underway at 4:00 p.m. With port engine running slow. Stopped again at 4:25 p.m.

Underway 5:05 p.m. Heading back to Frankfort as port engine heating up.

The *Arthur K. Atkinson* as seen from another Ann Arbor ship in 1963. *(Photo from the A. C. Frederickson Collection.)*

    Stuck at 6:05 p.m. Stopped working engines to run water in #1 and 2 holds 7:40 p.m.

March 7 Boat 5 got to us and broke us loose at 1:00 a.m. and started back for Kewaunee as the Chief had gotten the engine trouble corrected.

    Arrive Kewaunee 4:31 a.m. Delays: 23 hrs. 30 min. enroute a/c ice.

The *No. 5, No. 7,* and *Wabash* all suffered damage to their propellers in February. The *Atkinson*'s turn came on March 18 as she was turning around in Kewaunee harbor. She hit a submerged obstacle that damaged her starboard propeller and the variable-pitch propulsion system. Six days later she was on her way to a shipyard in Calumet City, Illinois, for repairs.[12]

As the month of March wore on, the delays lessened, even though the boats were still following the ice channel. On March 12 the *Atkinson* crossed from Kewaunee to Frankfort in normal time. The reprieve was short-lived but by March 22 ice delays were down to an hour or less. On April 6 the Ann Arbor decided it was time to return to Menominee. The *No. 5* did the honors in near normal time. The winter was over; but on May 16 the *No. 7* was treated to one last indication of just how severe it had been. On her way from Kewaunee to Frankfort she ran through newly frozen ice—not enough to be a hindrance but strong enough to support the ice chunks she was throwing off her bow.

There is no doubt that the winter of 1963 was the worst the Ann Arbor had encountered since 1917—even worse than 1936. It was colder; the company's best icebreakers got stuck with regularity several miles offshore; the severe conditions lasted a full two months, about twice as long as in 1936; and the Ann Arbor boats were shut out of Menominee for two months. Some asked why the Ann Arbor was shut out of Menominee for nine weeks in 1963 and not at all in 1936 when the temperatures in February were about the same. One factor may have been additional snow in 1936, which would have insulated the ice on Green Bay from the intense cold and caused it to freeze more slowly. Another could be that the *No. 5* was a better icebreaker in 1936 than any Ann Arbor ship in 1963. The *Atkinson,* which was much more powerful going forward, did not have sufficient power to back off, and the Ann Arbor did not send her to Menominee for that reason. A third could be that, while February was very cold in both years, January and March were colder in 1963.

Throughout the winter the crews never stopped fighting the weather and never stayed in port due to ice conditions. They fought round the clock, and when they were in the clutches of the ice they didn't give up. They pumped water into and out of the holds, moved railcars fore and aft, worked the engines, and helped each other. All of the ships suffered significant delays, but they kept the transportation route alive—and it was still much faster to ship across the lake than through Chicago.

The winter of 1977 resembled the earlier years of 1917, 1936, and 1963 in that it was very cold—the second coldest in the twentieth century and the fifth coldest since measurements were recorded—and again the lake froze shore-to-shore.[13] The big difference was in the Ann Arbor itself. In 1936 there were five boats to keep Frankfort Harbor open, in 1963 there were four; and in 1977 there was only one—the *Viking.* With her 6,120-horsepower diesel-electric propulsion system—which gave her over twice the power of the *No. 5*—she was the best icebreaker ever to cross the lake for the company. Her captains boasted that she could plow through four feet of sheet ice.

The *Viking* leaving the Frankfort stub piers in 1977. In this picture she is *not* stuck in the ice. *(Photo courtesy of Ned Edwards.)*

But times had changed. The Ann Arbor was a shell of its former self. Business was so slow that she was only averaging one and a half round trips a day to Kewaunee. Menominee and Manistique had been abandoned and Manitowoc embargoed. The problem the *Viking* faced was her inability to be in two places at once. When she crossed the lake to Kewaunee she could do nothing about the ice being shoved between the breakwaters and into the basin at Frankfort by powerful westerly winds. In the end, she would be defeated.

In late January Captain Bruce Jewell was interviewed by a reporter from the *Grand Rapids Press.* During the interview, he stated, "I'll lay odds that most of the lake is nothing but ice by mid-February if not sooner."[14] Little did he know how correct he would be or how much he would be affected by it. His battle with the lake began on Wednesday, January 26, when he took the *Viking* out of Frankfort bound for Kewaunee. There was a gale force wind blowing from the south, heavy snow, and essentially no visibility. As the *Viking* ventured farther into Lake Michigan it became obvious that she would not be able to get into Kewaunee. The entrance was narrow, and the huge waves would make any attempt to enter dangerous, even reckless, so Captain Jewell and the *Viking* returned to Frankfort.[15] In a few hours the wind veered to the west, which allowed Captain

Jewell to sail for Kewaunee, but it also brought on a condition that would work to his detriment. For the next several days, winds of twenty to thirty miles per hour with a westerly component shoved more and more ice into the basin between the Frankfort breakwaters and piled up ice outside the entrance as well.[16]

Captain Jewell completed his round-trip to Kewaunee without incident, but on the return from his second round-trip, on Thursday, January 27, he became stuck in the ice at the harbor entrance for about twenty-five minutes. He broke his way in and completed two more trips to Kewaunee while the westerly winds continued to shove ice against the harbor entrance. His good fortune was about to end. When he tried to leave Frankfort Harbor Saturday morning, January 29, he couldn't get past the breakwaters. Heavy pack ice with slush ice beneath it stood in the way. Ironically, the area inside the stub piers and the inner harbor itself, while covered with sheet ice, was passable. The narrow opening between the stub piers prevented large concentrations of ice from being pushed into the inner harbor. Captain Jewell took several runs at the entrance but could not break through. The rest of Saturday, Sunday, and Monday passed, but he was unable to free the *Viking*.

Well before sunrise on Tuesday, February 1, the *Viking* got help from an unlikely source, the Coast Guard cutter *Raritan*.[17] The *Raritan* was only 110 feet long, but she was powerful, and because of her small size her power was concentrated—a bullet compared to the *Viking's* sledgehammer—so she broke her way through the ice right up to the *Viking*. By 10:00 a.m. the *Viking* was under way, but instead of crossing the lake she returned to the slip because she had not been fully loaded when she left Saturday and there was more freight to be sent across the lake.

In Frankfort, Captain Leonard Kittleson relieved Captain Jewell. As he attempted to leave the harbor, Captain Kittleson got about 100 feet farther than Captain Jewell had and then hung up on the ice. The *Raritan* tried to tow the ship, but the tow line parted. The *Raritan* returned to Frankfort Harbor and moored at the Luedtke dock overnight while the *Viking* remained at the harbor entrance. During the evening the wind dropped and switched to the south, relieving some of the pressure at the harbor entrance. The *Viking* broke free around 2:00 a.m. on Wednesday, February 2, but was stuck again by 4:00. Just before sunrise, the *Raritan* returned to the *Viking* and broke her free. She cut a path into the lake for the big ship to follow, and soon the *Viking* was on her way to Kewaunee.

The mighty Coast Guard cutter *Raritan,* 110 feet of solid power. *(Photo courtesy of John Hunsberger.)*

The *Viking* near the spot where she got stuck in 1977. On the day this photo was taken, she was not stuck. *(Photo courtesy of Ned Edwards.)*

For the next several days, cross-lake service returned close to normal aided by light winds from the north that did not add to the congestion at the harbor entrance. The *Viking* made continuous trips across the lake, and it was good that she did because on February 8 the wind switched to the southwest at twenty to thirty miles per hour and her problems began in earnest. For the next eight days the wind had a westerly component. The *Viking* crossed the lake from Kewaunee on the eighth and tried to get into Frankfort Harbor but got stuck at the entrance. The *Raritan* was dispatched to the rescue, arriving in the early afternoon. She freed the *Viking* and began breaking a track into Frankfort but was called away from the scene to help the T/V *Amoco Wisconsin,* a tanker that was attempting to reach Traverse City. Heating oil was badly needed to heat homes and businesses there and drew a higher priority than freight. With no prospect of entering Frankfort, the *Viking* returned to Kewaunee.

The following day (February 9) the *Viking* returned to Frankfort, arriving at about 10:00 a.m., but she could not break through the ice at the entrance. By 2:00 she was stuck. She broke free early the following morning, Thursday, February 10, but still could not get into Frankfort. The *John M. Selvick,* a commercial tug, was dispatched from across the lake, but she was of little help. Before long she had damaged her rudder and was in need of assistance herself. The *Viking* remained at the harbor entrance until help arrived in the form of the *Raritan* about 9:00 p.m. The two vessels lay in the ice all night, waiting for daylight.

The *Raritan* began assisting the *Viking* early Friday morning, February 11, but made little progress. By midmorning she was called away to tow the *John M. Selvick* back to Wisconsin and was having some difficulty herself. She was running short of food. A Coast Guard helicopter made three drops of food and other supplies. Aboard the *Viking* matters were also getting complicated. Frank Chorley, an oiler, was suffering from an eye problem that was getting worse. He was airlifted off the boat and taken to a hospital.

The Coast Guard icebreaker *Westwind* arrived late in the day (February 11) and broke out the *Viking* about 10:00 p.m. but could not lead her into the harbor because she (the *Westwind*) drew too much water. Once free, the *Viking* returned to Kewaunee. Port Captain Bill Bacon requested a Coast Guard cutter to open Frankfort Harbor but was doubtful he would receive help soon. He told a newspaper it might take anywhere from four or five days to a week or more.[18]

This photograph of the Coast Guard cutter *Westwind* was taken from the *Viking*. The *Westwind* helped free the *Viking* but could not lead her into Frankfort Harbor because she (the *Westwind*) drew too much water. *(Photo courtesy of John Hunsberger.)*

Four days later, Tuesday, February 15, the *Viking* crossed the lake from Kewaunee and again attempted to get into Frankfort. This was the third attempt in eight days. She was expected at 12:30 p.m., but at midafternoon she was still well out in the lake. There was a current running, and Port Captain Bacon thought if the *Viking* could get inside the harbor and break up some of the ice the current might take it away. Late in the day, as she approached the breakwater, she became stuck. By now there were 110 freight cars piled up in Elberta and many more in Kewaunee.[19]

The *Raritan* arrived about 8:00 p.m. but was unable to help. Port Captain Bacon would have preferred the *Westwind* or the *Mackinaw* because both were much more powerful than the *Raritan,* but the *Westwind* was on her way to assist two Canadian tankers and another icebreaker in Whitefish Bay on Lake Superior while the *Mackinaw* was at River Rouge,

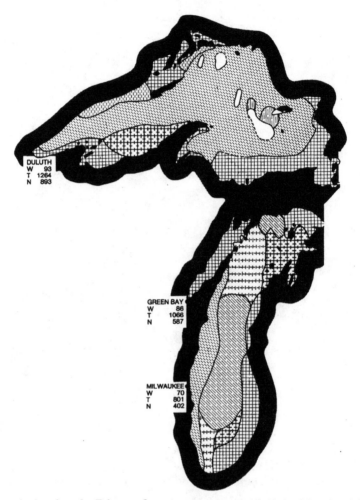

Composite ice chart for February 6, 1977. *(Chart courtesy of the National Oceanic and Atmospheric Administration, Great Lakes Environmental Research Laboratory.)*

Michigan, on her way north after completing repairs on her propeller and shaft in Lorain, Ohio.[20] Chief Petty Officer Larry Pierce, of the Coast Guard's Ice Navigation Division, said, "During the present fuel crisis, car ferries just don't have as high a priority in Coast Guard Rescue operations as oil and freight carriers."[21] His comment about oil is understandable, but he does not seem to have understood that car ferries carried little but freight.

At 3:35 a.m. on Thursday, February 17, the *Viking* got into Frankfort

LEGEND

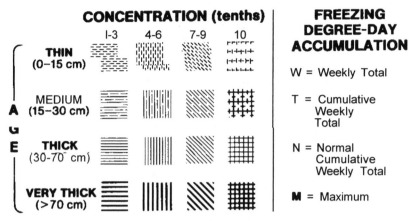

DASHED LINE INDICATES PROJECTED ICE BOUNDARY
CLEAR AREAS INDICATE OPEN WATER

The concentration legend (*left*) depicts ice thickness and concentration. Symbols near the upper left corner represent ice that is relatively thin and loosely concentrated; those near the lower right, ice that is thick and heavily concentrated. A freezing degree-day (FDD) value is defined as the difference between thirty-two degrees and the average daily temperature. When the average temperature on a given day is below thirty-two degrees, positive FDDs occur; when it is above thirty-two degrees, negative FDDs accumulate for the day. A comparison of cumulative weekly FDDs with normal cumulative weekly FDDs provides an indication of the severity of the winter. (*Legend courtesy of the National Oceanic and Atmospheric Administration, Great Lakes Environmental Research Laboratory.*)

with the help of the *Raritan* and a change in wind direction to the southeast. The *Raritan* tied up across the harbor at the Luedtke dock while the *Viking* unloaded and took on new cars for the trip back across the lake. Later in the morning, the *Viking* followed the *Raritan* out of the harbor and started across the lake to Kewaunee, but the situation had not significantly improved. That night the wind came out of the south at eighteen miles per hour, then the southwest and finally northwest. Late in the morning on Friday, February 18, the *Viking* returned from Kewaunee but was stopped well outside the harbor entrance even though the wind had abated. The *Westwind* arrived from Lake Superior and began helping. The *Mackinaw* had been dispatched but was delayed because she had received orders to go to Ludington, where two Chesapeake and Ohio car ferries were stuck. She left Ludington about 5:00 p.m., arrived near Frankfort about 7:30, and immediately began helping

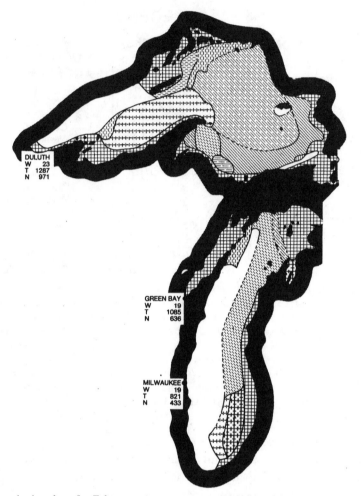

DULUTH
W   23
T 1287
N   971

GREEN BAY
W   19
T   1085
N   636

MILWAUKEE
W   19
T   821
N   433

Composite ice chart for February 13, 1977. *(Chart courtesy of the National Oceanic and Atmospheric Administration, Great Lakes Environmental Research Laboratory.)*

the *Westwind* free the *Viking*. After seven hours, they successfully got the *Viking* into port about 2:30 a.m., February 19.[22]

Once the *Viking* was safely in her home port, the *Westwind* was sent to Milwaukee, and by noon the *Mackinaw* was passing under the Mackinac Bridge en route to her home port of Cheboygan.[23] The Coast Guard had no interest in staying around to help the *Viking* another time. Instead, it supported a federal rerouting order, approved by the Interstate Commerce Commission, authorizing the line to keep the car ferry in port indefinitely.[24]

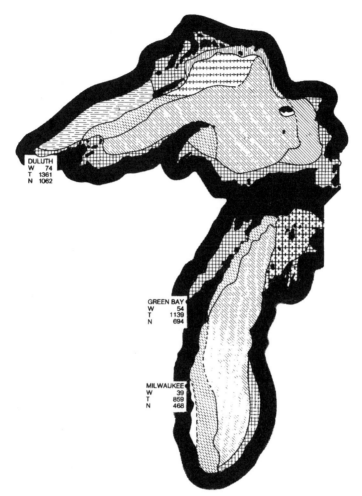

Composite ice chart for February 20, 1977. *(Chart courtesy of the National Oceanic and Atmospheric Administration, Great Lakes Environmental Research Laboratory.)*

So the fight was over. From February 8 through February 19 the *Viking* completed two round-trips to Kewaunee and was shut out of Frankfort for nine days—the longest stretch since the Ann Arbor fleet was held fast in the ice off Frankfort in 1917. Nearly all of that period was spent trying to get in or out of Frankfort. The *Viking* did not get into or out of the harbor once without help. The lake had won.

On Tuesday, February 22, the loaded freight cars in Elberta left for Chicago and then on to their western destinations. The empties left the next day. A Coast Guard representative described the ice as "arctic."

Three-quarters of the top layer was blue ice, or solid, while the rest was slush. Just outside the harbor, the ice was piled fifteen feet high and extended twelve to thirty feet below the surface.[25] Lake Michigan was 90 percent frozen.[26]

Within a week, conditions improved and the *Viking* could have gone back into operation, but that was not to be. While in port, during a routine inspection, the crew discovered a damaged bull gear.[27] The vessel could have operated safely, but the company elected to repair the faulty gear. The *Viking* did not get back into service until March 15, three weeks and four days after she fought her way into the harbor with the help of the *Mackinaw*.

SIXTEEN ❋ *Rebirth and Defeat: The Final Years*

After the bankruptcy filing in October 1973, the Ann Arbor continued to operate under the receivership of John M. Chase. The company was protected from creditors, but its economic position steadily worsened. Deficits increased each year, reaching $5,635,000 in 1975, while the business shrank.[1] In 1972 the Ann Arbor ferried 33,206 railcars across the lake; in 1975 the number was 14,777.[2] By 1976, the *Viking* was averaging less than one and a half full loads across the lake each day.

In June 1974 the receiver sold the *City of Green Bay* to Marine Salvage Ltd. of Port Colburn, Ontario. She was towed from Frankfort Harbor on June 13. Former officers and sailors watched as she cleared the stub piers, then the breakwaters, and headed north toward the Straits—gone forever. In August, she was sold to a company in Castellon, Spain, towed across the Atlantic, and torn apart for scrap.[3]

The *City of Green Bay* brought fond memories to the many people who had sailed her and others who had crossed the lake as passengers. As the *Wabash,* she was the flagship and largest ship of the line from 1927 until the rebuilt *No. 6* became the *Atkinson* in 1959. Her downfall probably occurred in 1962 when she was converted to oil-fired steam, rather than diesel-electric, as was the *No. 7* when she became the *Viking.* Nonetheless, she was the Ann Arbor's best from a passenger standpoint for thirty-six years and possibly her entire life.

At the time of the bankruptcy filing, there was no possibility that the

The *City of Green Bay* as she appeared in 1965. *(Photo from the A. C. Frederickson Collection.)*

entire Ann Arbor line could continue based on its profit potential. The Detroit, Toledo and Ironton had poured millions into the company with only disappointment and failure to show for its efforts. As Charles Towle stated, a receiver would face the same problems. But there were other forces at work. The Penn Central had been in receivership for over three years, and five other eastern railroads had declared bankruptcy. The seven railroads, including the Ann Arbor, served an area in which 42 percent of the nation's population lived and 50 percent of its industrial goods were produced.[4] Thus, the federal government was faced with the specter of losing a huge part of its rail infrastructure with devastating economic effects. House Majority Leader Thomas P. O'Neill Jr. said a shutdown of the Penn Central would double the nation's unemployment in sixty days. He added that Rhode Island would be bankrupt in four days and New York and New England in about two weeks.[5]

In December 1973 Congress passed the Regional Railroad Reorganization Act, and in early January 1974 President Richard Nixon signed it into law. The new law established the United States Railroad Association (USRA), a nonprofit association charged with the responsibility of designing a new rail system, including parts, though not all, of the seven bankrupt railroads. The USRA would finance the system, which would be operated by the Consolidated Rail Corporation (Conrail), a for-profit corporation also created by the law. The USRA would have money available to help state governments subsidize parts of the seven railroads not included in the system. The law required that the USRA submit a plan to Congress by July 28, 1975. Either the House or the Senate could veto the plan, but neither could amend it. If neither house acted before November 10, the plan would go into effect.

The state of Michigan was hopeful that the Ann Arbor would be included in the plan, but was quickly disillusioned when the Department of Transportation issued a study in February 1974 that included only the Toledo to Owosso part of the railroad.[6] Multiple hearings and plans followed, but none included the entire Ann Arbor Railroad and its car ferries. As it became evident that the final system plan would not include the entire Ann Arbor, the state became concerned that the USRA would include the profitable southern portion of the line, Ann Arbor to Toledo, making it even more difficult to keep the rest of the line (Ann Arbor to Frankfort and the car ferries) operating.[7]

In early 1976, Congress passed the Regional Railroad Reorganization and Revitalization Act, which funded the new Conrail and included an option to help states subsidize portions of the seven railroads not included in Conrail. The federal government would provide 100 percent of the subsidy the first year, 90 percent the second year, 80 percent the third year, and 70 percent for the fourth and fifth years. There was no provision beyond the fifth year.[8] An amendment was attached that allowed the state of Michigan to petition the USRA to remove the southern portion of the Ann Arbor from the plan.[9] The state was able to apply for a federal subsidy, which, added to its own, kept the railroad and car ferries running.

In mid-1975 the Northwest Michigan Regional Planning and Development Commission, a nonprofit planning body made up of representatives from nine northwestern Michigan counties, hired a Washington, DC, railroad consulting firm, V. M. Malanaphy and Associates, to study the Ann Arbor and other railroads serving the area and in danger of abandonment. In November, Vincent Malanaphy, president of the firm, submitted his report, in which he said the Ann Arbor was the only railroad worth saving. He also wrote a report for the Michigan Department of Highways on the effect the USRA plan would have on the Ann Arbor. By early 1976, he not only felt that the Ann Arbor was worth saving, he wanted to be the one to do it.

Vincent M. Malanaphy was well educated and uniquely qualified to attempt the revitalization of the Ann Arbor. A graduate of Columbia University and the College of Business Management, Malanaphy began his career in 1961 as an industrial engineer for the Pennsylvania Railroad. By 1968 he had become a systems industrial engineer on the staff of the

Vincent M. Malanaphy.
*(Photo courtesy of the
Traverse City Record-Eagle.)*

vice president with responsibilities for operational and economic analyses of all capital projects. He added to his business knowledge by attending the Wharton School of Business Advanced Management Program and in 1968 went to the Detroit, Toledo and Ironton Railroad as director of market research and planning. He later became the assistant vice president for marketing. Since much of his effort was directed toward marketing the services of the Ann Arbor, he became intimately acquainted with the railroad's strengths and weaknesses. In 1974 he left the railroad to form V. M. Malanaphy and Associates. Two years later he formed the Michigan Interstate Railway Company, with which he hoped to revive the Ann Arbor Railroad.

Malanaphy joined with four partners, two of whom took an active part in the business. George C. Betke took responsibility for the financial aspects of the business and was elected president while Charles W. Chapman assumed responsibility for legal matters. Malanaphy's plan was simple and logical. He knew that taken alone the car ferries were unprofitable, but he felt that in the short term he could use them to build overhead business (traffic that originated and terminated elsewhere but passed through the Ann Arbor) that would pay the bills and give him time to develop online business (business originating on the Ann Arbor) by attracting industry to locate along the Ann Arbor's right-of-way. The online business, more profitable than overhead business, would be the basis for long-term solvency. Malanaphy knew the car ferries would be obsolete within a few years (some said they were already), but he hoped by then to have options—either dropping the car ferries altogether and supporting the railroad with online business or investing in "super car ferries," vessels with greater capacity and lower operating costs.

Malanaphy told the state of Michigan of his interest in May 1976. By then the state had signed a contract with Conrail, the railroad created by the USRA, to operate the Ann Arbor. The Department of Highways had wanted the Detroit, Toledo and Ironton to continue operating the Ann Arbor, but the railroad was concerned that it might be responsible for providing the very generous Title V labor benefits mandated by the Regional Rail Reorganization and Revitalization Act of 1976. Conrail was already responsible for providing those benefits to its own employees.

Conrail began operating the Ann Arbor on April 1, 1976. Before long it became evident that the operator was not the ideal choice. It was in Conrail's interest to pursue east-west traffic through the Chicago gateway in direct competition with the Ann Arbor's cross-lake service. Recognizing the conflict of interest, Conrail included in its contract with the state a clause absolving it from blame for any traffic diverted from the Ann Arbor. While it was difficult to prove, Malanaphy told the state that Conrail had diverted seventeen to nineteen thousand cars of coal and had made no effort to support the Ann Arbor. He pointed out that in the *Official Railroad Guide,* a handbook shippers used to find information, Conrail listed nothing about the Ann Arbor other than the fact that it was operated by Conrail. A shipper reading the guide would have no idea what area the Ann Arbor served or that it provided cross-lake service. In its own advertising materials, including maps, Conrail made no mention of the Ann Arbor.[10]

It took a year and a half, but Malanaphy and his Michigan Interstate Railway Company received a three and a half year contract to operate the Ann Arbor starting October 1, 1977. The state would pay an operating subsidy based on projected revenues and costs in the contract to be adjusted as actual costs and revenues became known. Michigan Interstate would lease railcars, locomotives, and other items from the state. The state paid a management fee based on volume.

At first the new company enjoyed success. Through an aggressive marketing effort and attention to service, the company increased the number of carloads ferried across the lake from 8,807 in 1977 to 9,889 in 1978. This was still a very low number, but the downward trend that began in 1969 had been broken. With the increased revenues and economies achieved by the management, Michigan Interstate required less than the subsidy stipulated in the contract.

By the end of 1978 Malanaphy felt he needed to gain back more of the traffic lost while Conrail was operating the railroad. He knew that would not be an easy matter, but he took a calculated risk. In December the railroads were granted a general 7 percent rate increase by the Interstate Commerce Commission. Malanaphy picked twenty-two items for which the new rate was 50 percent or more over his cost and "flagged out" those items. In other words, he did not take the increase. That put him below the rates for shipment through the Chicago gateway and gave him an opportunity to compete with Conrail and others on price.

His competitors did not take the flag-out lying down. The flag-out not only put them at a disadvantage shipping through the Chicago gateway, it reduced the revenue they would receive shipping across the lake via the Ann Arbor. Conrail, the Grand Trunk and Western, and the Detroit, Toledo and Ironton all dropped their tariffs (schedules of shipping rates) for shipment via the Ann Arbor. Now, instead of increasing his traffic, Malanaphy was in danger of seeing it drastically reduced!

Malanaphy appealed to the Interstate Commerce Commission, which said it would investigate, but that could take up to two years and it did not order the railroads to restore the tariffs in the meantime. By the time the matter was settled, Michigan Interstate could be bankrupt.[11] Fortunately, Michigan governor William Milliken and Representative Guy Van der Jagt went to bat. By late January the tariffs had been restored and Michigan Interstate still had a future.

Michigan Interstate's first proposal and its contract with the state were based on a two-boat operation. Malanaphy felt that he needed to reopen service to Manitowoc in order to generate enough traffic to make the railroad viable. He was hoping to have the *Atkinson* repaired, but there were obstacles, so he leased the *City of Milwaukee* from the Grand Trunk and Western Railroad. The *City of Milwaukee*, built in 1931 at the Manitowoc shipyard, was of the same basic design as the *Ann Arbor No. 7*, built six years earlier. While she was essentially unimproved, with nowhere near the speed of the *Viking*, she was a solid ship, powered by oil-fired steam, that handled well. Also she was comfortable in winter. A seaman coming off watch could walk into the galley at all hours of the day and night and find the coal stove going, an urn of hot coffee, and genuine coffee mugs. By contrast, the *Viking* was heated by electricity. The same seaman returning from duty would find a galley that was stone

The *City of Milwaukee* presented a striking silhouette as she departed Frankfort Harbor in the early 1980s. *(Photo courtesy of Roy Nerg.)*

cold, with the electric stove turned off, and he would have to take his coffee in a Styrofoam cup. The *City of Milwaukee* began operating in January 1979. The company reopened Manitowoc in early February.[12]

The *City of Milwaukee*'s debut was not without incident. On her return to Frankfort from one of her first trips to Kewaunee, she entered the basin only to become stuck in ice that had been pushed between the breakwaters by a strong northwest wind. Unable to plow her way through to the inner harbor, she backed out into the lake. That would not have been a cause for concern except that the crew, on entering the basin, had begun releasing the jacks and turnbuckles that secured the cars in anticipation of docking. Shortly after the ship cleared the breakwaters, she took a heavy roll to port and the two 170-ton hopper cars of potash on the port side closest to the bow rolled over.

The car nearest the bow rested against the inside of the boat, but the second car rolled onto its side, leaving the trucks (wheels) on the track to roll back and forth. The crew got the trucks under control in short order, but that was just the beginning of their problems. Once the ship was docked and unloaded, they began the job of righting the cars. The car resting against the side of the ship was not difficult, but the one that rolled completely on its side was a huge problem. The yard crew began by wrapping chains around the car and leading them to a block on an adjoining rail, which allowed them to change direction and pull the chain with a locomotive. When they began pulling, the block snapped. It was now clear that they would have to remove the cargo (170 tons of potash) from the car before they could right it. They began by shoveling, but it soon became apparent that the process would take too long. The company rented a vacuum truck from Muskegon and transferred the potash into an empty car on an adjoining track. The process took days. Then the yard crew righted the car with the block and chains. The cars also bent three stanchions, which the Coast Guard stipulated must be replaced. The ship was out of commission for about two weeks.[13]

With the *Viking* and the *City of Milwaukee* operating, the Ann Arbor steadily increased its overhead business. Although the winter weather and ice created problems, they also offered a benefit for the Chicago gateway was even more adversely affected. In January 1979, 22 percent of the cars ferried across the lake were rerouted from the Chicago gateway due to weather delays. By July the company had ferried over twice the number of cars as in the first half of the previous year. In August and September the company ferried over four thousand cars, and by the end of the year it had ferried over twenty thousand, the most since 1973.

In late October the company had more cross-lake business than it could handle, and 364 cars were backed up in Kewaunee. To make matters more difficult, the *City of Milwaukee* was scheduled for its annual inspection on November 15. That would tie the boat up for about three weeks. Malanaphy badly needed another boat, but the *Atkinson,* which was to be rehabilitated, would not be ready before February 1980 at best.

Malanaphy contacted the Chesapeake and Ohio Railroad, which operated the car ferries out of Ludington; then he called the state. His plan was to lease the Chesapeake and Ohio's *Spartan,* a 393-foot coal-burning car ferry, and run all three boats to work down the backlog.[14] When the *City of Milwaukee* went into the shipyard, he would run the *Spartan* and the *Viking.* When the *City of Milwaukee* returned to service he would again run all three boats until the backlog was worked off or the *Atkinson* was ready.

The state agreed and told him to proceed, but it was not to be. Seven days later, the state sent Malanaphy a terse telegram canceling permission. Unstated was a concern that leasing the Chesapeake and Ohio boat would set off a union struggle with the state in the middle. The Chesapeake and Ohio boats were operated by members of the National Maritime Union while the Ann Arbor boats were operated by members of the Seafarers International Union.[15]

Malanaphy had no choice but to place a rerouting order on Manitowoc traffic and an embargo (with a reservation system) on Kewaunee traffic.[16] After months of hard work building the traffic to the level of two thousand cars a month, he was forced to violate the basic rule that had been known since the days of James Ashley—the need to be consistent. Malanaphy lost customers and found it very difficult to get them back.

Another problem that surfaced in the fall of 1979 turned out to be even more far reaching. In November state railroad inspectors found that 11.5 miles of the 15.5 miles of track between the small town of Diann and Toledo did not meet class II standards, which allowed a speed of twenty-five miles per hour. All trains, including those of the other lines that ran on the Ann Arbor tracks, were slowed to ten miles per hour. The problem was even more serious because the tie condition prompting the slow order created the potential for harmonic oscillation of railcars with a high center of gravity, such as those carrying automobiles, at speeds of seven to ten miles per hour. Malanaphy received calls from the Ford Motor Company and General Mills, voicing their concerns about safety.[17]

Michigan Interstate's contract with the state called for the state to bring all rail facilities (including track) up to the class II standard. Malanaphy felt (and those at the Michigan Department of Transportation agreed) that the track would have to be brought up to the class III standard, which allowed trains to run at forty miles per hour, if he was to operate without a subsidy. He had written the state in December 1977 with a plan to rehabilitate the track to that level but received no state money for rehabilitation in 1978. Michigan Interstate repaired the 11.5 miles of track, but by March the company was facing 38.5 miles of additional slow orders. The orders were coming faster than the company could repair the track. Part of the difficulty came from increased traffic, much of which was cement and heavy materials, which put more of a strain on the track—but railroads were supposed to be best suited to handle just such materials.

As 1980 unfolded, the *City of Milwaukee* continued to serve the Ann Arbor. The *Atkinson's* rehabilitation was further and further delayed. By now the country—indeed, the world—was in a recession brought on by Ayatollah Khomeini's overthrow of the shah of Iran in 1979. With sources of oil in the Middle East threatened, the price of petrochemicals skyrocketed, nearly doubling the cost of gasoline.[18] Americans turned to imported Japanese cars, which gave much better gasoline mileage than American-made autos and proved to be more durable. The result was a severe recession for the Big Three American manufacturers, all of which had major manufacturing plants in Michigan. The number of cars built in America dropped from 9,300,000 in 1978 to 8,162,000 in 1979. By 1982, the number had dropped to 5,049,184.[19]

Michigan Interstate felt the recession in two ways: reduced traffic and cost of fuel. By June 1980 the online traffic that Malanaphy needed so badly for his long-term solvency was down 40 percent and his fuel costs had nearly doubled. His cross-lake traffic was holding up, but he had another problem—a long list of items he had submitted to the state for reimbursement that had not been paid. The problem was not just lethargy on the part of the state. Many of the items involved uncharted territory in which the state's obligation was not clear; nor was it clear whether the state could get reimbursement from the federal government. Rail subsidies were still relatively new for both the state and the federal governments and the ground rules were not completely spelled out. Malanaphy forced the issue by threatening to shut down the car ferries on June 16, then delayed until June 30.

For his efforts Malanaphy netted $1.2 million to cover various items on the list and $648,000 in additional subsidies for the current year. It could be argued that money he received was intended for him all along. The state transferred funds out of contingency accounts provided for in the contract. At about the same time, the state bought the remaining Ann Arbor track and ferry facilities so that it owned all but the 32.5 miles of track from Durand to Owosso and the Owosso yard, which were owned by the Grand Trunk.

In mid-August the *Arthur K. Atkinson* was finally ready for service. Ceremonies were held in Manitowoc and Elberta. At last the Ann Arbor had two high-speed ships crossing the lake. The cross-lake business was improving, but the online business, 60 percent of which was automotive, was still very slow. Auto production through mid-August was 30 percent lower than it had been the previous year.

While Malanaphy and the Ann Arbor were fighting the recession, slow orders, high fuel costs, and lack of money to fix the track, the state of Michigan was grappling with broader transportation problems. Although the Ann Arbor (with 328 miles of track) was initially the largest railroad subsidized, the state elected to subsidize 465 miles of abandoned Penn Central track as well—much of it in small segments.[20] State transportation policy was determined by the Michigan Transportation

The rechristening of the *Arthur K. Atkinson* in Elberta, August 1980. Vincent Malanaphy is in the light suit to the left of Kristie Fought, the 1980 National Hang Gliding Queen, who broke a bottle of champagne across the ship's bow. *(Photo courtesy of Ned Edwards.)*

Commission, a board of six people appointed by the governor. Once policy was set, the Michigan Department of Transportation carried it out.

In late 1975 the state issued its Michigan Railroad Plan, which was submitted to the USRA to obtain subsidies. The plan demonstrated a good grasp of both the values and the problems of cross-lake car ferry service. It stated that the Ann Arbor acted as a feeder and trunk route that mostly benefited shippers in Ohio, Michigan, Wisconsin, and Minnesota. There was some traffic with destinations farther east and west, but the core was regional.[21] It claimed that such traffic was vital to the state and should be subsidized but suggested that there would need to be "route consolidation." Three companies, the Ann Arbor (Frankfort), the Chesapeake and Ohio (Ludington), and the Grand Trunk and Western (Muskegon) operated car ferries across the lake. Although the plan did not specifically call for shipment through a single port, it did infer that three carriers were too many.

The plan also recognized the inherent problems of cross-lake service.[22]

1. The boats were old and perhaps already obsolete. They would be useful for another ten years, but new vessels with greater capacity and lower costs were needed.

2. The boats were labor intensive. About thirty-five people comprised the crews of the *Atkinson* and the *Viking*, and the Chesapeake and Ohio car ferries, coal-burning steamboats, required over fifty.

3. Fixed capacity. Most car ferries carried 22 modern railcars. In the 1890s that was a train. Now it was a small fraction of one. Unlike a railroad, car ferries could not expand their capacity when conditions demanded. Trains could haul anywhere from 50 to 150 cars as needed without an appreciable change in crew.

4. To be viable, the railroads should be attracting high-rate traffic to maximize the return on their limited capacity. In fact, most of the traffic was comprised of low-rated commodities such as pulp, paper, and forest products.

5. Railroads other than the Ann Arbor had little incentive to compete with their own routes through the Chicago gateway. Not stated in the plan was the fact that the time it took to pass through the gateway had been greatly reduced since the late 1960s. While shippers might still save a day or two by using the cross-lake routes, they no longer enjoyed the advantage they had when it took a railcar a week to ten days to pass through Chicago.

6. It was very difficult to tell whether car ferries made money or not. Evidence was inconclusive and often put together for adversarial purposes.

7. Railroads had done little to promote supplemental use of the car ferries for trucks, autos, and passengers (much the same thoughts that David Smucker and John Chubb had when the Detroit, Toledo and Ironton took over the Ann Arbor in 1963).

When the state began its subsidy program in 1976 its goal was not simply to save the Ann Arbor but to buy time in which it could work out solutions to the problems it had identified. A major decision before the Transportation Commission became the selection of a single port for cross-lake service. The Grand Trunk discontinued its ferry service in late October 1978, leaving the choice between Frankfort and Ludington. The Chesapeake and Ohio operated three car ferries out of Ludington with daily trips to Milwaukee, Manitowoc, and Kewaunee. All three ships were coal-burning steamboats.[23] The ships required larger crews than the Ann Arbor boats and were subject to environmental concerns due to their burning coal.

The Chesapeake and Ohio was solvent but had been trying to get out of the cross-lake business for years. In 1963 the company aligned itself with the Baltimore and Ohio Railroad, which had a good connection in Chicago, reducing the need for the cross-lake route. Whether that was all that drove the decision to abandon cross-lake service is uncertain, but the company's actions left no doubt of its intent. Thus, the state had a solvent railroad that wanted to get out of the cross-lake business and an insolvent railroad that wanted to stay in it.

In September 1980 the Michigan Department of Transportation completed its Northwest Regional Rail Rationalization Report. The report, presented in Frankfort to a public meeting of the Appropriations Sub-committee for Transportation, gave three alternatives for selection of port and carrier (see p. 232).

1. The Ann Arbor operates Ann Arbor and Chesapeake and Ohio boats out of Frankfort.

2. The Ann Arbor is given trackage rights from Clare to Ludington and operates both companies' boats across the lake. The Ann Arbor is given trackage rights on the Chesapeake and Ohio from Clare to Cadillac and operates on its own track to Yuma to support the sand business with the Ford Motor Company.

3. The Chesapeake and Ohio operates trains to Ludington and operates both companies' car ferries across the lake. The Ann Arbor is given trackage rights on the Chesapeake and Ohio from Clare to Cadillac and operates on its own track to Yuma to support the sand business with the Ford Motor Company.[24]

The report also addressed the modernization of cross-lake service. Back in July 1979, the Transportation Commission signed a $35.4 million contract with the Upper Peninsula Shipbuilding Company (UPSCO), a newly formed company in Ontonagon, a small town on the Upper Peninsula of Michigan, to build one 136-foot tug and four barges.[25] The concept was to operate one tug, powered by two 4,000-horsepower diesel engines, which would notch into the stern of a barge that could hold

EAST-WEST ALTERNATIVES

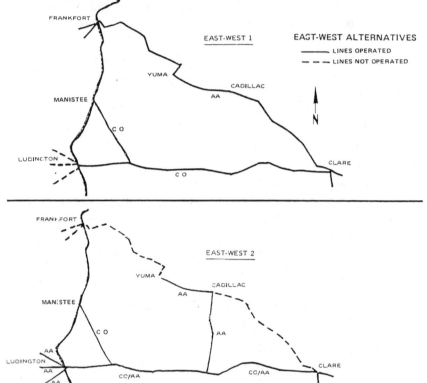

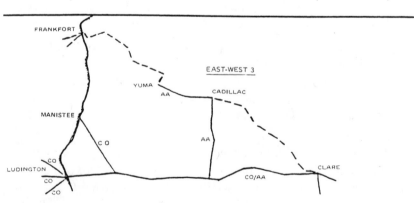

The three alternatives outlined in the September 1980, "Northwest Regional Rail Rationalization Report." *(From Archives of Michigan, Lansing.)*

twenty-eight 50-foot railcars and push it across the lake.[26] The tug would drop off the barge and pick up another (fully loaded) and push it back. The tug could operate with a crew of six and be very cost effective because it never had to wait for the barges to be loaded or unloaded. The report included the tug barge in the various alternatives and left the impression that operating tug barges would be the most cost-effective choice.

Questions arose concerning the ability of the tug barge system to handle November storms on Lake Michigan and heavy ice. Proponents countered that the system had been successful in the North Sea and the Sea of Japan, where waves were said to reach thirty feet in height. Skeptics pointed out that the structure of a thirty-foot wave in the Sea of Japan was much different from that of a thirty-foot wave in Lake Michigan and weathering one did not necessarily imply the ability to weather the other. Also sea ice was nowhere near as dense and hard as freshwater ice. Michigan Interstate issued a position paper in June 1979, pointing out the unknowns (performance in storms and ice). At the September 1980 meeting of the Appropriations Sub-committee on Transportation in Frankfort, Malanaphy told those assembled that the economies were flawed. The tug would require a crew of sixteen plus two galley personnel and could not make nearly as many trips as projected. He also pointed out what he called significant errors in the state's analysis of Michigan ports. He said that Ludington would require a much greater capital expenditure than Frankfort and that option 1 (Ann Arbor to Frankfort and the use of Ann Arbor car ferries) would be the most cost effective.[27]

Unknown to Malanaphy and probably the state as well, the tug barge project was already in jeopardy, even though two powerful legislators, Representative Dominic Jacobetti and Senator Joe Mack, were strongly pushing the project with the blessing of Governor Milliken. The idea was to build a new shipyard, which would bring about 350 jobs to the Upper Peninsula and allow the modernization of cross-lake service as well, but it was not well researched by the state. The Upper Peninsula Shipbuilding Company was grossly undercapitalized, with only six thousand dollars, put up by Charles Kerkman, president, Robert Rotundo, vice president, and Robert Fischl, each of whom had borrowed two thousand dollars to secure his share of the company.[28] There was no feasibility study, no competitive bidding, and no performance bond from the company, which would have guaranteed payments to suppliers and assured that the state would be able to take title to the vessels when they were completed.[29]

The UPSCO officers expected to receive aid from the U.S. Economic Development Administration to build the shipyard, but in April 1980 the U.S. Justice Department began an investigation of alleged irregularities in the awarding of the contract, which effectively dried up all sources of financing other than the state. The company, without informing the state, continued building the shipyard with $11 million of the $35.5 million the state had pledged to build the vessels. The construction was completed in January 1981, and shortly thereafter the Economic Development Administration informed the company that there would be no federal help. The company was living week to week on payments from the state with no way to replace the $11 million.[30]

While the tug barge saga and "route consolidation" discussions were going on, the Ann Arbor was being hit with more and more slow orders. In early October 1980 the railroad was restricted to ten miles per hour on 138.9 miles of track, and parts were judged by the Federal Railroad Administration to be unsafe even at that speed. Unless something was done the Ann Arbor would be subject to fines. The slow orders hurt the company in at least four ways.

1. More crews were required to operate the trains. A single crew could not go from Owosso to Frankfort. The trip took nineteen hours, and the Federal Hours Service Law allowed a crew to work a maximum of twelve hours.

2. There were boarding costs for crews. A crew could go from Owosso to Toledo in a working day but could not return.

3. "Foreign" cars stayed on the Ann Arbor track for a longer time, increasing the payments the company made to other railroads while their cars were in the railroad's possession.

4. There was a reduced level of service.

The Michigan Department of Transportation, the Federal Railroad Administration, and Michigan Interstate met and worked out a plan that allowed the Ann Arbor to continue operation. The state pledged $2.7 million.[31]

As though the lack of business and slow orders were not enough to sink the Ann Arbor, the federal government passed the Staggers Act in October 1980. The act was good for railroads nationwide and was an important step in their survival, but its immediate effect on the Ann Arbor was negative. It allowed railroads to be more competitive by permitting them to make contracts with individual shippers. Thus, railroads such as Conrail were able to contract for lower prices than the established rates through the Chicago gateway, allowing them to beat the Ann Arbor on price. Also the act made it easier for railroads to abandon unprofitable routes, which put more pressure on the state to protect threatened lines.[32]

On December 26 Malanaphy wrote John Woodford, the director of the Michigan Department of Transportation, stating that because the state had failed to adequately rehabilitate the track he could not exercise his option to lease the entire Ann Arbor line and operate it without a subsidy when the contract expired on March 31, 1981. He stated that he would exercise his option to lease and operate the portion from Ann Arbor to Toledo if the state brought the track up to the class II level (twenty-five miles per hour) by the end of the construction season (November 1981). His decision would have a significant impact on his company, and the state.

The spring of 1981 brought more discussions on which port would be selected. In April five hundred people from Benzie County drove to Lansing to protest at a meeting of the Transportation Commission, concerned that it might shut down the Ann Arbor from Clare to Frankfort and send the car ferries to Ludington. Also it became clear that the federal operating subsidies would end on September 30, 1981.[33] It is unlikely that anyone in the Michigan Department of Transportation or Michigan Interstate as recently as a year earlier had expected the subsidies to end. The belief (and experience) was that once a subsidy began it went on forever. President Ronald Reagan, however, saw no value in continuing to subsidize unprofitable railroads. The state legislature was also losing patience, and in its appropriations bill for 1981–82 it mandated that rail subsidies be decreased at the rate of 25 percent a year until they reached zero in 1986.

As though matters were not grim enough for both the state and Michigan Interstate, the Wisconsin Department of Transportation published a study of cross-lake service in July 1981 that signaled that the department wanted out of subsidizing the car ferries. Until then, Michigan and Wisconsin had split their matching portion of the federal car ferry subsidy 52 to 48 percent. The report began by stating that there were many valuable rail projects in the state that could not be financed because of the obligation to subsidize the car ferries. It went on to discuss at length the "resource cost" of cross-lake shipments regardless of who paid it. The report determined that cross-lake shipment was higher in cost than shipping through Chicago without any appreciable advantage and that shippers should be willing to pay extra for whatever advantage they derived by shipping across the lake.[34] Thus, there was one more pressure on the state of Michigan, whose unemployment rate was already 17 percent.

The Michigan Department of Transportation unveiled a new Statewide Rail Rationalization Plan in June 1981, which recognized that the state could no longer support all of the trackage it was currently subsidizing. The plan discussed the need to support a "core" system that would provide service to major industries rather than subsidizing individual railroads. The Ann Arbor north of Clare was not included in the core but was listed as a "gray" area whose fate would be decided in a later study. On June 22, John Woodford, the director of the Michigan Department of Transportation, sent a policy statement to the Transportation Commission suggesting that until the selection of a single port was accomplished the Ann Arbor track from Clare to Frankfort should be maintained at minimum levels—a major blow to Michigan Interstate's chances of survival.

In view of the diminishing federal and state funds for operating subsidies and the unlikelihood of federal funds for capital expenditures, the Michigan Department of Transportation was told to solicit five-year fixed-fee bids to run the subsidized railroads. Each operator was to submit a bid to operate its own railroad and another to operate all of the subsidized railroads. In August, the Attorney General's Office, which was required to approve contracts, rejected all of the bids. By now, Congress had passed the Northeast Rail Services Act of 1981, which allowed Conrail to abandon unprofitable lines.[35] Conrail operated about four hundred miles of track in Michigan and was now free to abandon unprofitable segments, adding to the state's burden of maintaining service.

On the tug barge front, UPSCO officers Rotundo and Fischl bought out Kerkman in March 1981. It was later reported that they offered him $250,000 (of the state's money) and stock options. Also it was reported that they used state money to purchase six automobiles for the company's officers. In April, Rotundo, now president, told the state he had to have accelerated payments or he would shut the yard down. The company hired a Virginia law firm to prepare a case against the state. In mid-

The Upper Peninsula Shipbuilding Company Plant in Ontonagon, Michigan, as it stood unused in 2007. *(Photo from the author's collection.)*

summer, an audit showed that UPSCO would not survive past the first of the year without new long-term financing. The audit showed that the state had already paid $30 million and would need to spend another $32 million to complete the project. To date, only the tug and one barge were under construction. The state wanted the company to finish construction of the tug and barge, but the company wanted to start another barge.

While the state was adjusting to its new set of problems, Malanaphy was trying to bring his costs down. He had already worked out a reduction from five-man crews to three for his trains. In August 1981 he negotiated a five-year labor contract under which wages would lag the national average by about 12 percent but the workers would participate in a profit-sharing program. He also began working on a way to secure capital funds from the federal government to rehabilitate the track.

Through mid-August 1981 the Ann Arbor overhead business was good with all three car ferries operating—indeed, they were keeping the railroad alive—but the automotive business was still weak and slow orders (on 138.9 miles due to poor track) were bleeding the company. In

Overhead business utilizing the car ferries was good in 1981. *(Photo courtesy of the Benzie Area Historical Museum.)*

early September the Transportation Commission told the Michigan Department of Transportation to issue new six-month contracts, beginning on October 1 with a 35 percent reduction in subsidies. In response, Malanaphy told the department he would shut down the railroad north of Ann Arbor and the car ferries at midnight on September 30. Heated negotiations went on until the last moment, when the state offered a six-month contract with the subsidy reduction delayed two months and the management fee cut in half. The railroad kept running. In November, the cut was delayed another two months.[36]

In December the Michigan Department of Transportation issued its new Michigan Railroad Rationalization Report, tier I, which utilized a very detailed (and confusing) method of dividing the subsidized railroads into segments relative to traffic levels and ranking them. While the method differed from the June 1981 report, the outcome was similar, with all of the Ann Arbor north of Whitmore Lake (about twelve miles north of Ann Arbor), including the car ferries, in the "questionable" category. The report made no direct statement about port selection.

As 1982 unfolded, the state government of Michigan was in a very difficult position. It had cut hundreds of millions in state services and programs but was still $300 million in the red. The legislature was considering an increase in the sales tax and a $101 million bond issue, but at present there was no additional money for the state-subsidized rail-freight program.[37] Federal funds for rail-freight operating subsidies were a thing of the past. The state continued to subsidize the Ann Arbor at the rate of $453,000 a month, a slightly higher amount than had been required just three years earlier but nowhere near enough.[38] Low traffic levels due to the depression in the automobile industry, the poor track, and the high cost of fuel were causing Michigan Interstate to lose money at an alarming rate.[39] In January Malanaphy laid off about 25 percent of his employees and initiated 15 percent wage deferrals for his management personnel for February and March.[40]

In early February the Michigan Department of Transportation told Malanaphy that it was going to use the *Viking* to transport passengers between Muskegon and Milwaukee during the summer months and that he should substitute the *Atkinson* for the *Viking* and the *City of Milwaukee* for the *Atkinson*. Malanaphy replied that in summer, when he would need at least two ships, that was tantamount to substituting the *City of Milwaukee*, his least efficient ship, for the *Viking*, his most efficient ship.[41] The department backed off. In late February the company laid up the *Atkinson* due to lack of traffic. The *City of Milwaukee* had already been laid up. The railroad was running one train to Frankfort every second day.[42]

Malanaphy was working with the Michigan Congressional Delegation to obtain earmarked funding to rehabilitate the track. He still felt that if he could raise the speed to forty miles per hour he could run the entire railroad at a profit without a subsidy. While the outlook was favorable, he needed a long-term contract (which he did not have) in order to apply and he would not receive funds until later in the year.[43] Meanwhile his company was bleeding. He was losing about twenty thousand dollars a day on his business north of Ann Arbor.[44] On March 3 he addressed the Michigan Transportation Commission, outlining his concerns and stating the conditions he felt must be met if he was to continue operating north of Ann Arbor (including the car ferries). There was no definitive response.

On March 19 Malanaphy wrote Hannes Meyers, the chairman of the

Michigan Transportation Commission. He discussed the latest Railroad Rationalization Plan's tier II, the reasons he felt Frankfort should be the single port for cross-lake service, his plans to secure federal funding for rehabilitation of the track, and the efforts Michigan Interstate had made to reduce costs through its labor contracts and deferments of management salaries. He said it was not possible to continue operations at the current rate of subsidy and that he must have a six-month contract at the subsidy rate prior to October 1, 1981, or he would be forced to cease operations north of Ann Arbor. The car ferries would be shut down as well. He said that if he did not hear from the commission by the end of the business day on Friday, March 26, he would begin notification to shippers and employees that the railroad would be shutting down.[45]

Malanaphy extended the deadline in order to speak at the April 2 meeting of the Transportation Commission but came away with no more than an offer of a two-month extension at the current subsidy rate. It may be that the commission had no choice. Donald Riel, speaking for the Department of Transportation Rail Freight Division, said simply, "We do not have any more money to give him."[46] At 11:59 p.m. on April 5, 1982, the entire line north of Ann Arbor shut down operations. Then the machinations began.

The following day, April 6, the Michigan Department of Transportation reached an agreement with Michigan and Western Railroad Company, a subsidiary of the Green Bay and Western Railroad Company, the Ann Arbor's trading partner on the Wisconsin side of the lake, to operate the Ann Arbor. The company did not take over because Malanaphy had obtained a temporary restraining order from Judge Stewart Newblatt in the Federal Circuit Court in Flint, Michigan, preventing the state from allowing another operator to run the Ann Arbor to Toledo portion of the line. Michigan Interstate had been running that portion without a subsidy since April 1, 1981, and was listed as the common carrier, the entity that actually contracted with shippers to transport goods, with the Interstate Commerce Commission. The state was listed as the common carrier for the rest of the line and Michigan Interstate the designated operator. Malanaphy had the right to continue operating from Toledo to Ann Arbor subsidy free and, as written in the contract with the state, felt he had the right of first refusal on any contract the state might sign with another operator for any other portion of the line, including the car ferries.

On April 8, attorneys from Michigan Interstate and the state met in the office of Judge Newblatt in Flint. In a phone call, a representative of the ICC said that Michigan Interstate might have shut down without adequate notice to shippers. There were 141 cars stranded on the line. Michigan Interstate agreed to resume operations until the matter could be straightened out.[47] On April 9, the trains began to run and the *Viking* resumed crossing the lake.

In less than two weeks the ICC determined that Michigan Interstate had shut down properly. Malanaphy was free to shut down again. On April 20, he wrote John Woodford, outlining four options for continuation of operation and setting a deadline for a decision of 9:00 a.m. on April 23. Woodford wrote back, requesting more time, but Malanaphy was not going to wait. He had watched his company lose almost two million dollars in just over a year.[48] He sent notices to shippers and employees, placed an embargo and reroute through Chicago on cross-lake traffic, and shut down on April 26, 1982.

Captain Bruce Jewell brought the *Viking* into Frankfort, expecting to load and return to Kewaunee. Instead he was told to stand by. The standby, with a skeleton crew, lasted over two months. In early July Captain Jewell returned to the ship, collected his master's license, his radio license, a few personal belongings he kept onboard, and left the ship. It was over. Ninety years (eighty-nine years and 153 days to be exact) of Ann Arbor ships crossing the lake through storms, ice, rain, snow, and fog—and countless indescribably beautiful days—had come to an end. The industry that had defined Frankfort/Elberta, and its trading partners on the Wisconsin side of the lake for nearly a century slipped into history.

Epilogue

⁂ ⁂ ⁂

The April 26, 1982, shutdown of the Ann Arbor set off a lengthy legal battle between Michigan Interstate and the state. Michigan Interstate wanted compensation for some two million dollars the company had lost due to what it considered an insufficient subsidy and millions more for nonreimbursement of capital expenditures. The state wanted to either force Michigan Interstate to operate the entire line, including the car ferries, or give up the Toledo to Ann Arbor portion. The latter was very important because the state could not find an operator to take over the Ann Arbor system without the profitable Toledo to Ann Arbor run. The Michigan Transportation Commission petitioned the ICC to force Michigan Interstate to operate north of Ann Arbor but was turned down. It was also turned down when it tried to prevent Michigan Interstate from operating between Ann Arbor and Toledo.

Michigan Interstate initiated an arbitration proceeding under the terms of the contract and was awarded $889,000 in July. The state filed in Ingham County Court to have the ruling vacated. Michigan Interstate initiated another arbitration proceeding, but the state declined to participate, stating that Michigan Interstate had voided the contract when it shut down. In November, the court ruled that the state had to participate, and in May 1983 the company was awarded $10.4 million. Again, the state filed to vacate. Michigan Interstate won most of what it sought in a third arbitration but received no funds.

The *City of Milwaukee, Arthur K. Atkinson,* and *Viking* tied up and awaiting their fate.
(Photo courtesy of the Traverse City Record-Eagle.)

While the arbitrations were proceeding, the company was running out of funds. On January 20, 1983, Malanaphy filed for bankruptcy under Chapter 11. The combination of uncollected funds from the state, shutdown expenses, and legal fees put the company under. The court appointed W. Clark Durant III as trustee. Durant kept Malanaphy as president, but within a few months their approaches to the problem of creating a viable railroad differed so much that they could not be reconciled. Durant was most concerned about creating a stand-alone, viable railroad, even if that meant operating only between Ann Arbor and Toledo, while Malanaphy was intent on winning the battle with the state. On August 30, 1983, Durant removed Malanaphy from the presidency.

Durant convinced Carol Norris, deputy director of urban and public transportation for the Michigan Department of Transportation, to sell the Ann Arbor to Toledo portion of the railroad to private investors with the understanding that they must sink or swim on their own. The sale was consummated, and the railroad has been successful ever since. The state contracted with other operators to run parts of the Ann Arbor system (Michigan Interstate operated a portion of it for a short time in

1982), but the car ferries were never reactivated and the Cadillac to Frankfort tracks were eventually torn up.

Vincent Malanaphy passed away of a suspected heart attack on July 3, 1987, at the age of fifty-three. Neither he nor his partners received any money in settlement with the state.

With the car ferries shut down, very few of the crewmen continued working on the lake. Captain Bruce Jewell had an offer that would have led to a captaincy on a bulk freighter, but he turned it down. Chuck Holtrey, a car handler on the *Viking* with sixteen years of experience, took a job on a bulk freighter and worked on the ships for another eighteen years. A few others went to the bulk freighters. Most found other jobs, and several left the area; few found employment commensurate with their jobs on the boats.

For several months the *Viking, Arthur K. Atkinson,* and *City of Milwaukee* rested in Elberta. When the state's lease on the *Viking* and *Arthur K. Atkinson* expired in October 1982, the owner, Penn Central, put the ships up for sale. In April 1983, the Peterson Shipbuilding Company of Sturgeon Bay, Wisconsin, purchased the *Viking* for four hundred thousand dollars. She was towed out of Frankfort Harbor on May 11. The ship that had brought so much pride to the Ann Arbor and Frankfort/Elberta residents was gone. Within a year, the same company bought the *Arthur K. Atkinson.* In time both ships passed into other hands for various purposes (cruise ships, casino ships, pulp hauling), but neither was ever activated.

In December 1983 the state of Michigan leased the *City of Milwaukee* to the city of Frankfort and allowed the city to purchase her for a dollar on December 13, 1984. She resided on the Frankfort side of the bay until early 1985 when she returned to Elberta. The city sold the vessel to the Society for the Preservation of the *City of Milwaukee* for two dollars in October 1988. In 1990 she was declared a National Historic Landmark. She also qualified as a member of the Historic Naval Ships Association by reason of her supporting role in World War II when she carried war materials across Lake Michigan. On May 18, 2004, she was moved to Manistee, where she is now a museum ship open to the public for seasonal tours.

Did the Ann Arbor car ferries have to end? Probably. If the state had fixed the track to a standard of forty miles per hour Malanaphy might have been able to follow through on his plan to develop online business and make the railroad self-supporting, but it is difficult to see how the

May 11, 1983, was a sad day as the *Viking* was towed out of Frankfort Harbor. *(Photo courtesy of the Benzie Area Historical Museum.)*

The *City of Milwaukee* is well preserved and currently serves as a maritime museum in Manistee, Michigan. *(Photo from the author's collection.)*

car ferries could have survived. Their limited capacity, high labor costs, and all the other obstacles identified by the state in 1975 stood in the way of long-term success. The industry started by James Ashley when he took the *Ann Arbor No. 1* across the lake in 1892 filled a very real need for a short route to the northwest for at least seventy years, but when traffic through Chicago was speeded up by the use of unit and run-through trains in the mid-1960s, the advantage largely disappeared.

The tug barge concept might have worked, but we will never know how the vessels would have stood up to the storms and ice conditions so predominant on Lake Michigan. The shipyard shut down on July 2, 1982. The state of Michigan had invested forty-three million dollars in the project. Charles Kerkman and Robert Fischl of UPSCO were indicted for defrauding the state in January 1984. Fischl was convicted; Kerkman was let off with a mistrial but re-tried and convicted in November 1986. No tug or barge manufactured at the Ontonagon shipyard ever saw service for the state.

So the boats have left; the captains and crews have moved on; the wives and parents who for so long kept one eye on the lake no longer agonize over the fog, the ice, and high winds of Lake Michigan. Their loved ones are ashore, and for them the battle with the lake—and their romance with the inland sea—is over.

Appendix:
Ann Arbor Ships
and Their Disposition

❈ ❈ ❈

Ann Arbor No. 1

Registry: US 106974.
Builder/Year of Construction: Craig Shipbuilding Company, Toledo, Ohio,
    1892.
Length Overall: 260.4 ft.
Beam: 53 ft.
Construction: Wood with five-inch oak planking near the bow for ice breaking.
    Sheathed in three-sixteenth-inch steel to four feet above and below the wa-
    terline.
Power: Two compound steam engines to drive the propellers at the stern. One
    identical engine to drive the propeller at the bow. Each engine rated at 610
    hp at 86 rpm.
Capacity: 24 railcars.
Disposition: Burned to the waterline at Manitowoc, Wisconsin, on March 8,
    1910. Sold to Love Construction Company, Manistee, Michigan, and used
    as an unregistered sand sucker.

Ann Arbor No. 2

Registry: US 106984.
Builder/Year of Construction: Craig Shipbuilding Company, Toledo, Ohio,
    1892.
Length Overall: 264.2 ft.

Beam: 53 ft.

Construction: Wood, with five-inch oak planking near the bow for ice breaking. Sheathed in three-sixteenth-inch steel to four feet above and below the waterline.

Power: Two compound steam engines to drive the stern propellers. One identical engine to drive the propeller at the bow. Each engine rated at 610 hp at 86 rpm.

Capacity: 24 railcars.

Disposition: Retired in 1913. Sold to Manistee Iron Works in 1914 and cut down to a barge. Her boilers were placed in the steamers *Petoskey* and *Marshall C Butters*. Sold in 1916 to Nicholson Transit Company, Detroit, converted to a sand sucker, and renamed the barge *Whale*. Dismantled as the result of an accident with the steamer *William E. Corey* in 1927.

Ann Arbor No. 3

Registry: US 107418.

Builder/Year of Construction: Globe Iron Works, Cleveland, Ohio, 1898.

Length Overall: 258.3 ft.

Beam: 52 ft.

Construction: Steel with a double bottom.

Power: Two horizontal compound steam engines, the engines that originally powered the bow propellers on the *No. 1* and *No. 2*.

Rebuilt and lengthened to 306.9 ft at the Manitowoc Shipbuilding Company, Manitowoc, Wisconsin, in 1922.

Power after Rebuilding: Two triple-expansion steam engines, each rated at 700 hp.

Capacity: 22 railcars as originally built, 24 railcars after rebuilding.

Disposition: Retired in 1960. Sold to Bultema Dredge and Dock Company, Manistee, Michigan, in 1962. Cut down to a barge and renamed the *Manistee*. Now owned by National Maintenance and Repair of Louisiana Inc. and used to support a crane at the company's repair facility in Harahan, Louisiana.

Ann Arbor No. 4

Registry: US 203695.

Builder/Year of Construction: Globe Iron Works, American Shipbuilding Company, Cleveland, Ohio, 1906.

Length Overall: 259 ft.

Beam: 52 ft.

Construction: Steel.

Power: Two triple-expansion steam engines, each rated at 600 hp.

Capacity: 22 railcars.

Disposition: Sold to the state of Michigan in 1937. Renamed the *City of Cheboygan*, and used as an auto ferry at the Straits of Mackinac. Sold to Edward Anderson in 1958. Her engines were removed in 1959, and she was renamed the *Edward H. Anderson.* Used as a potato barge at Washington Island and later near St. Joseph, Michigan. Towed across the Atlantic to Genoa, Italy, for scrapping in October–November 1973.

Ann Arbor No. 5

Registry: US 208261.

Builder/Year of Construction: Toledo Shipbuilding Company, Toledo, Ohio, 1910.

Length Overall: 360 ft.

Beam: 56.3 ft.

Construction: Steel.

Power: Two triple-expansion steam engines, each rated at 1,500 hp.

Capacity: 32 railcars.

Disposition: Sold to Bulk Food Carriers of San Francisco in 1966, then to Hudson Waterways Corporation, New York, New York. She came under the control of the U.S. Maritime Commission, Washington, DC, in 1967 and was sold to Bultema Dredge and Dock Company, Manistee, Michigan, in the same year. In 1969 she was used as a breakwater for a project off South Haven, Michigan. In the spring of 1970 her forward two-thirds were clamshelled for scrap and her aft third was towed into Lake Michigan where it accidentally sank.

Ann Arbor No. 6

Registry US 214656.

Builder/Year of Construction: Great Lakes Engineering Works, Ecorse, Michigan, 1917.

Length Overall: 338 ft.

Beam: 56 ft.

Construction: Steel.

Power: Two triple-expansion steam engines, each rated at 1,250 hp.

Rebuilt at the Manitowoc Shipbuilding Company, Manitowoc, Wisconsin, in 1958–59. Renamed the *Arthur K. Atkinson.* Cabin deck was raised to provide clearance for triple-deck railcars.

Length after Rebuilding: 372 ft.

Power after Rebuilding: Two Nordberg nonreversing diesel engines, each rated at 2,750 hp. Variable-pitch propellers allowed both forward and aft movement.

Capacity: 26 railcars as originally built. In later years, as cars became longer, 22 railcars.

Disposition: Sold to Peterson Builders, Inc., in 1984 and towed to Sturgeon Bay, Wisconsin. Sold to Contessa Cruise Lines, Inc., in 1994 and towed to Ludington, Michigan. In 2003 she was towed to De Tour Village, Michigan, where she has been abandoned at the Interlake Steamship Company dock.

Ann Arbor No. 7

Registry: US 224430.

Builder/Year of Construction: Manitowoc Shipbuilding Company, Manitowoc, Wisconsin, 1925.

Length Overall: 347.9 ft.

Beam: 56.2 ft.

Construction: Steel.

Power: Two triple-expansion steam engines, each rated at 1,350 hp.

Rebuilt at the Frasier Nelson Shipyard, Superior, Wisconsin, in 1965. Renamed the *Viking*. Cabin deck was raised to provide clearance for triple-deck railcars.

Power after Rebuilding: Four General Motors diesel engines, each rated at 1,760 hp. The engines turned generators rated at 1,205 kilowatts, 750 volts. Power from the generators was fed to four electric propulsion motors rated at 1,530 hp each, giving the ship diesel-electric power.

Capacity: 30 railcars as originally built. In later years, as cars became longer, 22 railcars.

Disposition: Sold to Peterson Builders, Inc., in 1983 and towed to Sturgeon Bay, Wisconsin. Sold to Contessa Cruise Lines, Inc., in 1996 and towed to Erie, Pennsylvania. Sold to K&K Warehousing in 2003 and towed to Menominee, Michigan.

Wabash

Registry: US 226597.

Builder/Year of Construction: Toledo Shipbuilding Company, Toledo, Ohio, 1927.

Length Overall: 366 ft.

Beam: 57.6 ft.

Construction: Steel.

Power: Two triple-expansion steam engines, each rated at 1,350 hp.

Modernized at the Manitowoc Shipbuilding Company, Manitowoc, Wisconsin, in 1962. Renamed *City of Green Bay*. Cabin deck was raised to provide clearance for triple-deck railcars.

Power after modernization: Oil-fired steam. Output unchanged.

Capacity: 32 railcars as originally built. In later years, as cars became longer, 22 railcars.

Disposition: Removed from service in May 1972. Sold to Marine Salvage Ltd. in 1974 and towed to Castellon, Spain, for scrapping.

City of Milwaukee

Registry: US 230448.

Builder/Year of Construction: Manitowoc Shipbuilding Company, Manitowoc, Wisconsin, 1931.

Length overall: 347.9 ft.

Beam: 56.2 ft.

Construction: Steel.

Power: Two triple-expansion steam engines, each rated at 1,350 hp. Converted from coal to oil-fired steam in 1947.

Capacity: 30 railcars as originally built. In later years, as cars became longer, 22 railcars.

Disposition: Owned by Grand Trunk–Milwaukee Car Ferry Company, 1931–80. Chartered to the Ann Arbor after Grand Trunk ceased operations in 1978. Sold to the Michigan Department of Highways and Transportation in 1980. Sold to the city of Frankfort, Michigan, on December 13, 1984, for one dollar. Sold to the Society for the Preservation of the *City of Milwaukee* on October 17, 1988, for two dollars. Moved to Manistee, Michigan, in 2004 where she is open to the public as a museum ship.

Notes

* * *

Introduction

1. C. Q. Parnell, *Ice Seamanship* (London: Nautical Institute, 1986), 4.

2. The exact capabilities of car ferries are difficult to categorize. Some captains have said that the car ferries could plow though three feet of sheet ice, but one has pointed out that three feet of very cold ice is very solid. The condition of the ice obviously makes a difference, and the statements should probably be given some room for variation.

3. Lawson W. Brigham, LCDR, USCG., *A Handbook of Ice Operations for the U.S. Coast Guard's WTGB Cutter* (Newport, RI: Naval War College, 1982), 129.

4. Parnell, *Ice Seamanship*, 56, reads, "Important Note: This is a dangerous procedure which should be used with the utmost discretion as heavy damage to the vessel could easily result. Particularly in heavy or hard ice it should never be attempted by vessels with low or no ice class and with a bulbous bow, except possibly in some extreme emergency."

Chapter 1

1. November 24, 1892, Frankfort Life Saving Station, MI, Life Saving Station Logs, Records of the U.S. Coast Guard (Record Group 26), National Archives and Records Administration—Great Lakes Region (Chicago).

2. Robert F. Horowitz, *The Great Impeacher* (New York: Brooklyn College Press, 1979), 166.

3. *New York Times*, September 24, 1899, 28; Henry Burger, "Building the Ann Arbor Railroad, Part One," *Double A*, no. 3 (1984): 4–5.

4. Henry Earle Riggs, *The Ann Arbor Railroad Fifty Years Ago* (Saint Louis: Ann Arbor Railroad, 1947), 18.

5. Ibid., 5–7.

6. Ibid., 6.

7. Ibid., 19, 20, 22, 23.

8. Henry Earle, Riggs, *Our Life Was Lived While the Old Order Changed: A Story for Our Children* (Ann Arbor: Bentley Historical Library, University of Michigan, 1971), 60.

9. In the 1890s the Toledo, Ann Arbor and North Michigan was often a subject of articles in the *New York Times,* especially when the car ferries began operating and issues evolved concerning control of the company.

10. *Ballast* refers to the crushed stones that are used to form the rail bed. Ballast helps keep the railroad ties in position, provides a consistent base, and allows water to drain. Rail weight is measured in pounds per yard. Heavier weight rails can handle heavier railcars (with more weight on each axle).

11. Riggs, *The Ann Arbor Railroad Fifty Years Ago,* 11–12.

12. Ibid., 13.

13. Ibid., 12–14.

14. Graydon Meints, "Building the Ann Arbor Railroad, Part Two," *Double A* 14, no. 1 (1998): 5. The original bondholders' agreement stated a goal of reaching the Indiana and Grand Rapids Railroad, but the owners changed their plans and constructed the line to Copemish. While one cannot be certain, it is logical to infer that they intended to meet Ashley and the Toledo, Ann Arbor and North Michigan.

15. Riggs, *The Ann Arbor Railroad Fifty Years Ago,* 26.

16. Toledo, Ann Arbor and North Michigan Railway Company, "Annual Report," Toledo, 1892, 5.

17. J. B. Mansfield, *History of the Great Lakes,* vol. 1 (Chicago: J. H. Beers and Company, 1899; reprint Cleveland: Freshwater Press: 1972), 330.

18. Ibid., 439.

19. Arthur C. Frederickson and Lucy F. Frederickson, *Early History of the Ann Arbor Carferries* (Frankfort, MI: Arthur C. Frederickson and Lucy F. Frederickson, 1949), 2.

20. Stan Mailer, *Green Bay and Western* (Mukilteo, WI: Hundman Publishing, 1989), 60. The Kewaunee, Green Bay and Western Railroad did not go all the way to Omaha. It connected with the Green Bay, Winona and St. Paul, which ran to St. Paul and connected with lines running to Omaha and Sioux City.

21. Kewaunee Chamber of Commerce Centennial Book Committee, *Kewaunee: A Harbor Community* (Kewaunee, WI: Kewaunee Chamber of Commerce), 1983, 9,10, 45–46.

22. Mailer, *Green Bay and Western,* 99–100.

23. Ibid., 100, 104.

24. George W. Hilton, *The Great Lakes Car Ferries* (Berkeley, CA: Howell-North, 1962), 56–57.

25. James, Clary, *Ladies of the Lakes II* (West Bloomfield, MI: Altwerger and Mandel, 1992), 17–18. The Russians also visited the *Ann Arbor No. 1* and *No. 2.*

26. Allen B. Blacklock, *Blacklock's History of Elberta* (Manistee, MI: West Graf, 1975), 37.

27. Hilton, *The Great Lakes Car Ferries,* 260.

28. Ibid., 70.

29. "Development of 75 Years Incorporated in New Ice Breaker Design," *U.S. Coast Guard Academy Alumni Association Bulletin* 2, no. 1 (April 1945): 24–27. This source traces the use of the bow propeller to the *St. Ignace* car ferry at the Straits of Mackinac. The *Mackinaw* also was designed with a swept back bow, allowing her to ride up on top of sheet ice, crushing it with her weight and power.

30. Frederickson, *The Early History of the Ann Arbor Carferries*, 3.

31. Captain Alexander L. Larson to Ann Arbor Railroad, Frankfort, 1940.

32. Frederickson, *The Early History of the Ann Arbor Carferries*, 3–4.

Chapter 2

1. Frederickson, *The Early History of the Ann Arbor Carferries*, 4.

2. *Kewaunee Enterprise*, December 2, 1892, 1.

3. *Door County Advocate*, December 3, 1892, 5.

4. W. E. May and Leonard Holder, *A History of Marine Navigation* (New York: W. W. Norton, 1973), 115–18.

5. Mansfield, *History of the Great Lakes*, 1:439.

6. F. H. Quinn, R. A. Assel, D. E. Boyce, G. A. Leshkevich, C. R. Snider, and D. Weisnet, "NOAA Technical Memorandum ERL GLERL–20, Summary of Great Lakes Weather and Ice Conditions, Winter 1976–77," Great Lakes Environmental Research Laboratory, Ann Arbor, October 1978, 31. The winter of 1892–93 ranked fifteenth. Only four years in the Ann Arbor's ninety-year history were colder: in descending order, 1903–4 (coldest), 1976–77, 1919–20, and 1917–18 (least cold). The vast majority of the top twenty were in the eighteenth and nineteenth centuries.

7. *Kewaunee Enterprise*, December 9, 1892, 4.

8. Frederickson, *Early History of the Ann Arbor Carferries*, 14.

9. *Kewaunee Enterprise*, January 13, 1893, 3.

10. Ibid. Weather conditions were taken from appropriate entries in the Frankfort, MI, Life Saving Station Logs, Records of the U.S. Coast Guard (Record Group 26), National Archives and Records Administration—Great Lakes Region (Chicago).

11. Frederickson, *Early History of the Ann Arbor Carferries*, 5.

12. *Kewaunee Enterprise*, January 20, 1893, 3.

13. *New York Times*, November 27, 1892, 17.

14. *Kewaunee Enterprise*, December 2, 1892, 1.

15. Ibid., February 3, 1893, 5.

16. Ibid., March 31, 1893, 5.

17. Ibid., January 27, 1893, 4.

18. Ibid., June 30, 1893, 4.

19. Ibid., February 17, 1893, 5.

20. Ibid., March 17, 1893, 5.

21. Record Group 21, Records of the District Courts of the United States, U.S. Circuit Court, Northern District of Ohio, Western Division, Civil Records, Mixed Case Files, Case no. 1146; National Archives and Records Administration—Great Lakes Region (Chicago).

22. *Toledo Blade*, April 29, 1893, 2.

23. Ibid.

24. Riggs, *The Ann Arbor Railroad Fifty Years Ago,* 36.
25. Alexander L. Larson to Ann Arbor Railroad Company, Frankfort, 1940.
26. The company initiated service to Manistique in 1902.
27. *Door County Advocate,* March 28, 1903, 1.
28. Frederickson, *Early History of the Ann Arbor Carferries,* 17–18.
29. Alexander L. Larson to Ann Arbor Railroad Company, Frankfort, 1940.
30. Ibid.
31. Hilton, *The Great Lakes Car Ferries,* 76–77.
32. Ibid., 77.
33. Frederickson, *The Early History of the Ann Arbor Carferries,* 5
34. Riggs, *The Ann Arbor Railroad Fifty Years Ago,* 33, 45. Although the company was in receivership for only four years and two months, Burt was responsible for the reporting of five fiscal years.
35. Ibid., 36.
36. Hilton, *The Great Lakes Car Ferries,* 78.
37. Ibid.
38. Frederickson, *Early History of the Ann Arbor Carferries,* 21.
39. Hilton, *The Great Lakes Car Ferries,* 82.
40. Ann Arbor Railroad Company, "Annual Report," 1902, 6.

Chapter 3

1. Hilton, *The Great Lakes Car Ferries,* 79.
2. Frederickson, *Early History of the Ann Arbor Carferries,* 15.
3. *Ann Arbor No. 3,* "Logbook," February 16–20, 1899, Historical Collections of the Great Lakes, Bowling Green State University, Bowling Green, Ohio.
4. While running aground does not in itself cause a ship to capsize, ice pressing against the side of a ship, once grounded, can easily roll it over.
5. Hilton, *The Great Lakes Car Ferries,* 76.
6. *Door County Advocate,* February 7, 1903, 1.
7. City of Menominee, *History of the City of Menominee, Michigan,* 34.
8. *Door County Advocate,* March 10, 1.
9. Ibid.
10. *Ann Arbor No. 3,* "Logbook," April 6, 1900.
11. *Door County Advocate,* April 14, 1900, 1.
12. Movements of the *Ann Arbor No. 3* on April 7–9, 1900, were taken from her logbook.
13. *Door County Advocate,* April 14, 1900, 1.
14. Ibid., 1.
15. *Kewaunee Enterprise,* February 12, 1904, 1. Weather observations were taken from the appropriate entries of the Kewaunee Life Saving Station, WI, Life Saving Station Logs, Records of the U.S. Coast Guard (Record Group 26), National Archives and Records Administration—Great Lakes Region (Chicago).
16. *Kewaunee Enterprise,* February 19, 1904. Weather observations and the quotation were taken from the appropriate entries of the Kewaunee Life Saving Station, WI, Life Saving Station Logs, Records of the U. S. Coast Guard (Record Group 26), National Archives and Records Administration—Great Lakes Region, (Chicago).

17. *Kewaunee Enterprise,* February 19, 1904, 1; February 23, 1904, 1.

18. Ibid., March 4, 1904, 1. Appropriate entries were taken from the Kewaunee Life Saving Station, WI, Life Saving Station Logs, Records of the U. S. Coast Guard (Record Group 26), National Archives and Records Administration—Great Lakes Region, (Chicago).

19. *Kewaunee Enterprise,* March 18, 1904, 1. Appropriate entries from the Kewaunee Life Saving Station, WI, Life Saving Station Logs, Records of the U. S. Coast Guard (Record Group 26), National Archives and Records Administration—Great Lakes Region, (Chicago).

20. Quinn et al., "NOAA Technical Memorandum ERL GLERL–20," 31.

21. *Marinette Daily Eagle Star,* December 29, 1904, 1.

Chapter 4

1. Frederickson, *Early History of the Ann Arbor Carferries,* 8.

2. Ibid.

3. Ibid., 10. Frederickson states that this incident occurred on January 2, 1905, but that is probably incorrect. The Frankfort Life Saving Station logbook recorded winds from the north-northeast with moderate surf. The information in the book is quite specific, leaving no doubt that the incident occurred, but probably at another time.

4. Ibid., 18–19. The date of this incident is probably not accurate. The Frankfort Life Saving Station logbooks indicate moderate weather on February 25 and 26. Nevertheless, the amount of detail in Frederickson's account leads one to believe that the incident occurred as described. Unfortunately, the logbooks from the *No. 1,* which Captain Frederickson used to write the story, are no longer available.

5. *Door County Advocate,* November 28, 1907, 1.

6. George Richey and Peter R. Sandman, *Frankfort's Royal Frontenac Hotel,* rev. ed. (Honor, MI: George Richey, 2002), 3–4, 11–12.

7. Ann Arbor Railway Company, "Annual Report," Toledo, year ending June 30, 1903, 8.

8. H. Roger Grant, *Follow the Flag: A History of the Wabash Railroad Company,* Railroads in America (DeKalb, IL: Northern Illinois University Press, 2004), 93.

9. Ibid., 94.

10. Ibid., 150.

11. Ann Arbor Railway Company, "Annual Report," Saint Louis, year ending June 30, 1903, 3, 6.

12. Grant, *Follow the Flag: A History of the Wabash Railroad Company,* 97, 99, 105.

13. Scott D. Trostel, *The Detroit, Toledo, and Ironton Railroad: Henry Ford's Railroad* (Fletcher, OH: Cam Tech Publishing, 1988), 66, 72, 74.

14. Frederickson, *Early History of the Ann Arbor Carferries,* 24.

15. Hilton, *The Great Lakes Car Ferries,* 206–7, 210, 211.

16. Ibid., 195, 196, 207.

17. Ibid., 114, 117.

18. *Menominee Herald Leader,* March 28, 1908, 1.

19. University of Wisconsin Sea Grant Institute, Wisconsin Historical Society,

Wisconsin's Great Lakes Shipwrecks, www.wisconsinshipwrecks.org/tools_deaths door.cfm. The Door was felt to be such a danger that it was one of the first locations to receive a lighthouse. A lighthouse on Plum Island was built in 1848 and another erected on Pilot Island in 1850.

20. Proposed Ship Canal at Sturgeon Bay, Wisconsin, http://memory.loc .gov/rbc/rbpe20/rbpe206/20605600/001dq.gif.

21. *Menominee Herald Leader,* April 2, 1908, 1.

22. Ibid., April 3, 1908, 1.

23. Ibid., April 9, 1908, 1.

Chapter 5

1. *Manistique Pioneer Tribune,* June 4, 1909, 1.

2. Hilton, *The Great Lakes Car Ferries,* 85.

3. Ibid.; *Manistique Pioneer Tribune,* June 25, 1909, 1; July 23, 1909.

4. Ann Arbor Railway Company, "Annual Report," Toledo, year ending June 30, 1910, 9.

5. *Manitowoc Daily Herald,* March 9, 1910, 1.

6. Hilton, *The Great Lakes Car Ferries,* 86.

7. Ann Arbor Railway Company, "Annual Report," Toledo, year ending June 30, 1910, 9.

8. There doesn't appear to be a town in Michigan named Okema, but the young man may have come from Onekama, a town about twenty-two miles south of Frankfort.

9. *Anchor News,* January, 1978, 3–7; Supervising Inspector General, Steamboat Inspection Service, "Annual Report to the Secretary of Commerce and Labor for the Fiscal Year Ending June 30, 1911," 343. This document states that the cause of the fire was unknown.

10. Arthur C. Frederickson and Lucy F. Frederickson, *Frederickson's History of the Ann Arbor Auto and Train Ferries* (Frankfort, MI: Daisy Butler, 1994), 56.

11. Ibid., 61.

12. Leonard L. Case, *The Crystal Gazer* (Benzonia, MI: Benzie Area Historical Society, 1985), 128–30; Charles M. Anderson, *Memos of Betsie Bay: A History of Frankfort* (Manistee, MI: J. B. Publications, 1988), 45.

Chapter 6

1. Horowitz, *The Great Impeacher,* 173 n. 3. There is some question concerning Ashley's middle name. It may have been Mitchell, Monroe, or Mansfield. I have settled on Mitchell, but the reader should understand that there are other possibilities.

2. *New York Times,* September 17, 1896, 5.

3. Horowitz, *The Great Impeacher,* 10–11.

4. *New York Times,* September 17, 1896, 5.

5. Horowitz, *The Great Impeacher,* 149, 156–59, 161–62.

6. Toledo, Ann Arbor and North Michigan Railway Company, "Profit Sharing and Stock Allotment of the Stockholders and Employees of the Toledo, Ann Arbor, and North Michigan Railway Company, 1889," in "Annual Report," Toledo, 1889, 18–20.

7. *Detroit Free Press,* January 5, 1886, 4.

8. Ibid., January 6, 1886, 4.

9. Ibid.

10. Ibid., January 8, 1886, 4.

11. The bulk of this story is taken from the sources cited and articles in the *Toledo Blade* from January 4 through January 14, 1886. A more exciting version, in which Ashley fought off the DL&N people with muskets and tangled with the Vanderbilt interests, appeared in the *New York Times* September 24, 1899, 28. The story most likely mirrored what he told a reporter, but there is no other evidence of its authenticity.

12. *New York Times,* April 26, 1893, 1.

13. Ibid., April 30, 1893, 2.

14. *Wall Street Journal,* April 29, 1893, 2.

15. Record Group 21, Records of the District Courts of the United States, U.S. Circuit Court, Northern District of Ohio, Western Division; Civil Records, Mixed Case Files, Case no. 1146; National Archives and Records Administration—Great Lakes Region (Chicago).

16. Horowitz, *The Great Impeacher,* 168.

17. *New York Times,* September 24, 1899, 28.

18. Riggs, *Our Life Was Lived While the Old Order Changed,* 68. State of Ohio Bureau of Vital Statistics, Certificate of Death, Registration District no. 769, File no. 64144, Ohio Historical Society.

19. Esther E. Shott, "Wellington R. Burt, Esquire," MA thesis, Wayne State University, 1938, 2, 5, 6; *Saginaw News Courier,* March 3, 1919, 8.

20. Shott, "Wellington R. Burt, Esquire," 7, 9, and 10.

21. Ibid., 11, 12, 13.

22. Ibid., 33.

23. *Saginaw News,* March 3, 1919 8.

24. Schott, "Wellington R. Burt," 14, 23, 24.

25. *Saginaw News,* March 3, 1919, 8; Schott, "Wellington R. Burt," 86.

26. Schott, "Wellington R. Burt," 31–33. Schott refers to the railroad as the Chicago, Mackinaw, and Saginaw, but that is incorrect.

27. Willis F. Dunbar, *All Aboard! A History of Railroads in Michigan* (Grand Rapids, MI: William B. Eerdmans, 1969), 148.

28. Riggs, *The Ann Arbor Railroad Fifty Years Ago,* 44.

29. Riggs, *The Ann Arbor Railroad Fifty Years Ago,* 28–29.

30. Riggs, *Our Life Was Lived While the Order Changed,* 108, 137.

31. Riggs, *The Ann Arbor Railroad Fifty Years Ago,* 29.

32. *Saginaw News Courier,* March 3, 1919, 8.

33. Schott, "Wellington R. Burt," 167, 168.

34. *Saginaw News,* December 30, 1959; Lorri Lea (librarian, *Saginaw News*), discussion with the author in fall 2007. Ms. Lea states that the inheritance is due to be distributed in 2011.

35. Grant, *Follow the Flag,* 94.

36. *New York Times,* July 8, 1916, 9.

37. Ibid.

38. Ibid., February 2, 1908, 11; February 4, 1908, 11.

39. Ibid., March 26, 1925, 23.

40. Ibid.

Chapter 7

1. A sand sucker is a barge used for dredging mud and sand off the bottom of a river or lake, thus sucking sand.

2. Hilton, *The Great Lakes Car Ferries,* 87, 89.

3. Ibid., 90.

4. Ibid , 261. She was rated at 2,500 horsepower, 500 less than the *Ann Arbor No. 5*. She also had less capacity (twenty-eight railcars compared to thirty-two for the *No. 5*) according to the 1917 Ann Arbor Railroad Company's "Annual Report," 8.

5. This and other log entries in this chapter involving the *Ann Arbor No. 6* are taken from the 1917 logbook of the *No. 6* as transcribed by A. C. Frederickson. Quotations involving the *No. 6* are also from the logbook. Firemen banked the fires by covering them with coal (a bank) and reducing the air, thus greatly reducing the rate of combustion and saving fuel. When the ship was ready to get under way, the firemen would break up the bank and increase the air, allowing the fire to burn more quickly and producing more steam in the boilers. For an excellent description of the duties of a fireman on a steamship, see Fred W. Dutton, *Life on the Great Lakes* (Detroit: Wayne State University Press, 1981).

6. Both vessels employed a bow propeller. The *Sainte Marie* was built in 1913 and replaced the original *Sainte Marie,* the vessel that so impressed the Russians in 1901. After visiting the straits, they contracted with a firm in England to build a similar vessel, dismantle it, and ship it to Siberia for reassembly. The newer version was smaller, only 250 feet in length, but very powerful for its size. Its engines were capable of 2,700 horsepower, 200 more that the *No. 6* in a vessel 88 feet shorter. It was a fearsome icebreaker.

7. *St. Ignace Enterprise,* January 25, 1917, 1.

8. There is conflicting information about exactly what happened. The *No. 6* logbook implies that the *Chief Wawatam* came to break her out, though an article in the January 27, 1917, *St. Ignace Republican News* states that the *No. 6* was stuck in the ice channel between Saint Ignace and Mackinaw City. The article further states that the *Chief Wawatam* got stuck because it was forced outside the channel by the presence of the *No. 6*.

9. Fred G. Nurnberger (state climatologist, Michigan State University Climatology Program) discussion with author, October 1999.

10. *St. Ignace Republican News,* January 27, 1917, 1.

11. *Ann Arbor No. 6,* logbook, January 30, 1917, as transcribed by A. C. Frederickson.

12. Ibid., January 31, 1917.

13. The chronology of the *No. 6*'s trip to Frankfort is taken from ibid.

14. A. C. Frederickson, personal notes on the history of the *No. 7* and the *Wabash. Tumblehome* refers to the inward curve of a ship's topsides. More simply, the upper part of the sides very gently slope inward toward the center of the ship.

15. Because of the delay in the Chadburn system of sending commands from the bridge to the engine room, the "working," or rocking back and forth of the

boat, was turned over to the engine room crewmen. They gave the engines full power ahead, and when they sensed that the ship had gone as far as it could they reversed the engines and applied ever increasing power astern. As close to the ice as they were in the bottom of the ship, they had little difficulty sensing when it was time to apply and release power.

16. *Ann Arbor No. 5*, logbook (as transcribed by Arthur Frederickson). This and other entries attributed to the *Ann Arbor No. 5* were taken from this source.

17. Ibid., February 13, 1917.

18. A snatch block is a single block (pulley) anchored to some point in the ice. The line (or cable) leaves a winch onboard the ship, extends to and around the block, and goes back to the ship. The loose end is attached to the ice blocks or some kind of netting that holds several blocks together. When the line is reeled in on the winch the ice is carried away from the ship toward the snatch block.

19. The *No. 5* logbook gives no indication of who the officials might have been, but it is likely that A. W. Towsley, the general manager, was present. It seems highly unlikely that he would have remained in Toledo while his entire fleet was marooned off Frankfort.

20. Information concerning the battle to enter Frankfort was taken from the *Ann Arbor No. 5* logbook (as transcribed by Arthur Frederickson); the Ann Arbor No. 3 logbook, Historical Collections of the Great Lakes, Bowling Green State University, Bowling Green, Ohio; and log entries for the period from Frankfort Life Saving Station, MI, Life Saving Station Logs, Records of the U.S. Coast Guard (Record Group 26), National Archives and Records Administration—Great Lakes Region (Chicago).

21. Arthur C. Frederickson and Lucy F. Frederickson, *Later History of the Ann Arbor Carferries No. 6 and 7* (Frankfort, MI: Arthur C. Frederickson and Lucy F. Frederickson, 1951), 6.

Chapter 8

1. Mark L. Thompson, *Graveyard of the Lakes* (Detroit: Wayne State University Press, 2000), 207–8

2. Frederickson, *Early History of the Ann Arbor Carferries,* 31. The bulk of the narrative in this chapter is taken from this source. Arthur Frederickson, as a wheelsman on the *No. 4,* was an eyewitness; however, as with any eyewitness account, there are some inconsistencies with other information. Parts of the narrative taken from other sources will be noted.

3. Arthur Frederickson's account in *Early History of the Ann Arbor Carferries* states that the wind was from the west-northwest, but the Frankfort Coast Guard Station logbook for February 13–14 states that the wind was from the west. Captain Frederickson's February 14, 1923, letter to Marine Superintendent R. H. Reynolds states that he did not deviate from his course to Kewaunee. Had the wind been from the west-northwest he would have taken an unnecessary amount of rolling on that course. It appears unlikely that he would have done so.

4. Mark L. Thompson, *Steamboats and Sailors of the Great Lakes* (Detroit: Wayne State University Press, 1991), 148; Thompson, *Graveyard of the Lakes,* 208.

5. The Toledo, Ann Arbor and North Michigan's advice to its captains in

1892 to keep their ships headed into the wind in a storm was only successful when the boat had the power to do so. Even then, if the waves were large enough the boats would take water at the stern.

6. Charles Frederickson, to R. H. Reynolds, (superintendent of marine), February 16, 1923, Historical Collection of the Great Lakes, Bowling Green State University, Bowling Green, Ohio. Arthur Frederickson states in his *Early History of the Ann Arbor Carferries* that the ship turned around at 1:00 a.m., a significant difference from the captain's letter. Since Captain Frederickson's letter is the official explanation, I am treating it as fact.

7. Frederickson, *The Early History of the Ann Arbor Carferries*, 32–33.

8. Blacklock, *Blacklock's History of Elberta*, 44. This publication contains several articles by Slyfield and others on the development of wireless at Elberta. Slyfield was a pioneer in the field, leaving Frankfort in 1929 to become the sound director for Walt Disney when sound was first being used in motion pictures.

9. Charles Frederickson to R. H. Reynolds, February 16, 1923, Historical Collections of the Great Lakes, Bowling Green State University, Bowling Green, Ohio.

10. A breeches buoy is a lifesaving device in which a pair of canvass "breeches" is suspended from a lifesaving ring attached by short lines to a block, which runs on a cable extending from ship-to-ship or shore-to-ship.

11. February 14, 1923, Frankfort Life Saving Station, MI, Life Saving Station Logs, Records of the U.S. Coast Guard (Record Group 26), National Archives and Records Administration—Great Lakes Region (Chicago).

12. *Benzie County Record Patriot*, December 13, 1978, 1.

13. Riprap is a collection of stones and/or chucks of concrete piled against a wall or breakwater to prevent erosion.

14. Ann Arbor Railroad Company, "Annual Report," Toledo, 1923, 6, 12.

15. Blacklock, *Blacklock's History of Elberta*, 42–43.

Chapter 9

1. Hilton, *The Great Lakes Car Ferries*, 95.

2. Ann Arbor Railroad Company, "Annual Report," Toledo, 1923, 6.

3. Frederickson, *Later History of the Ann Arbor Carferries*, 19.

4. *Door County Advocate*, December 26, 1924, 1.

5. The best year ever was 1924 when Menominee was shut down for forty-one days. The *Door County Advocate*, October 3, 1924, 11, estimated that the fifty-six-hour crossing in March 1924 by the *No. 5* and *No. 4* cost six thousand dollars.

6. From the western bridge in the town of Sturgeon Bay to Menominee is roughly twenty miles, about four of which are spent crossing Sturgeon Bay.

7. *Door County Advocate*, March 7, 1924, 1.

8. Ibid., March 28, 1924, 4.

9. Ann Arbor Railroad Company, "Annual Report," Saint Louis, 1934, 29.

10. Hilton, *The Great Lakes Car Ferries*, 261.

11. Historical Collections of the Great Lakes, Great Lakes Vessel Index, Bowling Green State University, Bowling Green, Ohio, www.bgsu.edu/col leges/library.cac/page39984.html.

12. Ann Arbor Railroad Company, "Annual Report," Saint Louis, 1929, 9, 29.

13. Ann Arbor Railroad Company, "Annual Report," Saint Louis, 1931, 12, 33.

14. *Benzie County Patriot*, March 15, 1923, 1.

15. Ibid., May 3, 1923, 1

16. Ibid., February 28, 1924, 1.

17. Ibid., August 11, 1982, 1.

18. Bruce K. Jewell (former Ann Arbor captain), discussion with the author, February 10, 2005.

19. Cooperative Institute of Meteorological Satellite Studies, "Wisconsin Weather Stories, Armistice Day Storm of 1940," http://cimss.ssec.wisc.edu/wi_weather_stories/stories/stories/ar.

20. Dana Thomas Bowen, *Memories of the Lakes* (Daytona Beach, FL: Dana Thomas Bowen, 1946), 271.

21. Ibid., 267, 269.

22. Ibid., 273.

23. The movements of the *Wabash,* the *No. 3, No. 5,* and *No. 7* were taken from the logbooks of the *No. 5, No. 7,* and *Wabash* for November 10–13, 1940.

24. The movements of the *Ann Arbor No. 6* were taken from the logbook dated November 10–13, 1940.

Chapter 10

1. Dunbar, *All Aboard,* 277.

2. Grant, *Follow the Flag,* 164–65; *Who's Who in America, 1946–47,* vol. 24 (Chicago: Marquis Who's Who, 1946).

3. Grant, *Follow the Flag,* 183.

4. Quinn et al., "NOAA Technical Memorandum ERL GLERL–20," 31.

5. *Benzie County Patriot,* January 16, 1936, 1.

6. *Manitowoc Herald Times,* February 18 1936, 1.

7. *Marinette Eagle Star,* January 23, 1936, 1.

8. Ibid., 9.

9. *Ann Arbor No. 6,* logbook, January 27, 1936.

10. *Manitowoc Herald Times,* February 7, 1936, 2.

11. The movements of the *No. 3* and *No. 6* described in this chapter are taken from their respective logbooks for February 1936.

12. The movements of the *Wabash* described in this chapter are taken from her logbooks for February and March 1936, as was this quotation.

13. *Marinette Eagle Star,* February 10, 1936 1; *Menominee Herald Leader,* February 10, 1936, 1.

14. *Benzie Record,* February 13, 1936, 1.

15. *Ann Arbor No. 6,* "Radio Log, WDCQ," February 23 and 24, 1936.

16. *Marinette Eagle Star,* February 22, 1936, 2.

17. The records of the *No. 3, No. 6,* and *Wabash* are taken from their logbooks. Logbooks for the *No. 5* and *No. 7* are not available, so it is not possible to

make a further comparison. Information concerning the *No. 5* comes from articles in the *Marinette Eagle Star.*

Chapter 11

1. Ann Arbor Railroad Company, "Annual Report," Saint Louis, 1940. The report showed a net income of $23,448.06. A year later net income climbed to $244,950.77.

2. Grant, *Follow the Flag,* 192–94.

3. The Chesapeake and Ohio absorbed the Pere Marquette Railroad in 1947.

4. Ann Arbor Railroad Company, "Annual Reports," Toledo, 1946–54.

5. The triple-deck railcars literally carried autos or small trucks on three levels.

6. The route was not exactly new. Shippers had the right to specify the same route before the lines were combined. The only new aspect was that the lines were now controlled by the same people.

7. Grant, *Follow the Flag,* 242–44.

8. John Schlosser (chief of operations for the Ann Arbor from 1963 to 1967), discussion with the author, January 24, 2006. Mr. Schlosser said that they moved the office to Frankfort to be closer to where the costs were incurred.

9. Some captains even used the bow thruster to help them enter the harbor in a crosswind.

10. *Duluth News-Tribune,* September 20, 1964, 44.

11. The Ann Arbor did not establish similar schedules for the chief engineers, although it probably should have. Chief engineers felt the same responsibility as captains to be awake and involved while the ship was in port. Their feeling was that should anything go wrong mechanically while the ship was maneuvering in the harbor immediate action would have to be taken. No one wanted to awaken to find the ship crushed against a seawall (or some similar mishap) due to some equipment malfunction.

12. *Benzie County Patriot,* November 23, 1967, 1.

13. Ibid., May 19, 1966, 1; ibid., October 5, 1967, 1; Historical Collections of the Great Lakes, Great Lakes Vessels Index, Bowling Green State University, Bowling Green, Ohio, http://www.bgsu.edu/colleges/library/hcgl/vessel.html.

14. *Benzie County Patriot,* January 27, 1949, 1.

15. Edward Ericksen (former Ann Arbor car ferry captain), discussion with the author, December 14, 1999.

16. As noted earlier, the *Atkinson,* with its 5,500 horsepower, was superior at breaking ice, but it had difficulty backing off. The diesel-electric *Viking* was superior in all respects and was a better icebreaker than the *No. 5* had been at any time in its career.

17. John H. Bultema, discussion with the author, February 25, 2006; Valerie van Heest (cofounder of Michigan Shipwreck Research Associates), discussion with the author February 4, 2007. For an entertaining and informative description of the use of the *No. 5* as a breakwater and its fate thereafter, the reader may want to view *Planes, Trains, and Ships: Ann Arbor No. 5 Discovered,* a film produced by Valerie Olson van Heest and Robert Gadbois, at www.michiganshipwrecks.org.

Chapter 12

1. Interviews with the adult children of former Ann Arbor captains and mates.

2. Ann Arbor Railroad Company, "Annual Report," Saint Louis, 1949. The report stated that the car ferry employees began working a forty-hour week on October 1, 1949. That meant they worked four (five-day) weeks straight (twenty days) and then took their "weekends" off (eight days). There was no overtime pay for working twenty straight days.

3. Dolores Bigelow (daughter of Jack Carter), discussion with the author, September 25, 2007.

4. Joan Olsen (daughter of Captain Carl Jacobsen), Barbara Johnson (daughter of Captain Edward Ericksen), John Peterson (former owner of the *Benzie County Patriot*), and others, discussions with the author (Joan Olsen, May 16, 2000; Barbara Johnson, February 18, 2000; John Peterson, February 11, 2000).

5. Joyce Kirkoff (former owner of the Villa Marine Restaurant, Frankfort), discussion with the author, March 12, 2003.

6. Charles Holtrey (former car handler on the Ann Arbor); John Peterson, and others, discussions with the author (Charles Holtrey, February 27, 2002; John Peterson, February 11, 2000).

7. While it does not appear in any of the company records I have seen, this story was confirmed by many crew members who to this day do not want their names divulged.

8. *Benzie County Patriot*, March 3, 1955, 1; March 10, 1955, 1.

9. Ibid., July 22, 1965, 1; John Schlosser (former chief operating officer of the Ann Arbor Railroad Company), discussion with the author, January 24, 2006.

10. *Benzie County Patriot*, November 27, 1947. The allusion to poor coal was not without precedent. In 1947 the crews struck for three days because of what they claimed was the poor quality of the coal. They stated that the coal didn't burn hot enough so it was not possible to generate enough heat in the boilers to build the needed steam pressure. The problem was particularly acute on the *No. 3*, which had only two boilers.

11. *Benzie County Patriot*, August 9, 1951, 1.

12. Ibid., August 2, 1951, 1.

13. Ibid., August 16, 1951, 1.

14. John Hunsberger (former engineer on the Ann Arbor car ferries and chief engineer on the *Viking*), discussion with the author, January 24, 2006.

15. *Benzie County Patriot*, April 10, 1952, 1.

16. Ibid., June 26, 1952, 1.

17. Ibid., August 21, 1952, 1.

18. Ibid., September 18, 1952, 1.

19. Ibid., February 12, 1953, 1.

Chapter 13

1. Several crew members tell of a time when the *Atkinson* was brought

around slowly in a big sea and as a result a cement car crashed on its side. Had anyone been in the way, he would have been crushed. The captain had little excuse since the *Atkinson* allowed direct control of the power from the pilothouse.

2. Captain Dority's biography is taken from Mansfield, *History of the Great Lakes*, vol. 2; *Milwaukee Journal*, June 29, 1953; and Marriage Records, Benzie County, 1892.

3. *Benzie County Patriot*, December 23, 1954, 10; Peter Sandman and Florence Bixby, *Port City Perspectives* (Frankfort, MI: State Savings Bank and Frankfort/Elberta Area Chamber of Commerce, 2000), 47–48.

4. *Benzie County Patriot*, September 12, 1940, 1; Sandman and Bixby, *Port City Perspectives*, 41.

5. *Benzie County Patriot*, March 13, 1952, 1; *Benzie County Patriot*, November 12, 1953, 1; Sandman and Bixby, *Port City Perspectives*, 41; Fran Larson (daughter-in-law of O. T. Larson, Captain Larson's brother), discussion with the author, September 12, 2001.

6. Axel Frederickson was a mate at the time and later became a captain for the Ann Arbor.

7. Daisy Butler (granddaughter of Captain Frederickson), discussion with the author, December 8, 2001; Carol Stack (granddaughter of Captain Frederickson), discussion with the author, December 12, 2002. Both granddaughters provided biographical information on Frederickson.

8. *Benzie County Patriot*, April 5, 1956, 1.

9. *Benzie County Patriot*, July 1, 1937, 1; *Benzie County Patriot*, September 18, 1947, 1; Record of Marriages, Manistee County, Book 3, 146.

10. Sandman and Bixby, *Port City Perspectives*, 68; *Benzie County Patriot*, March 8, 1943, 1; Joan Olsen (Captain Anton Jacobsen's granddaughter), discussion with the author, May 16, 2000.

11. Joan Olsen, discussion with the author, May 16, 2000; Sandman and Bixby, *Port City Perspectives*, 69. I also obtained biographical information about Captain Carl Jacobsen from a number of crew members who served with him.

12. *Benzie County Patriot*, March 14, 2007, 6; Barbara Johnson and Sharon McKinley (daughters of Captain Ericksen), discussion with the author, February 18, 2000. I also obtained biographical information about Captain Ericksen from crew members who served with him.

13. A third book on the Ann Arbor, titled *Frederickson's History of the Ann Arbor Auto and Train Ferries*, a combination of the Fredericksons' works, was published by his daughter, Daisy Butler.

14. Daisy Butler, discussion with the author, February 23, 2002; Carol Stack, discussion with the author, December 12, 2000. I also obtained biographical information about Captain Frederickson from crew members who served with him.

15. Bruce K. Jewell, discussions with the author, May 18, 2001, and February 10, 2005. I also obtained biographical information about Captain Jewell from crew members who served with him.

Chapter 14

1. *Benzie County Patriot*, February 10, 1966, 1.

2. John Schlosser (chief operating officer of the Ann Arbor Railroad from 1964 until 1967), discussion with the author, January 24, 2006. Schlosser was onboard the *Arthur K. Atkinson* on the initial trip from Manistique to Frankfort.

3. *Benzie County Patriot,* October 26, 1967, 1; March 14, 1968, 1.

4. Ibid., February, 15, 1968, 1.

5. Ann Arbor Railroad Company, "Annual Report," Dearborn, 1963, 5.

6. Ibid., 1964, 5; 1965, 3.

7. *Benzie County Patriot,* November 18, 1967, 1; November 25, 1965, 1.

8. Ann Arbor Railroad Company, "Annual Report," Dearborn, 1966, 3, 4, 6.

9. *Benzie County Patriot,* June, 29, 1967, 1.

10. Ann Arbor Railroad Company, "Annual Report," Dearborn, 1968, president's letter.

11. Ibid., 1967, notes; 1968, president's letter and income statement.

12. This was another recommendation made by John Chubb before his departure.

13. Charles L. Towle (president of the Ann Arbor Railroad Company and Detroit, Toledo, and Ironton Railroad), and M. H. Weisman (assistant comptroller, Ann Arbor Railroad Company and Detroit, Toledo, and Ironton Railroad), testimony at ICC hearing, Finance Docket no. 25658, September 15–16, 1969.

14. Ann Arbor Railroad Company, "Annual Report," Dearborn, 1969, president's letter, income statement, and notes.

15. Joseph R Daughen and Peter Binzen, *The Wreck of Penn Central* (New York: Little, Brown, 1971), 240.

16. Ibid., 310. In his testimony to the Senate Commerce Subcommittee on July 29, 1970, Alfred E. Pearlman, president of Penn Central, stated that rate increases historically followed wage increases by about a year and often longer. He also said that a recession in the industries that supplied the railroad traffic and an inflationary spiral in wages and costs—issues Charles Towle discussed in the Ann Arbor Railroad Company's annual report for 1970—were instrumental in Penn Central's demise.

17. Charles L. Towle, "Remarks before the Board of Directors Meeting of the Ann Arbor Railroad Company, Philadelphia, Pennsylvania," March 25, 1970, 1, Bentley Historical Library, University of Michigan, Ann Arbor.

18. Charles L. Towle, "Remarks before the Board of Directors Meeting of the Ann Arbor Railroad Company, New York, New York," December 21, 1970, 3–4, Bentley Historical Library, University of Michigan, Ann Arbor.

19. Charles L. Towle, "Remarks before the Board of Directors Meeting of the Ann Arbor Railroad Company, New York, New York," July 7, 1971, 5, Bentley Historical Library, University of Michigan, Ann Arbor.

20. Chapter 77 allowed the railroad to continue operations under the guidance of a receiver but protected it from creditors.

21. Ann Arbor Railroad Company, "Annual Report," Dearborn, 1970, president's letter and notes.

22. Towle, Charles L. "Remarks before the Board of Directors Meeting of the Ann Arbor Railroad Company, Dearborn, Michigan," December 15, 1971, 4, Bentley Historical Library, University of Michigan, Ann Arbor.

23. Ibid., 4–6.

24. Charles L. Towle, "Remarks before the Board of Directors Meeting of the Ann Arbor Railroad Company, New York, New York," July 7, 1971, 3, 5, 6, Bentley Historical Library, University of Michigan, Ann Arbor.

25. Charles L. Towle, "Remarks before the Board of Directors Meeting of the Ann Arbor Railroad Company, New York, New York," September 22, 1971, 2, 3, Bentley Historical Library, University of Michigan, Ann Arbor.

26. Ann Arbor Railroad Company, "Annual Report," Dearborn, 1971.

27. Ann Arbor Railroad Company, "Annual Report to the Interstate Commerce Commission," Dearborn, 1972, 300.

28. John M. Chase Jr. (Trustee of the Property of the Ann Arbor Railroad Company, debtor, to the Interstate Commerce Commission), "Annual Report," 1973, 93.

Chapter 15

1. Frederickson, *Later History of the Ann Arbor Carferries*, 18.

2. Ibid., 28. The *No.* 7 traveled 293 miles and ended up back in Frankfort, where she started, with the same cargo.

3. The movements of the *No.* 5, *No.* 7, and *Wabash* were taken from their respective logbooks.

4. Quinn et al., "NOAA Technical Memorandum ERL GLERL–20," table 3.

5. *Benzie County Patriot,* January 24, 1963, 1.

6. Movements of the *No.* 7 and the *Wabash* were taken from their respective logbooks. The *Wabash* left Frankfort at 7:50 p.m. on February 4, arrived in Menominee at 4:50 p.m. on February 6, and reached Frankfort on her return trip at 2:25 a.m. February 7.

7. *Ann Arbor No.* 7, logbook, January 21–31. Entries for ten of the eleven days following January 20, 1963, record winds from the west, northwest, or southwest.

8. Movements of the *Atkinson* and the *Wabash* were taken from their respective logbooks.

9. *Benzie County Patriot,* February 28, 1963, 1.

10. *Ann Arbor No.* 5, logbook, February 21, 1963; February 25, 1963.

11. *Benzie County Patriot,* February 28, 1963, 1.

12. *Arthur K. Atkinson,* logbook, March 18, 1963; March 24, 1963.

13. Quinn et al., "NOAA Technical Memorandum ERL GLERL–20," table 3.

14. *Grand Rapids Press,* January 30, 1977, B2.

15. Movements of the *Viking* were taken from the mate's logbook, January 26, 1977, through February 19, 1977.

16. Wind speeds and direction in this chapter are taken from the logbook of the *Raritan* and the mate's logbook of the *Viking.*

17. Movements of the *Raritan* are taken from logbook entries from the vessel.

18. *Benzie County Advisor,* February 16, 1977, 1.

19. *Benzie County Record Banner,* February 17, 1.

20. *Manitowoc Herald Times Reporter,* February 16, 21; U.S. Coast Guard cutter *Mackinaw,* logbook entries, February 15–16, 1977.

21. *Traverse City Record-Eagle,* February 16, 1977.
22. *Benzie County Advisor,* February 23, 1977, 1; U.S. Coast Guard cutter *Mackinaw,* logbook entries; *Viking,* mate's logbook.
23. USCG Cutter *Mackinaw,* logbook.
24. *Traverse City Record-Eagle,* February 21, 1977.
25. *Benzie County Advisor,* February 23, 1977, 1.
26. Raymond A. Assel, John E. Janowiak, Sharolyn Young, and Daron Boyce, "Winter 1994 Weather and Ice Conditions for the Laurentian Great Lakes," *Bulletin of the Meteorological Society* 77, no. 1 (January 1996): 80–81. This article states that the winter of 1979 was even worse, with 99 percent ice coverage. While the Ann Arbor did have to call the Coast Guard for help that year, the boats were not kept out of Frankfort for anything like nine days.
27. William C. Bacon (former port captain), discussion with the author, January 28, 2007.

Chapter 16

1. John M. Chase Jr. (trustee of the property of Ann Arbor Railroad Company, debtor to the Interstate Commerce Commission), "Annual Report," 1975, 18, 20, Bentley Historical Library, University of Michigan, Ann Arbor.
2. Vincent M. Malanaphy and the staff of the Michigan Interstate Railway Company, "The Economic Implications of the Ann Arbor Railroad System's Flag-Out on 22 Selected Commodities in Ex-Parte 357," prepared for the Michigan Department of State Highways and Transportation and the Wisconsin Department of Transportation, submitted November 17, 1978, exhibit 1, Archives of Michigan, Lansing.
3. *Benzie County Patriot,* June 19, 1974, 1; October 16, 1974, 20.
4. *Congressional Quarterly Almanac, 1975* (Washington, DC: Congressional Quarterly 1976), 752.
5. Ibid., 753. These statements were made while urging the passage of HR 2051 in February 1975. The bill provided funds to keep Penn Central and the other bankrupt railroads running until the new Conrail Corporation could begin operations.
6. *Traverse City Record-Eagle,* February 2, 1974, 1.
7. *Benzie County Patriot,* February 25, 1976, 1.
8. *Congressional Quarterly Almanac 1975,* 758.
9. *Benzie County Patriot,* December 10, 1975, 1.
10. Malanaphy, Vincent M., "Presentation to the Michigan Department of Highways," March 1977, 2, 6–7, Archives of Michigan, Lansing.
11. Malanaphy was blindsided by the ICC decision. The Michigan Northern Railway Company had similarly flagged out an increase, and its action had been upheld by the ICC (I&S Docket nos. 9179 and 9179, sub. no. 1). Malanaphy had reason to expect the same treatment, but that did not happen.
12. *Ann Arbor Trail by Rail and Lake* 79–1, no. 2 (1979). This is a publication of the Ann Arbor Railroad Historical Society.
13. Ibid.; *Traverse City Record-Eagle,* January 17, 1979; Jed Jewarski (crew member on the *City of Milwaukee*), discussion with the author, January 15, 2007;

James Gilbert (former yardmaster on the Ann Arbor Railroad), discussion with the author, June 26, 2002.

14. The 393-foot length is the distance between the perpendiculars, or approximately the waterline length. The overall length is about 410 feet, which is the length currently advertised by the company that operates the *Badger,* her sister ship.

15. Donald E. Riel (former acting administrator, Freight Division, Michigan Department of Transportation), discussion with the author, December 1, 2006.

16. An embargo is an order by a common carrier (the entity that contracts with the shipper to ship the item) or regulating agency prohibiting or restricting freight transportation.

17. V. M. Malanaphy to V. Goodman (administrator of rail and port facilities, Urban and Public Transportation, Michigan Department of Transportation), November 5, 1979, Archives of Michigan, Lansing.

18. "Retail Motor Gasoline and on Highway Diesel Fuel Prices, 1949–2003," www.fueleconomy.gov.

19. Willis F. Dunbar and George S. May, *Michigan: A History of the Wolverine State,* 3rd ed. (Grand Rapids, MI: William B. Eerdmans, 1995), 632.

20. Michigan Transportation Commission, "Annual Report," 1978, 12, Library of Michigan, Lansing.

21. "Preliminary Copy Michigan Railroad Plan, Phase II, Revised," December 9, 1975, 222, Archives of Michigan, Lansing.

22. Ibid. The seven points were taken from ibid., 224–25, 238.

23. The company owned three ships: the 389-foot *City of Midland,* built in 1941, and the *Badger* and *Spartan,* both 393 feet in length, built in 1952 and 1953, respectively.

24. Bureau of Transportation Planning, Michigan Department of Transportation, "Northwest Regional Rail Rationalization Report, Preliminary Draft," September 24, 1980, 48–51, Archives of Michigan, Lansing.

25. Michigan Transportation Commission, "Annual Report," 1980, 11, Library of Michigan, Lansing.

26. *Benzie County Record Patriot,* June 29, 1979, 1.

27. Vincent Malanaphy, "Statement on Northwest Regional Rail Rationalization Report, Frankfort, Michigan," September 12, 1980, Archives of Michigan, Lansing.

28. *Traverse City Record-Eagle,* March 12, 1984, 5.

29. *Detroit Free Press,* March 11, 1984, A15.

30. Ibid., A14.

31. *Ann Arbor Trail by Rail and Lake* 80–4, no. 10 (1980).

32. Donald E. Riel, discussion with the author, December 1, 2006.

33. *Detroit News,* February 13, 1981, A6.

34. Division of Planning and Budget, Division of Transportation Assistance, Wisconsin Department of Transportation, Madison, "Analysis of Cross Lake Transportation Services," July 24, 1981, 1, 21, Archives of Michigan, Lansing.

35. Carol C. Norris (deputy director, Urban and Public Transportation, Michigan Department of Transportation) to Michigan Transportation Commission, November 7, 1984, 5, photocopy in possession of the author.

36. *Ann Arbor Trail by Rail and Lake,* 81–5, no. 16 (1981): 8.

37. *Owosso Argus Press,* October 3, 1981, 4; May 1, 1982, 1.

38. The operating subsidy for 1978–79 averaged $443,831 a month. In 1979–80 the figure rose to $582,609 a month. For the eighteen months from April 1, 1980, through September 30, 1981, the average was $575,390. These figures were taken from the "Michigan Statewide Rail Rationalization Report," June 1981, table 3, Archives of Michigan, Lansing. The later figures do not necessarily reflect the amount Michigan Interstate thought it was due.

39. *Owosso Argus Press,* 1, January 20, 1982. Traffic in December was off 50 percent from the previous year. In January it was off 35 percent.

40. Ibid; V. M. Malanaphy to Hannes Meyers (chairman, Michigan Transportation Commission), March 19, 1982, Archives of Michigan, Lansing.

41. *Muskegon Chronicle,* February 10, 1982, 1; Ivan Bartha (acting administrator, Rail Freight and Water Transportation, Michigan Department of Transportation) to V. M. Malanaphy, February 22, 1982, Archives of Michigan, Lansing; V. M. Malanaphy to Ivan Bartha, March 2, 1982, Archives of Michigan, Lansing.

42. *Ann Arbor Trail by Rail and Lake* 82–1, no. 17 (1982): 2.

43. Hugh Scott (Barnett and Alagia law firm, Washington, DC) to William G. Milliken (governor of Michigan), March 22, 1982, Archives of Michigan, Lansing.

44. *Detroit News,* May 7, 1982, B6; *Owosso Argus Press,* May 7, 1982, 7.

45. V. M. Malanaphy to Hannes Meyers, March 19, 1982, Archives of Michigan, Lansing.

46. *Lansing State Journal,* April 1, 1982, B1.

47. *Benzie County Record Patriot,* April 14, 1982, 1; *Owosso Argus Press,* April 27, 1982, 2.

48. Michigan Interstate Railway Company, "Financial Statements," year ended March 31, 1982, exhibit B, National Archives and Records Administration—Great Lakes Region (Chicago); *Detroit News,* May 7, 1982, B6.

Bibliography

❋ ❋ ❋

Anderson, *Memos of Betsie Bay: A History of Frankfort*. Manistee, MI: J. B. Publications, 1988.

"The Ann Arbor No. 1 Carferry Burns!" *Anchor News*, Manitowoc, Wisconsin Maritime Museum, January 1978.

Ann Arbor Railroad Company. "Annual Reports," Toledo, 1900–1905; Detroit, 1909; Toledo, 1910–24; Saint Louis, 1925–62; Dearborn, 1963–71.

Ann Arbor Railroad Company, John M. Chase Jr., Trustee, "Annual Reports to the ICC," Dearborn, 1972–1976. Bentley Historical Library, University of Michigan, Ann Arbor.

Ann Arbor Trail by Rail and Lake 79–1, no. 2 (1979); 80–4, no. 10 (1980); 81–5, no. 16 (1981); 82–1, no. 17 (1982).

Assel, Raymond A., John E. Janowiak, Sharolyn Young, and Daron Boyce. "Winter 1994 Weather and Ice Conditions for the Laurentian Great Lakes." *Bulletin of the Meteorological Society* 77, no. 1 (January 1996): 71–87.

Blacklock, Allen B. *Blacklock's History of Elberta*. Manistee, MI: West Graf, 1975.

Bowen, Dana Thomas. *Memories of the Lakes*. Daytona Beach, FL: Dana Thomas Bowen, 1946.

Brigham, Lawson W. *A Handbook of Ice Operations for the U. S. Coast Guard's WTBG Cutter*. Newport, RI: Naval War College, 1982.

Burger, Henry. "Building the Ann Arbor Railroad, Part One." *Double A* 3 (1984): 4–6.

Case, Leonard L. *The Crystal Gazer*. Benzonia, MI: Benzie Area Historical Society, 1985.

Clary, James. *Ladies of the Lakes II*. West Bloomfield, MI: Altwerger and Mandel, 1992.

Congressional Quarterly Almanac, 1975. Washington, DC: Congressional Quarterly, 1976.

Cooperative Institute of Meteorological Studies. "Wisconsin Weather Stories, Armistice Day Storm, of 1940," http://weatherstories.ssec.wisc.edu/redi rect.html.

Daughen, Joseph R., and Peter Binzen. *The Wreck of Penn Central.* New York: Little, Brown, 1971.

Dunbar, Willis F. *All Aboard! A History of Railroads in Michigan.* Grand Rapids, MI: William B. Eerdmans, 1969.

Dunbar, Willis F., and George S. May. *Michigan: A History of the Wolverine State.* 3rd ed. Grand Rapids, MI: William B. Eerdmans, 1995.

Dutton, Fred W. *Life on the Great Lakes.* Detroit: Wayne State University Press, 1981.

Frederickson, Arthur C., and Lucy F. Frederickson. *Early History of the Ann Arbor Carferries.* Frankfort, MI: Arthur C. Frederickson and Lucy F. Frederickson, 1949.

Frederickson, Arthur C., and Lucy F. Frederickson. *Frederickson's History of the Ann Arbor Auto and Train Ferries.* Frankfort, MI: Daisy Butler, 1994.

Frederickson, Arthur C., and Lucy F. Frederickson. *Later History of the Ann Arbor Carferries No. 6 and 7.* Frankfort, MI: Arthur C. Frederickson and Lucy F. Frederickson, 1951.

Frederickson, Charles O., to R. H. Reynolds (superintendent of marine), February 16, 1923, Historical Collections of the Great Lakes, Bowling Green State University, Bowling Green, Ohio.

Grant, H. Roger. *Follow the Flag: A History of the Wabash Railroad Company.* Railroads in America. DeKalb, IL: Northern Illinois University Press, 2004.

Hilton, George W. *The Great Lakes Car Ferries.* Berkeley, CA: Howell-North, 1962.

Historical Collections of the Great Lakes. *Great Lakes Vessel Index.* Bowling Green, OH: Bowling Green State University.

Holmes, Daryl. Address delivered at the Benzie Shores Library, Frankfort, Michigan, September 16, 2004.

Horowitz, Robert F. *The Great Impeacher.* New York: Brooklyn College Press, 1979.

Kewaunee Chamber of Commerce Centennial Book Committee. *Kewaunee: A Harbor Community.* Kewaunee, WI: Kewaunee Chamber of Commerce 1983.

Larson, Alexander L., to Ann Arbor Railroad Company, Frankfort, Michigan, 1940. Photocopy in possession of the author.

Mailer, Stan. *Green Bay and Western.* Mukilteo, WI: Hundman Publishing, 1989.

Malanaphy, Vincent M., to Hannes Meyers (chairman, Michigan Transportation Commission), March 19, 1982, Archives of Michigan, Lansing.

Malanaphy, Vincent M., to Edward V. Goodman (administrator of rail and port facilities, Urban and Public Transportation, Michigan Department of Transportation), November 5, 1979, Archives of Michigan, Lansing.

Malanaphy, Vincent M., Presentation to the Michigan Department of Highways, March, 1977, Archives of Michigan, Lansing.

Malanaphy, Vincent M., and the staff of the Michigan Interstate Railway Company. "The Economic Implications of the Ann Arbor Railroad System's Flag-Out on 22 Selected Commodities in Ex-Parte 357." Prepared for the Michi-

gan Department of State Highways and Transportation and the Wisconsin
Department of Transportation, submitted November 17, 1978, exhibit 1,
Archives of Michigan, Lansing.

Mansfield, J. B. *History of the Great Lakes*. Chicago: J. H. Beers and Company,
1899; reprint, Cleveland: Freshwater Press, 1972. 2 vols.

Michigan Interstate Railway Company. "Annual Report," Michigan Department
of Commerce, Owosso, 1978, Archives of Michigan, Lansing.

Michigan Interstate Railway Company. "Financial Statements for the Year Ended
March 31, 1982," exhibit B, Owosso, National Archives and Records Administration—Great Lakes Region (Chicago).

Michigan Transportation Commission, "Annual Report," Lansing, 1978, Library
of Michigan, Lansing.

Norris, Carol C., to Michigan Transportation Commission, November 7, 1984.

Parnell, C. Q. *Ice Seamanship*. London: Nautical Institute, 1986.

"Preliminary Copy, Michigan Railroad Plan, Phase II, Revised," December 9,
1975, Archives of Michigan, Lansing.

Quinn, F. H., R. A. Assel, D. E. Boyce, G. A. Leshkevich, C. R. Snider, and D. Weisnet. "NOAA Technical Memorandum ERL GLERL–20, Summary of Great
Lakes Weather and Ice Conditions, Winter, 1976–77," Great Lakes Environmental Research Laboratory, Ann Arbor, October 1978.

Radio Logbook, WDCQ, *Ann Arbor No. 6*, February 23–24, 1936.

Richey, George, and Peter Sandman. *Frankfort's Royal Frontenac Hotel*. Honor, MI:
George Richey, 2002.

Riggs, Henry Earle. *The Ann Arbor Railroad Fifty Years Ago*. [St. Louis?]: Ann Arbor
Railroad, 1947.

Riggs, Henry Earle. *Our Life Was Lived While The Old Order Changed: A Story For Our
Children*, Bentley Historical Library, University of Michigan, 1971.

Sandman, Peter, and Florence Bixby. *Port City Perspectives*. Frankfort, MI: State
Savings Bank and Frankfort/Elberta Area Chamber of Commerce, 2000.

Scott, Hugh, to William G. Milliken (governor of Michigan), March 22, 1982,
Archives of Michigan, Lansing.

Shott, Esther E. "Wellington R. Burt, Esquire." MA thesis, Wayne State University,
1939.

Thompson, Mark L. *Graveyard of the Lakes*. Detroit: Wayne State University Press,
2000.

Thompson, Mark L. *Steamboats and Sailors of the Great Lakes*. Detroit: Wayne State
University Press, 1991.

Toledo, Ann Arbor and North Michigan Railway Company, "Annual Reports,"
Toledo, 1889, 1890, 1892.

Toledo, Ann Arbor and North Michigan Railway Company. "Profit Sharing and
Stock Allotment of the Stockholders and Employees of the Toledo, Ann Arbor
and North Michigan Railway Company, 1889." In Toledo, Ann Arbor and
North Michigan Railway Company, "Annual Report," Toledo, 1889, 18–20.

Towle, Charles L. (president, Ann Arbor Railroad Company and Detroit, Toledo
and Ironton Railroad), testimony at ICC hearing, Finance Docket no. 25658,
September 15 and 16, 1969.

Trostel, Scott D. *The Detroit, Toledo, and Ironton Railroad: Henry Ford's Railroad.* Fletcher, OH: Cam Tech Publishing, 1988.

Weisman, M. H.(assistant comptroller, Ann Arbor Railroad Company and Detroit, Toledo, and Ironton Railroad), testimony at ICC hearing, Finance Docket no. 25658, September 15–16, 1969.

Wisconsin Department of Transportation, Division of Planning and Budget and Division of Transportation Assistance "An Analysis of Cross-Lake Transportation Services," Madison, July 24, 1981, Archives of Michigan, Lansing.

Index

✳ ✳ ✳

277

Van der Jagt, Guy, 224
Viking, 59, 191, 219, 226, 241; comparison of crew requirement to C&O car ferries, 230; comparison with ice-breaking abilities of other car ferries, 2, 208, 264n16; comparison to *City of Milwaukee,* 224–25; converted from *Ann Arbor No. 7,* 156–58; effect of higher speed on captains, 158–59; only car ferry operating, 1973–78, 197, 208; sale to Peterson Shipbuilding Company, 1983, 244; state of Michigan's attempt to use in Muskegon, 239; in winter of 1977, 208–18
Villa Marine, 168
Vorce, L. E., 31

Wabash, 127, 129, 159; in Armistice Day storm, 135–36; comparison with ice-breaking abilities of other car ferries, 2, 130, 139, 200–201; constructed 1927, 130; first to have gyrocompass, 130, 134; remodeled, 1962, 156; renamed *City of Green Bay,* 156; sold and scrapped (see *City of Green Bay*); in winter of 1936, 142–44, 146–49, 151; in winter of

1959, 199–200; in winter of 1963, 202, 204, 206–7
Wabash Railroad Company, 66, 129–30, 138, 152–53, 155, 173–74
Washington Island, WI, 69, 131
Webber, John, 120–21
Westwind, 212–13, 215–16
Whale, 98
Whitmore Lake, MI, 238
William B. Davock, 135
William E. Corey, 98
Wilson, Mrs., 73
windrows, 4–6, 43–44, 48, 50, 54, 56, 71, 76, 81–82, 100–101, 105, 107, 109–11, 147–48, 195, 206, 210, 218
Wisconsin Central Railway Company, 36, 68
Wisconsin Department of Transportation, 235
Wisconsin Maritime Museum, Manitowoc, WI, 79
Woodford, John P., 235–36, 241

Yuma, MI, 197

Zimmerman, Eugene, 67, 94–96, 156